New Proclamation

NEW PROCLAMATION

Series A, 1998–1999

Advent through Holy Week

ADVENT/CHRISTMAS

Robert Kysar

EPIPHANY

Robert H. Smith

LENT

William H. Willimon

HOLY WEEK

Gail R. O'Day

FORTRESS PRESS
Minneapolis

NEW PROCLAMATION
Series A, 1998–1999
Advent through Holy Week

Cover and book design: Joseph Bonyata
Illustrations: Tanja Butler, *Graphics for Worship,* copyright © 1996 Augsburg Fortress.

ISBN 0-8006-4239-2

The paper used in this publication meets the minimum requirements of American National Standard for Information Sciences—Permanence of Paper for Printed Library Materials, ANSI Z329.48-1984.

Manufactured in the U.S.A. AF 1-4239

02 01 00 99 98 1 2 3 4 5 6 7 8 9 10

Contents

The Season of Epiphany
Robert H. Smith

The Season of Lent
William H. Willimon

Holy Week
Gail R. O'Day

PUBLISHER'S FOREWORD

TWENTY-FIVE YEARS AGO Fortress Press embarked on an ambitious project to produce a lectionary preaching resource that would provide the best in biblical exegetical aids for a variety of lectionary traditions. This resource, *Proclamation,* became both a pioneer and a standard-bearer in its field, sparking a host of similar products from other publishers. Few, however, have become as widely used and well known as *Proclamation.*

Thoroughly ecumenical and built around the three-year lectionary cycle, *Proclamation's* focus has always been on the biblical text first and foremost. Where other resources often have offered canned sermons or illustrations for the preacher to use or adapt, *Proclamation's* authors have always asserted the best resource for the preacher is the biblical text itself. *Proclamation* has always been premised on the idea that those who are well equipped to understand a pericope in both its historical and liturgical context will also be well equipped to compose meaningful and engaging sermons. For that reason, *Proclamation* consistently has invited the cream of North American biblical scholars and homileticians to offer their comments because of their commitments to the text.

New Proclamation represents a significant change in Fortress Press's approach to the lectionary resource, but it still retains the best of the hallmarks that have made it so widely used and appreciated. Long-time users of the series will immediately notice the most major change, that is, the switch from eight to two volumes per year. The volume you are holding covers the lectionary texts for approximately the first half of the church year, from Advent through Holy Week, which culminates with the Great Vigil of Easter. By going to this two-volume format, we are able to offer you a larger, workbook-style page size with a lay-flat binding and plenty of white space for taking notes.

Because the Evangelical Lutheran Church in America adopted the Revised Common Lectionary as its recommended lectionary source several years ago, the lectionary from the Lutheran Book of Worship no longer appears in *New Proclamation.* This allows our authors to write more expansively on each of the texts for each of the three lectionary traditions addressed here. When a text appears in less than all three of these lectionaries or is offered as an alternative text, these are clearly marked as follows: RC (Roman Catholic); RCL (Revised Common Lectionary); and BCP (Episcopal, for Book of Common Prayer).

Although they are not usually used as preaching texts, *New Proclamation* offers brief commentary on each assigned psalm (or, as they are listed, the Responsive Reading) for each preaching day so that the preacher can incorporate reflections on these readings as well in a sermon. Call-out quotes in the margins help signal significant themes in the texts for the day.

New Proclamation retains *Proclamation's* emphasis on the biblical text but offers a new focus on how the preacher may apply those texts to contemporary situations. Exegetical work is more concise, and thoughts on how the text addresses today's world and our personal situations take a more prominent role. Throughout most of the book, exegetical comments are addressed under the heading "Interpreting the Text," and the homiletical materials come under the heading "Responding to the Text." Readers will note, however, that sometimes there is not an easy division between exegesis and application; thus in his comments on the Epiphany texts Robert H. Smith instead gives the reader more creative headings that help address the themes of the day.

Each section of this book is prefaced by a brief introduction that helps situate the liturgical season and its texts within the context of the church year. Unlike *Proclamation,* which was not dated according to its year of publication, this volume of *New Proclamation* is dated specifically for the years 1998–1999 when the texts for Series A next appear. Although preachers may have to work a bit harder to reuse these books in three years' time, they will also find that the books should coordinate better with other dated lectionary materials that they may be using at the same time. When feast or saint's days land on a Sunday (such as St. John the Evangelist) in 1998 and 1999, the texts for those days are commented on so that preachers have the option of celebrating those days appropriately. Those traditions that follow the numbering of propers or days in Ordinary Time will find those listed as well.

Other conveniences also appear in *New Proclamation.* Preachers who conduct services at different times on Christmas Eve and Christmas Day will find Robert Kysar has commented on three different sets of texts that are appropriate for each of those times. Readers will also note that both William Willimon and Gail O'Day offer comments on the texts for Palm/Passion Sunday. Willimon's comments, however, focus primarily on the processional—Palm Sunday—texts while O'Day's work centers on the Passion Sunday texts. Bibliographies and notes accompany most of the sections as well.

For all its changes, *New Proclamation* does not claim to reinvent the preaching lectionary resource. It is, in many ways, a work in progress and readers will see even more helpful changes in future volumes. One thing that has not changed, however, is the commitment to offer preachers access to the ideas of the best biblical scholars and homileticians in North America. Robert Kysar, Robert H. Smith, William H. Willimon, and Gail R. O'Day—all veterans from previous *Proclamation* volumes—have each risen to the occasion to address these texts in fresh ways and to make *New Proclamation* truly new. We are grateful to them for their contributions to this new effort.

Appreciation also goes to the panel of preachers and homileticians who served as a focus group for producing *New Proclamation:* Reverend Mary Halvorson (Grace University Lutheran Church, Minneapolis) Reverend Susan Moss (St. James Episcopal, Minneapolis), Father Jim Motl (St. Paul Seminary, St. Paul), Reverend Rob Englund (Lebanon Lutheran Church, Minneapolis), and Dr. Michael Rogness (Luther Seminary, St. Paul). Cynthia Thompson and David Lott served as textual editors; Joseph Bonyata designed and produced the volume. Thanks also goes to Frank Stoldt, Samuel Torvend, and Dennis Bushkofsky for their editorial assistance.

THE SEASON OF ADVENT

ROBERT KYSAR

THE SEASON OF ADVENT awakens our anticipation of the future. It prepares us for the nativity of our Lord but also stirs expectations of what God might do in our futures. Advent is rooted in the basic human longing for a better time, a longing as ancient as the Hebrew prophets. After a long season of Ordinary Time, the Sundays before the Nativity excite the human imagination with hope and strengthen us to trust a future in which God meets us.

The assigned readings for Advent exemplify this future orientation. The four Gospel lessons begin with Jesus' words concerning the last day (First Sunday in Advent) before turning to John the Baptizer and his role as a forerunner of Jesus (Second and Third Sundays in Advent). Finally, the assigned reading for the Fourth Sunday in Advent recounts the promise of Jesus' birth. The readings from Isaiah express Israel's profound hope for God's future activity, supported by the liturgical voices of selected Psalms. The second lessons for the first three Sundays represent the Christian hope and climax on the Fourth Sunday in Advent in Paul's words about Christ's place in God's redemptive plan.

ADVENT IS A TIME FOR PREACHERS TO NAME THE CONTEMPORARY LONGING FOR A NEW FUTURE AND PROCLAIM A RELIABLE HOPE. THE ADVENT PROCLAMATION UNLEASHES A POWER THAT RECREATES THE HUMAN SPIRIT WITH ITS WORDS OF EXPECTATION.

Ours is a day in which hopelessness often prevails and the prospects of the future appear dim. The biblical passages not only exhibit a yearning comparable to our own but announce a promise that empowers our faltering capacity to hope. Advent, then, is a time for preachers to name the contemporary longing for a new future and proclaim a reliable hope. The Advent proclamation unleashes a power that recreates the human spirit with its words of expectation.

FIRST SUNDAY IN ADVENT

NOVEMBER 29, 1998

REVISED COMMON	EPISCOPAL (BCP)	ROMAN CATHOLIC
Isa. 2:1-5	Isa. 2:1-5	Isa. 2:1-5
Ps. 122	Ps. 122	Ps. 122:1-9
Rom. 13:11-14	Rom. 13:8-14	Rom. 13:11-14
Matt. 24:36-44	Matt. 24:37-44	Matt. 24:37-44

EACH OF THE READINGS turns us toward the future but without neglecting the present. In the Isaiah passage hope for the future contrasts with present conditions and calls us to faithfulness now. The psalm invites consideration of hope for a home of peace and goodwill. In Romans Paul suggests how the impending future propels us into Christian living in the present. The Gospel lesson stresses our ignorance of the future while it encourages trust in God's promise and alertness to the coming of the divine at any moment. In every reading, hope for the future recreates the present.

FIRST READING
ISAIAH 2:1-5

Interpreting the Text

The prophet of eighth-century Judah wastes no time in offering a desolate people new hope. Depictions of the nation's plight surround the vision in these verses, first in the scathing words of chapter 1 and then with subsequent threats of judgment in 2:6—4:1. The passage's promise, therefore, stands in sharp contrast with social conditions. What God will do does not evolve out of inherent human possibility but in spite of it.

The passage begins with "in days to come," a typical prophetic way of speaking of an undetermined future time. It then moves through four distinct stages. The first is a figurative transformation of the landscape in which Jerusalem is made the world's pinnacle (v. 2). Then the world's people come to the mountain to learn and to live differently, for the "Word of the Lord" is found there (v. 3). Third, the people are transformed by God's administration of true justice. Divine justice brings an end to violence and war, and tools for productive living are fashioned from now useless instruments of war. Justice here does not mean judgment on the nations but the arbitration of disputes (v. 4). The final stage is an exhortation for the people to respond now in faithful living to the proclamation of what God will do in the future (see Micah 4:1-4 for a nearly identical passage). The whole passage stirs the imagination to see a transformed world in which humans as well as the landscape are recreated.

Responding to the Text

Where do we pin our hopes? We may naturally tend to hope for what might be implicit in the possibilities of the present situation, else prospects for the future seem illusory. But Isaiah insists that hopes pinned on God arise precisely in spite of present possibility. Hence, Christian hope is very different from cultural ambitions. We hope against what seems possible, for the ground of the future is not in ourselves but in the Lord of history.

How, then, shall we imagine such a future, if it contradicts the possible? The passage invites us to see a mountain swelling up out of the horizon and people swarming to that mountain. Maybe what our world needs is a "mountain" amid the flat and desolate landscape of human failure and evil—a high place where we can see beyond human differences and disputes. Our mountains have been successively leveled, flattened by the dissolution of human possibilities.

In our personal travels, my wife and I have always found ourselves attracted to mountains. Invariably we want to ascend a mountain to glimpse the view from the top. On a clear day, from the mountaintop you can see forever, and the view always puts things in proper perspective. The experience is like those pictures of our world shot from an orbiting spacecraft. From such a vantage point, justice looks different than it does when one is immersed in the crowds below.

THE HIGH GROUND FOR WHICH WE YEARN IS THE VANTAGE POINT OF THE DIVINE WORD AND ITS POWER TO MAKE OUR LIVES NEW. SUCH IS THE MOUNTAIN GOD RAISES FROM THE FLATLANDS OF OUR SOCIAL AND PERSONAL LIVES—A MOUNTAIN ON WHICH STANDS A CROSS RADIATING WITH THE JUSTICE OF LOVE.

But the vantage point of "the mountain of the Lord's house" is unique, for there God's justice reigns. The mountain we seek is one where our vision is transformed by true justice, not a human imitation. The high ground for which we yearn is the vantage point of the divine Word and its power to make our lives new. Such is the mountain God raises from the flatlands of our social and personal lives—a mountain on which stands a cross radiating with the justice of love.

Advent occasions our examination of the basis of our hopes, and lures us to pin our hopes on a mountain perspective that illumines our lives and our world with light.

Responsive Reading

PSALM 122

Interpreting the Text

This psalm is one of the "Songs of Ascent" and pictures a community in pilgrimage toward Jerusalem. It has three distinct parts, beginning with the individual's joy in being invited to go to the Temple and into the divine presence (vv. 1-2), and ending with a prayer for the community's welfare (vv. 6-9). Between those two parts is a declaration of praise for Jerusalem (vv. 3-5). "Jerusalem" functions as an image for the community, and its peace is the community's solidarity and mutual support.

Responding to the Text

Many of us have sought "to make a house a home" and have pursued the ingredient that transforms a place into an environment of peace and security. For we know dwelling places can be places of warmth and love or of hostility and abuse.

The psalm speaks of the reasons Jerusalem is "home" for the pilgrim. What makes it a home is that here worshipers "give thanks to the Lord," justice is done (v. 5), and inhabitants pray for one another's peace and well-being. The psalm is about community, our lives together in church and society. God invites us to our "home" in relationship with our Creator in Christ. In that relationship we will be made a community that seeks peace and goodness for one another.

Second Reading

ROMANS 13:8-14

Interpreting the Text

This reading is part of Paul's depiction of the life in Christ, the consequences of God's act on our behalf that he has described in earlier portions of the letter. The epicenter of the passage is the apostle's assertion that believers "know what time it is . . . night is far gone, the day is near" (vv. 11-12a). That assertion is sandwiched between two sections in which Paul urges faithful Christian living. On one side is the plea to love others, since that love fulfills the purpose of the Law (vv. 8–10). His summary of the commandments with the love commandment unites the ancient law with Jesus' teachings. On the other side of the passage's center comes the exhortation to "put on the Lord Jesus Christ," contrasting practices of darkness with those that are "honorable" (vv. 12b–14).

The heart of the passage emphasizes the importance of the present. The words *time* (Greek, *kairos*, meaning crucial time), *moment* (literally, *hour*), and *day* (vv. 11–12a) all imply the decisive time of divine activity for humanity's restoration. The image of awakening from sleep suggests that a conclusion of God's plan is as near as the dawn that begins the day. "Salvation" here refers to the completion of God's purpose for our lives. To empower his exhortations, Paul appeals to how critical the believers' present is in the light of God's work in Christ. The future that God has promised casts the present in a new light that calls forth Christian living.

Responding to the Text

What time is it? We wear or carry watches and surround ourselves with clocks so that we can always know the time. I once found myself befuddled because my watch stopped working, and I was reduced to having to ask others what time it was. Knowing the time is crucial.

GOD'S PROMISE FOR THE FUTURE CASTS OUR PRESENT IN NEW LIGHT. PROMISE IS LIKE THAT; IT MAKES THE PRESENT SACRED.

But the question "What time is it?" sometimes goes deeper for us. The "time" may not be a chronological point but an urgency summoned by a situation in which we find ourselves. We speak of certain "times" of our lives when we had to make tough decisions, bear heavy responsibilities, or work through difficulties. The time of day and the time of our lives are two quite different matters.

Paul asks his readers to consider what time it is, for he believes the present is one of those urgent periods in our lives. The present is conditioned by something that lies close at hand in the future; the present becomes crucial by virtue of what the future holds. God's promise for the future casts our present in new light. Promise is like that; it makes the present sacred.

A single parent I once knew understood the importance of a promise for the present. She struggled financially to raise a son on her minimum-wage job and nearly gave up. The task was too great, the burden too heavy. Then she was given a promise. If her son could graduate from high school, a benefactor would cover all his expenses to attend the local college. That promise empowered her to continue her struggle; her present task became possible. In due time, her son did graduate and was able to go to college.

Paul reminds us of God's promise to complete the process of restoring humanity and the world. He urges us to remember what time it is, to recall the promise of God and what that means for our present lives. Christian living seems too great a burden, too much of a task. But "the night is far gone, the day is near." That makes the present a time of promise and empowers us for faithfulness.

Gospel

MATTHEW 24:36-44

Interpreting the Text

Matthew 24 is this evangelist's version of Jesus' words concerning the last days, that is, Christ's appearance in glory and final victory over evil. The RCL introduces the lesson with verse 36, which states the mystery of the exact date of Christ's reappearance. The substance of the lesson includes two parables on the theme of preparedness (the days of Noah, vv. 37-39, and the householder, v. 43) along with a number of lessons drawn from them (vv. 40-42 and 44). "The coming of the Son of Man" refers to the glorious reappearance of Christ to complete God's rule in the world (see Dan. 7:13-14 where "Son of Man" is translated "a human being").

The parable of the days of Noah suggests how God's final act would catch humans unprepared (vv. 37-39). They were swept up in business as usual ("eating and drinking, marrying and giving in marriage"). The point is not their sinfulness but their neglect of what God was about to do. With comparable surprise the coming of the Son of Man threatens to find us inattentive to God's plan. The twin sayings concerning pairs, one of which is taken and one left (vv. 40-41), drive home the possibility of being unprepared. In each pair two people are about the same task, but one benefits from the event and the other does not. That possibility issues in an appeal to remain alert, since the decisive moment is unknown (v. 42).

LIKE A LASER BEAM, JESUS' WORDS CUT INTO OUR SOULS TO LAY OPEN THE LIMITS OF OUR KNOWLEDGE AND FORCE US TO ACKNOWLEDGE THE ABSOLUTE BOUNDARIES OF OUR VISION.

The tiny parable of the householder and the thief furthers the same point (v. 43). Like the people of Noah's time, the house owner lacks knowledge of when the thief would come. Since the disciples do not know the crucial time, they must live as if any moment might be the occasion for their Lord's coming (v. 44).

Throughout the lesson one theme is reiterated: You do not know the time; therefore, you must be ready at all times. Readiness is expressed in commands to "keep" or "stay awake" (vv. 42-43) and "be ready" (v. 44).

The theme of this lesson (and the whole of chapter 24) probably addressed the first readers with particular relevance. There may have been growing uncertainty about Christ's final appearance and opponents who attacked Christians with the charge that the delay of God's final victory demonstrated the error of their faith. Maybe some tried to calculate the exact date of such an event (for example, 24:23-24). Matthew's message was as important for the first century as it is for our own.

Responding to the Text

Samuel Beckett's play *Waiting for Godot* pictures two pitiful characters awaiting the arrival of a mysterious Godot. But Godot never comes. The waiters squander their time in pointless conversation and trivial concerns. Toward the end of the play, weariness overtakes them, and one of them asks, "Was I sleeping . . . Am I sleeping now? . . . At me too someone is looking, of me too someone is saying, 'He is sleeping, he knows nothing, let him sleep on.'" In the last scene, the same character asks his companion, "Well? Shall we go?" The other responds, "Yes, let's go."[1] But they do not move. And the play ends.

Beckett powerfully demonstrates the futility of waiting for the future to the neglect of the present. Like the lamentable characters waiting for Godot, we have no sure knowledge of the future, even though we thirst to know it. Horoscopes, fortune tellers, crystals, and angels—we use them all in hope of some inkling of the future. But the future remains shrouded in mystery, always surprising us with the unexpected.

The Gospel lesson accents the fact that no one knows when God will act. The people of Noah's day did not know, nor did the householder whose home was robbed while he slept. Not the disciples, not even the angels of heaven nor the Son know the day and hour. Only God knows! Like a laser beam, Jesus' words cut into our souls to lay open the limits of our knowledge and force us to acknowledge the absolute boundaries of our vision. Our unquenchable thirst to know the future goes unsatisfied. We are destined to live in a present without assurance of what may follow.

But there is more to the Gospel lesson. God promises to complete the divine rule in our world. The Son of Man will come, however mysterious may be the day and hour of his coming. In his coming, God will finally end the horrors of suffering, cut down the perennial forces of evil, vindicate Jesus' life and death, and enact the divine will.

The promise is permeated with God's freedom; God is totally free of our plans for the future. Consequently, we are left with nothing but pure trust. We trust the promise, not because we can calculate a time and place for its fulfillment, but only because it is God's promise. We trust the promise without the props of our reason or cleverness of mind. We trust it because it comes from One who has sacrificed his life out of love for us.

So, how shall we live in the meantime? Shall we wait at the side of the road endlessly, fiddling away the present for the sake of a mysterious future? Jesus weaves together the fact that we cannot know the future with the command to be alert in the present. We do not know the future, but we know God is here right now and appears to meet us in the present moment.

Jesus asks of us not the pointless waiting Beckett describes in his play, nor the kind of waiting I remember as a child, when I sent off for my radio hero's very own famous decoder ring. My life stopped, suspended in waiting for its delivery. Actually, I can't remember if the ring ever arrived. Jesus asks of us a different and active kind of anticipation. He never uses the word *wait* in our lesson. Instead, he urges us to "keep awake," "stay awake," and "be ready." The lesson encourages us to live faithfully in active trust, ready to meet God in every moment.

SECOND SUNDAY IN ADVENT

DECEMBER 6, 1998

REVISED COMMON	EPISCOPAL (BCP)	ROMAN CATHOLIC
Isa. 11:1-10	Isa. 11:1-10	Isa. 11:1-10
Ps. 72:1-7, 18-19	Ps. 72 or 72:1-8	Ps. 72:1-2, 7-8, 12-13, 17
Rom. 15:4-13	Rom. 15:4-13	Rom. 15:4-9
Matt. 3:1-12	Matt. 3:1-12	Matt. 3:1-12

GOD PROMISES AND DOES what is promised. Isaiah pictures God's raising up an ideal king and the peace resulting from his reign. The psalm complements that picture with the people's prayer for a truly just king. Paul turns our attention to the God of hope who is the source of such a future. In the Gospel lesson, John the Baptist declares that God's new reign is near, warns of the judgment it brings, and invites repentance. Together the lessons provoke our vision of God's rule, our commitment to that vision, and our readiness for its actualization.

FIRST READING
ISAIAH 11:1-10

Interpreting the Text

Whatever its historical setting, this passage offers hope in a time of uncertainty. It moves from the description of an ideal Davidic king (vv. 1-5) to a vision of peace throughout all nature (vv. 6-9).

The Davidic dynasty has been reduced to a mere stump, out of which comes a new king who fulfills all that Judah had dreamed possible for David's successors. He is gifted with "the spirit of the Lord," which lavishes distinct features on him (v. 2). "Counsel and might" refer to gifts of negotiation and diplomacy, while "fear of the Lord" suggests his humility and utter dependence on God. He will practice a true justice devoid of superficial impressions and without curry to the rich and powerful. "The rod of his mouth" and "the breath of his lips," however, depict declarations of punishment for the deserving (v. 4b). He wears "righteousness" and "faithfulness" like daily garments (v. 5).

The presence of such justice brings the entire creation to peace, depicted in a series of snapshots. The concord stretches from relationships among animals to those between humans and nature. Predators live in harmony with their prey, and any mere child leads them about like domesticated animals. The weakest of humans is safe with such pacified creatures (vv. 6-9).

Filled with "knowledge of the Lord," the whole world becomes Jerusalem, God's "holy mountain." God invites all the world's people to come to this exemplary king and benefit from his rule (vv. 9-10).

Responding to the Text

Among John Lennon's legacies is the song "Imagine," in which he invites listeners to visualize a world at peace. He offered it to us amid warfare abroad and division at home. And who among us can resist such imagining? We yearn for a pervasive peace rooted in justice and righteousness almost as much as we yearn for food and drink. Yet do we dare allow ourselves to dream such dreams? To protect ourselves from the pain of disappointment we may turn our eyes away from such a vision.

Isaiah invites us to take the risk and dream God's own dream for the world. In that divine dream all of our own longings are articulated. Justice, equity, righteousness, harmony, and knowledge of God are all there in ten verses. In his own day Israel's monarchy was weakened, the nation at war with a mighty enemy, its moral fabric tattered. Isaiah shares God's own dream in order to defeat hopelessness and empower determination.

Dreams are powerful, and imagination broadens possibility. Michael Ende's novel *The Never-Ending Story* describes the efforts of a little boy to save the land of Fantasia from the forces of nothingness. Fantasia was born from and sustained by the human capacity to imagine possibilities, and Fantasia's demise would mean the death of human imagination. The little boy could rescue the land and its inhabitants by imagining and crying out a new name for the princess. But he meets opposition from others in the forms of indifference, self-doubt, resignation, and fear. Finally, with only fragments of Fantasia remaining, the little boy cries out the princess's name and restores the world of dreams and hope.

ISAIAH INVITES US TO TAKE THE RISK AND DREAM GOD'S OWN DREAM FOR THE WORLD WHERE ALL OF OUR OWN LONGINGS ARE ARTICULATED: JUSTICE, EQUITY, RIGHTEOUSNESS, HARMONY, AND KNOWLEDGE OF GOD.

The death of imagination threatens to engulf our world and all human hope in nothingness. But dreams are powerful. Isaiah knew what dreams could do!

God's dream, however, is more than a figment of imagination. It is a promise, and we can trust this dreamer. But the divine dream requires commitment as well as trust. Dreaming God's dream empowers us to work now and here for what God wants for creation and will accomplish fully in the future.

Responsive Reading

PSALM 72

Interpreting the Text

With Psalm 72 (one of the "royal psalms") the community prays for their king. Most striking about this prayer is its attention to social justice and human welfare. It begins with this theme (vv. 1-4) and circles back to it again (vv. 12-14). The psalmist focuses on the "poor," "needy," "oppressed," and "weak." The prayer is another vision of the future as a time of true justice and peace that concludes by blessing God as the Lord who can bring this vision to reality.

WE JOIN OUR VOICES WITH ISRAEL'S BECAUSE OUR LORD BECAME POOR ON OUR BEHALF, SUFFERED INJUSTICE THAT WE MIGHT BE MADE JUST, AND ENDURED OPPRESSION THAT WE MIGHT BE FREED.

Responding to the Text

The city prepared for an onslaught of visitors from all around the world by systematically moving all its homeless from the center of activity and demolishing the shanty-type homes in the area. For the festive occasion the poor and the needy were made invisible.

But such people are not invisible to God. Our psalm concludes by blessing God, for God promises to right society's offenses against the oppressed. With this psalm we too bless God's compassion for the needy with our prayers and our acts. We join our voices with Israel's because our Lord became poor on our behalf, suffered injustice that we might be made just, and endured oppression that we might be freed.

SECOND READING

ROMANS 15:4-13

Interpreting the Text

This fragment of Paul's letter bridges two sections of the final exhortations to the Roman Christians. "Hope" glues the lesson together (vv. 4, 12, and 13).

The reading begins in the midst of Paul's pleas to care for the weak (vv. 1-6). Having quoted Psalm 69:10 (v. 3), the apostle then suggests the purpose of Scripture. The Hebrew Scriptures continue to incite hope among Christians. Endurance in difficulty, coupled with the encouragement of Scripture, breeds confidence in the future. Paul concludes this section with a prayer for the community's harmony in Christ (vv. 5-6).

Paul continues by encouraging readers to "welcome one another" the way Christ accepts us. The argument of verses 8-9 seeks to justify the place of Gentiles in the Christian community by offering three reasons for Jesus' ministry to only Jews: To demonstrate God's faithfulness to Israel ("the truth of God"); to "confirm the promise to the patriarchs," which included Gentiles (for example, Gen. 12:1-3); and to evoke Gentile thankfulness for their inclusion in God's work. "Although Jesus' ministry was directed to the Jews of Palestine, Gentiles were to be included eventually in God's kingdom, as even the Old Testament promises indicate."[2] Paul supports his argument with four citations of Scripture in verses 10-11. The last quotation ends with the declaration that the Gentiles receive hope by virtue of the Davidic king. This sparks the prayer of verse 13. God is the source of hope for all Christians and nurtures that hope through the Holy Spirit.

Responding to the Text

What source of hope do we have? We have tried them all in recent decades when hope has been so precious. Basic human goodwill, governments of every sort, well-intended enterprises—they have all let us down. Many of us have known the experience of utter hopelessness, times when all our resources have been exhausted and we have nowhere else to turn.

In just such times Paul's benediction for the Roman Christians speaks a new word to us. He claims that God alone is the source of our hope. God demonstrates faithfulness to promises made to the mothers and fathers of the Old Testament tradition and in Scripture provides us with a means of encouragement. Paul names God "the God of hope," the initiator of confidence in the midst of distress and uncertainty. Jesus himself modeled that reliance on God as the God of hope. When the religious and political establishments conspired against him, his family sought to take him home because he was out of his mind, his followers scattered like frightened rabbits, but Jesus prayed to God and went to the cross.

But today where do we find God's hope in a life of hopelessness? Paul helps us in the second part of his benediction: "so that you may abound in hope by the power of the Holy Spirit." The Spirit moves within and through the community of Christians, channeling God's hope to us through our sisters and brothers in faith. It is not their own hope they share but their God of hope who speaks and acts through them. Such was the case when one whom I shall call Albert reached the bottom after his wife had died. A friend from his congregation, who himself had lost his wife only a few years ago, visited Albert. That conversation rekindled a spark of hope in Albert's drab life—enough that he could go on. The God of hope, through the Spirit, enables us to abound in hope.

THE SPIRIT MOVES WITHIN AND THROUGH THE COMMUNITY OF CHRISTIANS, CHANNELING GOD'S HOPE TO US THROUGH OUR SISTERS AND BROTHERS IN FAITH. IT IS NOT THEIR OWN HOPE THEY SHARE BUT THEIR GOD OF HOPE WHO SPEAKS AND ACTS THROUGH THEM.

Martin Luther was right when he wrote, ". . . where there is hope, there [God] is worshiped."[3] God is our source of hope!

GOSPEL

MATTHEW 3:1-12

Interpreting the Text

The holy family has returned to Nazareth (2:19-23) and now the story leaps to a later time. The lesson begins with a brief introduction of John the Baptist (vv. 1-6), then recounts his words to religious authorities (vv. 7-10), and concludes with a messianic announcement (vv. 11-12).

John pops up "in the wilderness," a setting for the announcement of God's salvation (see v. 3). In announcing that God's reign is near, John anticipates Jesus' own message (see 4:17). The new reign of God calls for repentance, a turning away from immoral acts. Isaiah 40:3 announces God's coming to rescue Israel from exile, and now God is about to come to rescue humanity from its exile in sin. Turning to God (repentance) is now possible, because God is turning to us.

The description of John in verse 4 recalls Elijah (see 2 Kings 1:8), since for Matthew, John is Elijah returned (11:14 and 17:13). Elijah had not died but was taken into heaven (2 Kings 2:11-12), igniting a belief that he would return as the forerunner of the Messiah (see Mal. 4:5). John evokes quite a response (vv. 5-6). People were ready to confess their sins, and for them the Jordan had associations connected with both Elijah and Elisha (see 2 Kings 5).

The evangelist readies us for the role of the religious authorities in the Jesus story by having them step onstage in this early scene. The combination of Pharisees and Sadducees is curious, since they represent two of the major divisions in first-century Judaism and were opponents for the most part. John is none too easy on them. With cutting images reminiscent of the ancient prophets, he challenges them. Like "vipers" they have poisoned the people, and now the tree they have nourished must be axed. A new tree must produce "fruit," behavior that results from new character. Their heritage is no security against this judgment, since God—not lineage—makes children.

John completes his preaching (vv. 11-12) by distinguishing himself, both in terms of his baptism and identity, from the one who is yet to appear. He is not worthy to be Jesus' slave and carry his sandals. Jesus' baptism is with "the Holy Spirit and fire." In Matthew, Jesus never bestows the Spirit; the emphasis is on the identity of the Spirit with Jesus himself (see 1:18, 20; 3:16; and 28:19). Fire is an ancient symbol for judgment, and the picture in verse 12 recalls Isaiah 34:10 and 66:24. Our response to Christ is the beginning of the judgment.

Responding to the Text

Warning signs are everywhere today—on our highways, on buildings, and on the products we buy. Medical science warns of deadly diseases like skin cancer, stroke, and heart disease. Warnings alert us to what may await us in the future, and they make us accountable for our actions. We need warning signs on our journey through life to give us some sense of what the future might hold. We can then take responsibility for ourselves.

John the Baptist is a kind of warning sign. He alerts his listeners to the fact that something drastic is coming in the near future and warns them that they should prepare themselves. Our Gospel lesson is a bit strange in this sense. John announces that God is about to initiate a new reign in the world and rescue us from the rule of evil. The announcement of God's coming is good news, not bad news! So, what's all this about judgment?

Could it be that the other side of the good news of the gospel is the bad news of judgment? God is about to give us a gift of divine presence and rule. Might such a gift cut both ways? Strangely, a gift has the effect of calling us into question. Have you ever received an unearned gift and felt uncomfortable?

Such a gift is at the heart of the story told in the movie *Grand Canyon*. An upper-middle-class, white, suburban businessman finds himself on the receiving end of a free gift from an urban, blue-collar, African American tow-truck driver. In the middle of the night, the businessman's car breaks down in a deserted, deteriorating part of the city, where a gang of thugs finds him and threatens his life. The tow truck arrives, and its driver convinces the thugs to leave the scene. This act calls the man's whole life into question. He tries to repay the truck driver, who will have none of his charity. What unfolds in the story is a radical about-face in the lives of this fellow and his family as they come to grips with the gift of life they have received.

Such is the case with the gift of God's presence and rule. Divine generosity turns our lives upside down. That is what John was getting at in his harsh words to the religious authorities. Don't appeal to your ancestors! God is able to make children of Abraham from a bunch of rocks! The words shake their very identity. Our Creator's rule challenges our own creations of security and safety.

REPENTANCE, THEN, IS LETTING GO OF THE SECURITIES WE HAVE CREATED FOR OURSELVES IN ORDER TO ACCEPT GOD'S GIFT AND ITS SECURITY.

There is only one response to the coming of God: repentance. Not repentance in the simple sense of feeling sorry for our wrongs, but in the sense of turning around. Turning is the ancient meaning of the word *repentance*—a turning to face God, who in Christ turns to come among us. Repentance, then, is letting go of the securities we have created for ourselves in order to accept God's gift and its security.

When Christ comes among us, we are judged even more radically than when we are the objects of any gracious and undeserved gift. The advent of Christ means asking who we are, and nothing can insulate against this divine intrusion into our lives. But judgment is part of God's saving activity, integral to the good news.

John gives us fair warning! That in itself is merciful. We know who is coming; now we take responsibility for ourselves.

THIRD SUNDAY IN ADVENT

DECEMBER 13, 1998

REVISED COMMON	EPISCOPAL (BCP)	ROMAN CATHOLIC
Isa. 35:1-10	Isa. 35:1-10	Isa. 35:1-6a, 10
Ps. 146:5-10 or Luke 1:47-55	Ps. 146 or 146:4-9	Ps. 146:6-10
James 5:7-10	James 5:7-10	James 5:7-10
Matt. 11:2-11	Matt. 11:2-11	Matt. 11:2-11

THE THEMES OF THE READINGS form a triangle. At the pinnacle is who God is what God does. The two base points are how God (1) transforms our world and (2) implants patient trust. Isaiah speaks of God's recreation of all the world, while Matthew focuses on humanity's rehabilitation in God's dominion. The psalm witnesses to God's actions as reason to seek help and hope in the Lord, and in the Magnificat Mary praises God's habitual way of showing mercy. James encourages patience since Christ's coming is near. Promise empowers our trust because of who the Promiser is and what the Promiser does.

FIRST READING
ISAIAH 35:1-10

Interpreting the Text

Look what happens when God comes! With vivid scenes this passage sketches the impact of divine presence on humans and nature. "Here is your God" (v. 4a) is the centerpiece from which the four sketches emerge like spokes of a wheel. The divine coming will simultaneously bring judgment ("terrible recompense") and salvation.

The first sketch (vv. 1-2) depicts the conversion of the wilderness. When divine presence ("glory") permeates the land, the arid country blossoms and glows with the luxury of lush environments like Lebanon, Carmel, and Sharon. The second sketch shifts to the personal (vv. 3-4a) to show how the divine presence engenders strength in the fearful and weak. The pronouncement "Be strong, do not fear!" evokes new confidence.

In the third sketch the healing of the afflicted is shaded with the transfiguration of nature. The blind, deaf, lame, and speechless represent how all human afflictions are made whole (vv. 5-6) just as the desert is enriched with lavish vegetation (v. 7).

The concluding sketch displays the return of the dispersed to Jerusalem (vv. 8-10). They travel on a divinely constructed thruway safe from the dangers of both beasts and evil humans. It is so clearly marked that even directionless fools can find their way to Jerusalem. Along the way joy and gladness drive out all the sadness of suffering. "The Holy Way" represents both the pilgrims' passage to Jerusalem and the "way" of life possible with God present.

Responding to the Text

As with all traveling of great distances, the Christian journey is tiring. Like children in the back seat, we pray, "God, are we there yet? How much farther, Lord?" The journey wears us down. Dangers also surround us on our travel. We have to be careful. The way is not always clearly marked; we are liable to miss a turn and get lost. Along the way, wild beasts leap out at us. The beast of self-doubt screams its threats, and we must dodge the craws of greed and ambition. It's a dangerous road we Christians travel.

ISAIAH CALLS OUT TO US WITH WORDS OF HOPE IN OUR WEARINESS AND WITH AN ASSURING PROMISE IN OUR FEAR. GOD WILL COME; THE JOURNEY'S DESTINATION IS IN SIGHT, ISAIAH ASSURES US.

Maybe Isaiah's first readers were also weary from following God's path and frightened by the beasts along their way. As it did for the people of Israel, the passage calls out to us with words of hope in our weariness and with an assuring promise in our fear. God will come; the journey's destination is in sight, Isaiah assures us. Soon the road will become as smooth as silk and as straight as an arrow. Even those of us who have no sense of direction will easily find our way.

To endure—even survive—our journey we need confidence that there is a destination. The companions of an amateur mountain climber left him for dead in a vicious blizzard on Mount Everest. But he awoke knowing the base camp was somewhere below him and that he would die where he was if he did not move. Driven by a sheer instinct to survive, he dragged his frozen feet down the mountain until he staggered into the cluster of tents. There his colleagues ran out to meet him and take him back to his loved ones. He made the journey because he knew there was rescue in his destination where others would care for him.

God promises a destination for our journeys and comes out to meet us along the way. Much like the father goes out to meet his prodigal son in Jesus' parable, God comes in Christ to care for us. Christ's advent calls to us, "Here is your God," coming out to save you. The promise is sure, so "Be strong, do not fear!"

Responsive Reading
PSALM 146

Interpreting the Text

Where we seek help matters, the psalmist declares. After denying that help is found in mortals (vv. 3-4), the passage counsels us to seek help and hope in God (v. 5). The argument for this counsel is in who God is and what God has done: creator of "all that is"; liberator of the imprisoned, the blind, the lowly, and the abandoned; destroyer of evil; and Lord who forever reigns. The psalm implants trust by appealing to what we know about God.

Responding to the Text

We want to know the credentials of anyone who purports to be able to help us, otherwise we may entrust ourselves to the inept or dishonest. The psalmist reminds us of God's credentials as evidence that we can have hope in and seek help from our Lord. How we understand God is the key that unlocks our trust and hope. A God who is too small, too self-occupied, too fickle, and too narrow will not do. So, we remember the story of the One who proved to be the compassionate and faithful Lord of all, even the story of a love that suffered on our behalf. Our own faith is aroused by God, "who keeps faith forever."

LUKE 1:47-55 (RCL)

Interpreting the Text

Mary's song of praise transposes from a personal testimony to what God has done for her (vv. 47-49) into a communal affirmation of Israel's experience of God (vv. 50-55). In Mary's own experience of God's "favor" in her humble state she finds her Lord's habitual behavior, dethroning the proud and powerful in favor of the lowly, and satisfying the hungry. The marvelous role in which God casts her in bearing the Messiah triggers the memory of Israel's history of benefiting from divine mercy.

Responding to the Text

Like Psalm 146, Mary's Magnificat reminds us of the holy habits—who God is and what God does. God's way with the world is to show mercy on those who most need it and upset the world's standards with new ones. Mary advises us to view our experience of God through the lens of God's own history. God's habits are clear, when seen in this perspective. If God has always "looked with favor" on the lowly, we can trust that our own lowliness will not escape divine attention. When we feel lowly and are hungry is precisely when God is near.

SECOND READING
JAMES 5:7-10

Interpreting the Text

Patience and endurance are the last of the virtues this author encourages. The theme is patience while waiting for the divine advent. The words *patient* and *patience* play the leading role in the passage, appearing at the beginning and the end of the passage, as well as in the middle (v. 8). But those words are coupled with references to God's "coming" (vv. 7 and 8; see also 9). "Coming" translates the Greek word used for Christ's glorious appearance *(parousia).*

> JAMES WEDS PATIENCE WITH PROMISE. IF THE PROMISE IS WORTH WAITING FOR, PATIENCE IS POSSIBLE. THE QUALITY OF THE PROMISE DETERMINES THE MEASURE OF OUR PATIENCE.

The first verse immediately announces the theme of patience, supported by an analogy of the farmer, who must wait through the seasons of rain to see the benefits of his labor (see Deut. 11:14 and Jer. 5:24). But Christians can find new strength for the intervening time (literally, "erect our hearts" on hope), since we stand on the brink of the harvest and the advent is near (v. 8).

This is no time to be complaining about each other. The author jogs our memory of Jesus' words about judging another (Matt. 7:1), emphasizing their power by reminding us that Christ's coming results in judgment as well as salvation. "The Judge stands at the doors" suggests the immediacy of Christ's coming (v. 9; see also Rev. 3:20). But the tone quickly shifts back to patience, coupled this time with suffering, and is supported with an example. Although the author does not specify a particular prophet, Jeremiah comes immediately to mind because he suffered such contempt before history vindicated his message.

Responding to the Text

Do you know the definition of an "instant"? It is the time that lapses between when the traffic light turns green and the car behind you sounds its horn. We have become an impatient people. Instant food from the fast food establishments and microwave ovens, instant pain relief with medication, and instant pleasure with the push of the television's power button have all nurtured our impatience. We are not good "waiters." How are such impatient people going to learn patience? What is the secret to patience?

We have no patent on impatience, as James suggests. The early Christians were impatient for Christ's reappearing and the completion of God's new reign in the world. Even more, the references to suffering make it clear the first readers were experiencing tribulations and hardships. James advises us to cultivate patience especially for life's painful periods.

Patience is all the more difficult during times of hardship. The concluding scene of Isaac Bashevis Singer's novel *Shosha* shows two men pondering the foolishness of suffering.

> "What do you think, Tsutsik, is there an answer somewhere or not?"
> "No, no answer."
> "Why not?"
> "There can't be any answer for suffering—not for the sufferer."
> "In that case what am I waiting for?"
> Genia opened the door. "Why are you two sitting in the dark, eh?"
> Haiml laughed. "We're waiting for an answer."[4]

Often we may find ourselves sitting in the darkness, waiting impatiently for answers when we know that there are no answers—not for now at least. We yearn for that day when the darkness is penetrated by God's light and the answers materialize. We long for God's completion of the divine dominion in our world. Until then we must learn patience by enduring our difficulties.

But our question remains: How do we learn patience? James weds patience with promise. If the promise is worth waiting for, patience is possible. The quality of the promise determines the measure of our patience (for example, waiting through pregnancy for a child's birth). God's promise of the divine advent transforms our waiting. The promise that the Lord is coming strengthens our hearts for patience.

GOSPEL

MATTHEW 11:2-11

Interpreting the Text

Matthew has just begun a new section (see v. 1) and returns us to John and his ministry, a unit that continues through verse 19. John's question to Jesus from prison, followed by Jesus' reply (vv. 2-6) and his words concerning John (vv. 7-11) comprise this pericope.

We do not know why John now wants confirmation of Jesus' identity when he had seemed so confident (3:11-14). But from the confines of his prison he inquires if Jesus is the Messiah. (John's arrest is noted in 4:12 and his execution narrated in 14:1-12.) Jesus' response startles us. See for yourselves, he seems to say. His actions speak for themselves, or at least point to the answer John seeks. What is important is that human lives are being transformed under the sway of God's reign (see Isa. 35:5-6 and 61:1). Jesus' ministry starts no revolution against Roman oppression but nonetheless impinges on the total condition of people—physical, social, and economic—not just their spiritual welfare. All the evidence John needs is the fact that a grand reversal of human conditions has begun through Jesus. If God's rule over evil has begun, then Jesus is "the one who is to come."

JESUS' MINISTRY STARTS NO REVOLUTION AGAINST ROMAN OPPRESSION BUT NONETHELESS IMPINGES ON THE TOTAL CONDITION OF PEOPLE—PHYSICAL, SOCIAL, AND ECONOMIC—NOT JUST THEIR SPIRITUAL WELFARE.

With John's question answered, Jesus speaks about the Baptizer (vv. 7-11). He first assures the crowd of John's prophetic character (vv. 7-10). Why was he so popular that you went into the wilderness to see him? He was no wealthy king (remember his garments—3:4), nor some flimsy branch bent by the winds of conformity (finally arrested for disturbing the peace). His prophetic character drew you like a magnet, and now he suffers the fate of the prophets. But he is more than a prophet. He is one spoken of by the prophets as the messenger who prepares the path for the Messiah (Mal. 3:1; Exod. 23:20).

If John is the "super prophet," what then is his relation to the new kingdom God is inaugurating (v. 11)? "Truly" translates *amen* and signals a solemn and important utterance. Jesus claims that there is no one greater than John before the period of God's new reign; but now in this novel age even the lowliest person is greater than John. He stands on the other side of the division of ages, in the time of God's preparation for the new age. Participation in God's new rule sets one beyond the reach of even John (whom Jesus explicitly calls Elijah in v. 14—see Mal. 4:5).

Responding to the Text

"Go and tell John what you hear and see!" That is Jesus' answer to John's question. What do you hear and see? That is the evidence that God is doing something radical in Jesus' ministry and that God has intruded into our world to begin a new age. It is so new that even John himself is left out—left standing on the other shore. So new, in fact, that it drastically upsets life and ends business as usual. Astronauts must learn a totally new way of life outside the power of gravity, and scientists worry about the effects of such an environment on the physical body. The new age of which Jesus speaks is comparable to such an extreme change. The rule of God in heaven has intruded into our world below.

But what do we hear and see today? Jesus points John's disciples to how human afflictions are being healed and how the poor now hear some good news. If that is evidence of Jesus' identity as the Messiah, where do we see and hear such news today? What we see and hear may be very different. The sighted are blinded; the healthy stricken; the hearing deafened; the innocent murdered; and the poor kept poor.

Psychologists tell us that seeing and hearing is selective. We cannot absorb all the sensations with which we are bombarded, so we filter some out in order to perceive only a few. But maybe it's our perspective that determines seeing and hearing; maybe what matters is the vantage point from which we look and the octaves for which we listen. Some see and hear only the unfavorable sensations and hence become cynical about life. On the other hand, Siddhartha saw the river "always the same and forever new" until finally he said: "I sat there and listened to the river. It told me a great deal, it filled me . . . with thoughts of unity."[5] He saw and heard the unity of all reality where others saw and heard constant change.

What do we as Christians see and hear? In an episode of the television series *M*A*S*H* Hawkeye is temporarily blinded. For a week he lives with his eyes bandaged. Toward the end of the week, he confides to his friend Trapper that something marvelous has happened to him. His blindness has forced him to listen more carefully than ever before. "Did you know," he asks Trapper, "that the sound of rain is just like the sound of steaks cooking on a grill?" Hawkeye experienced a whole new world of sound revealed to him by the loss of his sight. The ears of faith hear new tones in the familiar sounds around us. What do *we* see and hear?

Jesus does more than try to present John with proof that he is the Messiah. He is not simply asking John's messengers to copy down the facts of what they witnessed. Jesus invites John and you and me to see and hear with the eyes and ears of faith—to perceive God at work in our world in a fourth dimension and in another range of sounds.

In Vermont some congregations instituted "The Good News Garage," an enterprise that uses volunteers to repair and rebuild old cars for those who cannot afford the expense of having it done in a repair shop. The goal is to enable people to get and keep jobs that require them to drive some distance. What do you see and hear? "The poor have good news brought to them."

FOURTH SUNDAY IN ADVENT

DECEMBER 20, 1998

REVISED COMMON	EPISCOPAL (BCP)	ROMAN CATHOLIC
Isa. 7:10-16	Isa. 7:10-17	Isa. 7:10-14
Ps. 80:1-7, 17-19	Ps. 24 or 24:1-7	Ps. 24:1-7, 10
Rom. 1:1-7	Rom. 1:1-7	Rom. 1:1-7
Matt. 1:18-25	Matt. 1:18-25	Matt. 1:18-24

TAKEN TOGETHER, THE READINGS ask us to consider what happens when God comes among us. The Isaiah story describes stubborn Ahaz who tries to ignore the sign of God's coming and its assurance. But Matthew depicts Joseph as welcoming and obeying a sign of divine advent that demands new righteousness. Psalm 80 prays for the shining face of God's presence, and Psalm 24 asks how we ready ourselves for such a presence. Paul presents God's act in Christ as the keeping of an ancient promise so as to bestow a new relationship with God and offer a call to new life.

FIRST READING
ISAIAH 7:10-17

Interpreting the Text

Judah's stubborn king is between a rock and a hard place. Assyria is at war with Israel (Ephraim) and Damascus (about 735 B.C.E.). Isaiah presents Ahaz a sign of God's will that Ahaz should remain neutral in the conflict (7:1-9). Now God offers to present the king another sign, and he refuses it (vv. 10-12); nonetheless, Isaiah announces another indication of the Lord's will (vv. 13-17).

God is willing to do whatever is necessary to convince Ahaz, but the king does not want to hear the message. He has already heard and rejected it (7:1-9), so he masks his refusal to listen in a pious unwillingness to "put the Lord to the test" (vv. 10-11).

But here comes Isaiah with God's sign (vv. 12-17). A "young woman" is pregnant with a child who shall be named "Immanuel" (that is, "God is with us"—v. 14b). The "sign" is a child whose name assures the king that God is with the nation and that he should not fear the foreign powers. Before the child is eating solid foods and able to distinguish good from evil, the military forces that the king faces will be annihilated. We do not know who this "young woman" is. The queen or the prophet's own wife? The Hebrew word means only a female who has reached the age of marriage but is not necessarily a virgin. But Isaiah knows the king will reject this sign and Judah is in for a devastating time (v. 17).

Responding to the Text

"My mind is made up; don't confuse me with the facts!" Sometimes we do not want to hear the truth. Many of us have an amazing capacity for denying truth, even when it stares us in the face. A lay leader continued to insist that women could not be competent pastors. He had to admit, however, that his own very skillful and effective pastor, who happened to be a woman, was an exception.

Some of us are like King Ahaz. He doesn't want to believe the prophet's message that God would protect the nation against their enemies. He refuses to ask God for a sign but nonetheless gets one. Isaiah declares that a child named "Immanuel" would be born, and before he would be old enough to discern right from wrong these foreign powers would be a thing of the past. But Ahaz probably didn't believe even then. Like Ahaz, some of us don't want to believe the sign.

In the popular 1989 movie *Field of Dreams,* the crazy farmer builds a baseball field on his farmland. Famous ballplayers of the past come out of the cornfield once again to play their game. But the farmer's brother-in-law, Mike, doesn't want to believe such a wild reality. Only when one rookie sacrifices his role on the team to save the life of the farmer's little daughter does Mike the doubter become a believer.

What must God do to convince us skeptics? In Christ, God becomes present in the flesh. It is indeed a fact that may confuse us when we have already made up our minds. Christ is Immanuel—God with us—even when we don't see that presence and the whole thing seems a crazy field of dreams. We humans can be a stubborn lot.

But God is patient beyond our stubbornness, so the divine advent happens again and again. We celebrate the divine coming every year—not simply as a remembrance of something long ago and far away—but as an acknowledgment of God's continuous presence and Christ's endless comings to be with us. If you think your mind is made up, think again.

Responsive Reading
PSALM 80 (RCL)

Interpreting the Text

This community lament begins with the flock crying to their shepherd to exercise strength on their behalf (vv. 1-2). "How long?" laments God's anger that makes tears the community's daily food and drink (vv. 4-6). Why would God establish and then destroy their land (vv. 8-13)? They implore God to care for them again by empowering the king ("at your right hand"—vv. 14-17). Then they will become faithful (v. 18). "Let your face shine" (vv. 3, 7, and 19) asks for God's favor and protection (see Lev. 6:25).

Responding to the Text

Faces are amazingly expressive, aren't they? The face says it all, and words are unnecessary. The child is worried, knowing that he has offended his parents, but a smiling face radiating love tells him all will be OK. Faces give access to personality and character.

In the people's cry for help the psalm repeats the refrain, "Let your face shine, that we may be saved." That prayer captures our own longings to see and know God's love. Like helpless sheep we seek the shepherd's protection; like wayward children we yearn for our divine parent's smile. God has heard our prayers and in Christ's advent the divine face enlightens our world. The light of Christ is God's face shining on us.

PSALM 24 (BCP/RC)

Interpreting the Text

Other lectionaries turn to Psalm 24 on this occasion, since it sketches the character of the community that enters the Temple. The whole "earth is the Lord's," but God focuses divine presence in this sacred place (v. 1-2). Those who enter are righteous in their inner being—"pure hearts" committed to truth. But they are also right in their relationship with others—"clean hands" and without deceitful speech. Such persons are ready to welcome their King (vv. 3-7).

Responding to the Text

When guests were coming, my Mom would always tell me to wash my hands especially well. But no matter how I scrubbed, she always found stains I had not removed.

How are we to prepare to welcome our guest this Advent? The psalm emphasizes that our righteousness is to be both within us and in our daily relationships. But we Christians know our hearts are never pure and our hands never clean; we know sin has dirtied us both inwardly and outwardly. Our guest in whom God focuses divine presence (Immanuel—God with us) enters the gates of our sanctuary to offer us a purity we never achieve on our own. To him we present our hearts and hands!

WE CHRISTIANS KNOW OUR HEARTS ARE NEVER PURE AND OUR HANDS NEVER CLEAN; WE KNOW SIN HAS DIRTIED US BOTH INWARDLY AND OUTWARDLY.

SECOND READING
ROMANS 1:1-7

Interpreting the Text

Paul begins by saying "this is who I am and the gospel I preach." The salutation names the sender (vv. 1-6) and the recipients (v. 7a), and offers a greeting (v. 7b).

Paul is committed to servanthood not by his own decision but by God's decision "called" to be an "apostle" (one sent) of the "gospel." That good news centers in Christ, the fulfillment of God's promise to Israel. On the physical plane, he is of Davidic descent; on the spiritual level ("according to the spirit of holiness"), he is established "Son of God" by his resurrection. Davidic kings are "sons of God," but Jesus is God's empowered agent ("Lord," used of "God" in Hebrew Scriptures) by virtue of God's having rescued him from death (vv. 1-5).

The gospel also concerns Christ's personal benefits for Paul (vv. 5-6). Chief among them is "grace"—God's unconditional love—which issues in a concrete calling, apostleship. The gospel creates both a new relationship with God and a new purpose for living. Paul's new purpose is the incorporation of the Gentiles (including many of the Roman readers) into God's family, where they obediently enact a grace-filled life.

The readers are "saints" made holy by God's love in a specific locale (v. 7a). The greeting comes from God, our ultimate parent, and Christ, our ultimate authority. Both intend readers to participate in divine favor and the wholeness and harmony ("peace") that originate from it.

Responding to the Text

An ancient promise kept creates new life! Tracing our family roots intrigues many of us today. We follow a map of generations back as far as records allow. Invariably we bump into ancestors who migrated to this nation compelled by its promise of a new life—perhaps captured in something as simple as land to farm. Or maybe such an exploration jolts us with the fact that our ancestors came here under duress and miraculously fashioned promise out of servitude. In either case, we unearth promise buried somewhere in our histories, and that casts our lives in new perspectives. Alex Haley's memorable book *Roots* did that for many African Americans. The old promise enlivens the present.

In introducing himself and his understanding of the gospel to Christians in Rome, Paul names this as the first feature of the message he brings: "the gospel of God . . . promised beforehand through his prophets in holy scriptures." In Christ, God keeps the ancient divine promise, and that act yields a new life. For Paul the new life is grace and apostleship—a new relationship with God because of divine love and a new purpose for living. He unearths the ancestral promise and its fulfillment as the basis of a new life for us today.

THE CELEBRATION OF GOD'S ADVENT IN CHRIST AWAKENS THE PROMISE THAT WE ARE DESTINED TO BE GOD'S FAMILY.

Martin Luther King Jr. and other leaders in the African American community have done a similar thing in our nation. They have claimed the venerable promise of America as their own, and through their effort to see that promise kept they have created new possibilities for our society.

Running throughout Paul's first words to the Roman Christians is the marriage of God's reclamation of us as children and the life of faith. For the apostle, God's grace brought his calling. But the same is true for all Christians, for we too are called into a new relationship with our Creator and then into the "obedience of faith." An ancient promise kept creates new life belonging to Jesus and new life in living our faith.

In our Lord's nativity God keeps the promise. The celebration of God's advent in Christ awakens the promise that we are destined to be God's family.

GOSPEL

MATTHEW 1:18-25

Interpreting the Text

Joseph takes the spotlight in this scene. The genealogy concludes with Jesus (1:16) then tells how his birth "took place." The story follows a simple narrative plotline moving from conflict to resolution.

The conflict (vv. 18b-19): Betrothal entailed a legal agreement to marry, and constituted a bond that could be broken only through the process of formal divorce. Hence, Joseph is called Mary's "husband." A woman's pregnancy by another during betrothal constituted adultery and was grounds for divorce (see 5:32). Chagrined though he might be when he learns Mary is pregnant, Joseph is a "just man" and wishes his betrothed no harm. A "quiet divorce" is planned. The narrator, of course, tips us off with the news that the pregnancy is the result not of human but divine activity (v. 18).

The resolution (vv. 20-25): God upsets Joseph's plans. Like many Old Testament stories, God resolves the situation through an angel appearing in a dream. Angels provide the hotline between the transcendent realm and humans, while dreams are often taken to be a medium of divine communication. The angel addresses Joseph as "son of David," underscoring Jesus' messianic credentials as a descendent of David, and quiets his emotions with the words "do not be afraid." This evangelist rivets attention on Jesus' conception through the Spirit's work. "Jesus" is a shortened form of the Hebrew *Joshua,* which means "Yahweh helps," but help is equated with rescue or salvation. The angel lets Joseph in on God's plan for Jesus in humanity's salvation.

Through a series of fourteen fulfillment passages (for example, 2:15-16) Matthew accents the continuity of God's work in Christ with divine activity in the Old Testament. *Fulfill* is a rich word that in this case means "to bring to completion." In these passages the Gospel writer taps the richness of Scripture to mean something more than its original historical reference. That is clearly the case in the use of Isaiah 7:14 (see the first lesson, above). The Hebrew word (translated "young woman") is rendered here "virgin" in accord with the Greek translation of the Old Testament. The title "Immanuel" takes us to the heart of Matthew's view of Christ (see Matt. 28:20, Isa. 8:8 and 8:10).

Abstinence from "marital relations" highlights both Mary's virginity (Jesus' conception by the Spirit) and Joseph's faithfulness. Complying with the angel's command, they name the child Jesus. Joseph's conflict is eased through his obedience to divine revelation (vv. 24-25).

Responding to the Text

Joseph is in a corner! What is he to do? His betrothed is pregnant with a child that is not his own. Like any of us would, he resorts to what he thinks to be right and proper. He would divorce her quietly—no public show, no tabloid stories. It is the suitable thing to do. But then he gets a message. This is a special child conceived by God. He is told to go against his own sense of righteousness and wed Mary.

The best any of us can do is be faithful to what we know is right and good, to what we think we know of God's will. But sometimes God surprises us; sometimes God challenges our knowledge and questions our actions. Then we discover what Joseph learned: Our knowledge of God's will is but a tiny speck in the vast divine mind. What are we to do then? That becomes Joseph's second dilemma. Shall he trust his dream, this new assertion of the divine will? Or shall he stick with what he knows best?

God surprises us with a new righteousness, and our sense of the right and good is shattered. Dietrich Bonhoeffer, the famous German Christian of the mid-twentieth century, understood that experience. He wrote, "all thought remains in itself so long as existence remains in itself. But revelation, the Word, leads existence out of itself into a state of self-criticism."[6] He practiced his words when the Nazi regime drew him out of his sense of righteousness. In a daring act of Christian conscience, Bonhoeffer participated in a plot to end Hitler's life. For Bonhoeffer the situation called for a new righteousness, and he trusted what he discerned to be God's will at the time. His decision cost him his life.

WE ALL FIND SITUATIONS CHALLENGING OUR OWN SENSE OF GOD'S RIGHTEOUSNESS AND CATCH GLIMMERS OF A NEW RIGHTEOUSNESS FOR OUR DAY.

Most of us may not find ourselves in situations as unique as Joseph's or Bonhoeffer's. But we do find situations challenging our own sense of God's righteousness and catch glimmers of a new righteousness for our day. A woman learns that divorce is necessary, even though she was always taught otherwise. A man sits in the pew with a gay couple, although his past led him to think homosexuality violated divine will. The congregation welcomes a new member in the baptism of a child born out of wedlock, even if they never thought God welcomed such children.

God is always inviting us to new righteousness and confounding us with grace, as Amos Wilder's poem says:

> He came when he wasn't expected
>   as He always does . . .
> He is always one step ahead of us;

> the space-age calls for new maps
> and its altars and holy places are not yet marked.[7]

In the birth of Immanuel, God again comes unexpectedly to confound us with divine grace. Where will this child lead us? What new map for our day will this child chart? What new altars and holy places will he mark for us? Following him invites us out of contentment and complacency into an unknown land. He is always a step ahead of us.

A gift of love such as this pulls us into its draft. It pulled one person I know out of his depression and into a new confidence, out of an old life into an adventure with a new lifestyle. Because God valued him in Christ, he learned to value himself. Like Joseph, he obeyed and followed the divine message he received. In this Advent, God asks us for trust and obedience and gives us salvation and love.

THE SEASON OF CHRISTMAS

ROBERT KYSAR

UNSUPPORTED PROMISES ARE A dime a dozen! We hear endless promises in our society, too many of which go unfulfilled. God's promise is of a different sort. Unlike human promises, the divine promise is rooted in God's faithfulness.

The Christmas season is an expression of God's enduring commitment to humanity. The expectations stirred in Advent find their reason in a single historical event that gathers up all the divine promise for the future and thrusts us on in trust into what may lie ahead. The nativity event stands at the pinnacle of history, drawing on the past and leading us into the future. As we gather around that manger, we begin our pilgrimage with Christ to the cross and the empty tomb.

Christmas confronts us with the scandal of Christianity's particularity—that God would reveal the divine self in a single human life at a particular time and place in the world's history. Faith is born within us as that particularity challenges reason and contradicts logic. In the Christmas season we celebrate the nucleus of Christian faith.

CHRISTMAS CONFRONTS US WITH THE SCANDAL OF CHRISTIANITY'S PARTICULARITY—THAT GOD WOULD REVEAL THE DIVINE SELF IN A SINGLE HUMAN LIFE AT A PARTICULAR TIME AND PLACE IN THE WORLD'S HISTORY.

But Christmas happens in a real world where evil does battle with God's will. So the lessons for the season include not just the nativity story but the sobering word of Christ's rejection. In Series A that rejection is represented in Matthew's story of Herod's slaughter of the innocents and in John's reference to the world's refusal of the divine Word. The season acknowledges human condition.

The Christmas proclamation is saturated with promise, but promise held in faith. While society is content to celebrate the sentimentality of the season and to revive human goodwill, Christ's nativity recenters the faith community in the whole Christian story in all its realism and particularity.

NATIVITY OF OUR LORD 1

CHRISTMAS EVE DECEMBER 24, 1998

REVISED COMMON	EPISCOPAL (BCP)	ROMAN CATHOLIC
Isa. 9:2-7	Isa. 9:2-4, 6-7	Isa. 9:2-7
Ps. 96	Ps. 96 or 96:1-4, 11-12	Ps. 96:1-3, 11-13
Titus 2:11-14	Titus 2:11-14	Titus 2:11-14
Luke 2:1-14 (15-20)	Luke 2:1-14 (15-20)	Luke 2:1-14

THE WAITING IS OVER. God begins a new dominion in the world. Luke's story of Jesus' ordinary birth is accompanied by an extraordinary announcement of its meaning. Isaiah declares that a reversal has begun with a new king who enlightens a people engulfed in darkness. Psalm 96 invites a new song of joy that expresses an unprecedented perspective on life. God's grace has appeared, the epistle lesson asserts, and Christ has begun forming his own new people. In the context of the nativity celebration, the lessons gather around the manger, each displaying one of the colors in the Christmas spectrum.

FIRST READING
ISAIAH 9:2-7

Interpreting the Text

A reversal has begun. The lesson is part of 8:23—9:7. The unit's historical setting is debated, but it promises a prince who will rescue the people. The reading first describes the new reality (vv. 2-5) before announcing its cause (vv. 6-7).

An atmosphere of mystery fills verse 2 that invokes the ancient symbolism of light and darkness. "Walked" and "lived" cut to the heart of how people are to conduct their lives. The "light" illumines the path and eliminates the dangers of life's journey. The details of that illumination are specified in vv. 3-5. The nation acknowledges that it is God who multiplies their strength and joy. Oppression is defeated as Gideon had done (see Judges 6). Warfare becomes a thing of the past.

The new reality is the result of the birth of a very special prince whose rule is authorized beyond himself (v. 6). His dominion will earn him new throne names, each of which is comprised of two words—an adjective and a noun. "Wonderful Counselor" names his just and wise decisions; "Mighty God" describes his skill in battle; "Everlasting Father" epitomizes his commitment to the people's welfare; and "Prince of Peace" designates him as the origin of wholeness within the nation. So equipped he will gradually transform the nation with his rule—not temporarily but for all time.

But the new king comes as the result of more than political maneuvering. God's faithful commitment to the people ("zeal") alone accomplishes it.

Responding to the Text

Darkness awakens fear within us. The child's apprehension of darkness speaks a primary insecurity deep in all humans. Darkness is dangerous! In darkness we stumble when we try to walk. Without light, we become vulnerable to all life's dangers.

Sometimes our lives seem like we are trying to walk in darkness. We cannot see the accident that is about to happen, the disease that is about to strike, or the circumstance soon upon us. But the darkness also can be within us. Arthur Miller's *Death of a Salesman* recounts the last years of Willy Loman. At Willy's funeral, one of his sons remarks, "the man never knew who he was."[8] The darkness of never knowing who we are threatens many of us.

But the prophet claims that God will not allow us to live within a pit of darkness. He claims a light has shone, the darkness has been penetrated, and a new reality created. All this because of the birth of a child who shall be the source of light to overcome life's darkness.

We know how light can rescue us when we are captured in the darkness. Finding the light switch on the wall can make all the difference in the world. In Christ's birth God lights the way for us. This baby born in Bethlehem is the prism through which the truth of God's love shines within our darkened lives.

A cyclist entered a tunnel with her sunglasses on. At first it seemed no problem. She focused on the silhouette of her companion ahead of her. But then suddenly that image disappeared, and she was engulfed in darkness. She became disoriented. Where was the center line of the highway? How far was she from the tunnel walls on either side? As panic swept through her, from the corner of her eye she glimpsed a splinter of light. The tunnel had curved, taking her companion out of her eyesight. But now she saw the light of the tunnel's end and could find her way out. Christmas is the splinter of light from the end of the tunnel that lightens our path.

Responsive Reading
PSALM 96

Interpreting the Text

Verses 1-4 and 11-12 are a call to praise, and 13 gives reason for praise. The whole psalm pivots around God's universal kingship (vv. 3 and 10).

The call to praise invites a new perspective on the world in light of its ruler, who is the source of salvation for the nations and nature. Such an orientation evokes a "new song" from all people and all things as the expression of new life—all because God comes as the righteous judge to bring justice to all.

Responding to the Text

"What's new?" They are words of greeting that also pose a fundamental question. Amid all the innovations of our time, injustice and brokenness seem never to change. So, what's new this Christmas?

The psalmist declares that God's coming creates a new reality. In Christ, God comes to reveal what is real, true, and lasting amid the flux of our world, and our lives become new songs. On the occasion of the demolition of the Berlin Wall, Richard Bernstein put new words to Beethoven's Ninth Symphony making it an ode to freedom. What is new this Christmas is our ode to freedom from the interminable brokenness our world, for now there is One who "judges the world with righteousness" and "truth."

Second Reading
TITUS 2:11-14

Interpreting the Text

In these verses the epistle's author roots all of chapter two's exhortations to new life in God's act in Christ. The lesson begins with the disclosure of God's grace and its implications for behavior (vv. 11-13); it climaxes in Christ's making us his own people (v. 14).

God's unmerited love is the source of a new relationship between all humans and their Creator ("salvation"). God's gracious nature was not a new attitude but "appeared" in Christ. That grace becomes our tutor in righteous living during the interim before Christ's triumphant reappearance. Grace and hope are sources of a specific lifestyle, for they evoke new behavior fitting both what God has done and will yet do. That behavior is both a rejection of worldly standards and an enactment of God's own graciousness. Christ is named "Savior" and even "God"—the latter representing a rare equation of God and Christ in the New Testament (vv. 11-13).

Christ is both "God" and "Savior" by virtue of what he accomplished for us. In his self-giving death he frees us from sin so that we can be "a people of his own." Purification draws on the vocabulary of religious sacrifice to suggest our readiness to offer ourselves to God. Our restoration, then, seeks a divine goal. It forms us into a community whose life is in and for Christ himself and whose behavior is passionately devoted ("zealous") to "good deeds" for others (v. 14).

GRACE AND HOPE ARE SOURCES OF A SPECIFIC LIFESTYLE, FOR THEY EVOKE NEW BEHAVIOR FITTING BOTH WHAT GOD HAS DONE AND WILL YET DO.

Responding to the Text

Amid all the preparations for Christmas day, do you sometimes ask yourself, "What's the purpose of all of this?" *What's the purpose?* is a perfectly proper question, for we want our actions—even our lives—to be purposeful. *What's the purpose?* is an important question to ask on the occasion of Christ's nativity.

God goes about all the effort preparing us for this day, of bringing about the birth of the divine Son in Bethlehem, and of sending angels and directing shepherds. What's the purpose of it all? Yes, in one sense it is to bring peace to a troubled world. In another sense it is to let us in on God's love and solicit our love.

But the author of today's second lesson sees another purpose to Christ's advent. The goal God has in mind in Christ's coming is to make us Christ's own people. In Christ, God intends to gather a community, to form a family, and to nurture citizens of another realm, for God knows that we often feel like orphans who have no parents and belong to no family. Many of us know the loneliness of being in a crowd and belonging to no one. Our very identity seems woven into our belonging to a community.

The movie *Toy Story* is the account of an imaginary community of toys that live in the bedroom of a boy named Andy. When Buzz Lightyear, a new toy, is introduced to Andy's family, he insists that he is a real space ranger. After finally learning he is actually only a toy, he is at first depressed. But then the family of toys must cope with a series of crises. Through them, Buzz discovers his real identity and his purpose as a member of Andy's community of toys.

Christmas offers the good news that God is forming a new people in Christ and that our identity and purpose reside in belonging to God. We are a people who understand that we owe our lives and all that is good and right to God's love that appears in that Bethlehem manger. Christmas is the invitation to us all to become a part of Christ's own people.

Gospel
LUKE 2:1-20

Interpreting the Text

The account of Jesus' birth is starkly simple, especially after the events of chapter 1. The lesson has three components: a setting (vv. 1-5), the birth itself (vv. 6-7), and the shepherds' visit to the manger (vv. 8-20).

The historical setting is important, since Jesus' birth is not to be confused with mythological accounts of the origin of the gods (see also 1:5). Luke dates the event by naming the current rulers (vv. 1-2) and then gives the specific occasion—a registration probably for the purposes of taxation. That occasion emphasizes Joseph's Bethlehem roots and Davidic descent. Engagement constituted a legal relationship, so the pregnant Mary must accompany Joseph on the journey. The reader expects a marvelous birth scene but finds it reduced to only two succinct verses. The untimely delivery is complicated by the family's homelessness. (On "firstborn" see 2:23.)

The shepherds' experience, however, contrasts sharply to the simplicity of the birth itself. "Shepherds" trigger recollections of David (1 Sam. 17:15), of Israel's king (for instance, Jer. 3:15), and even of God (for instance, Ezek. 34:15). But by the first century shepherds had become suspicious migrants who lived on society's margins. Yet they are the first to hear the announcement of the birth, for they represent the lowly and despised who are blessed by this birth (see 1:52). They are the poor to whom "good news" is preached (4:18), but it is welcomed news for "all people." The angel's announcement uses three titles, each filled with promise: "Savior" (used of God in 1:47), "Messiah," and "Lord," all attributed to one born in David's hometown (v. 11). The angel's message ends with a "sign" to enable the shepherds to find this extraordinary baby.

The "heavenly host"—the community that surrounds God—interprets the meaning of the event. The whole of reality is affected. In heaven there is praise, and on earth, peace (v. 14). "Those whom he favors" puts emphasis on what

God does. Goodwill is neither a requirement for the peace Christ brings nor a manifestation of that peace. "Favors" designates God's gracious and free regard (see 12:32).

The shepherds immediately seek the child whose identity has been revealed to them. They share their experience with all who will listen, and all are surprised ("amazed") by their witness. Mary preserves their words and considers their meaning (vv. 16–19). The story concludes with the shepherds returning to their daily task filled with gratitude for the divine pleasure bestowed on them and the world (v. 20).

Responding to the Text

Beware of the ordinary! Watch out for the mundane! Surprises often come packaged in the dull, brown-paper wrapping of everyday events! Isn't that often the case? Most accidents, we are told, happen in the home amid daily chores. The most precious gifts are often surprise interruptions of our daily routines.

The birth of Jesus, as told by Luke, has that flavor to it. Two ordinary and common people journey together to fulfill a legal requirement. The birth is routine and without distinction. They wrap the new baby in cloth as was the custom of the time. Nothing at all extraordinary about it. Even the shepherds are about their daily chore on a nearby hillside—just another night of tending the flock. But then the surprise pops out. An angel with a startling message. The heavenly host singing the meaning of this "ordinary" birth. Suddenly the announcement of who this child really is transforms the commonplace features of the story.

THE CHRISTMAS STORY WARNS US TO WATCH OUT FOR THE ORDINARY, FOR GOD MAY BE PRESENT THERE.

The Christmas story warns us to watch out for the ordinary, for God may be present there. In an imaginative sermon, Allen Oliver speaks on behalf of the donkey, whose stall is invaded by the holy family in Bethlehem. The disgruntled donkey is impressed that this is an undistinguished birth, but then the shepherds enter and tell their story.

> This angel talks to strange people. First, he talks to these two—a carpenter and his wife. Then he talks to shepherds. Boy, that's some weirdo angel! You'd think with news like that he'd talk to kings and princes, prophets and priests, and people like that. No, he talks to carpenters, shepherds, and women. That's sure some weirdo angel![9]

"Weirdo angel," indeed! God intervening in ordinary circumstances and communicating good news to the likes of shepherds and common folk. Christmas alerts us to God in the commonplace, to the divine fondness for inhabiting the common. But there is more: The news is that God visits humanity in the form of a flesh-and-blood baby! This occasion sensitizes us to divine presence in our daily routines and to watch for angelic messages concealed in human dress.

After the shepherds have visited the manger and told their story, Luke tells us they "returned" to their flock and their regular chores. But their lives would never be the same, for now they will forever be attentive to God's intrusion into the common. So, too, will we return from this place and from this season watching for the divine where we expect only the human. As one mother said, after some hunters had rescued her son from certain death, angels are real but do not have wings.

As Christ is present in ordinary bread and wine, so God always meets us in life's banal realities.

Might God's love be in the simple smile, handshake, or hug of a friend? Might the divine will be concealed within the advice of a sister or brother in Christ? Might Christ meet us in our needy neighbor asking for food, shelter, or clothing? Years after I first heard them, I realized that a friend's unwelcomed comments about me were exactly true, even though I resisted them. I now know God spoke truth to me through a wingless angel in that ordinary conversation.

We Christians celebrate the divine habitation in the commonplace each time we break bread and pour wine together around this table. As Christ is present in ordinary bread and wine, so God always meets us in life's banal realities. God inhabits flesh and blood in the Christ child and continues to be there in and under the daily events of our lives.

Beware of the ordinary!

NATIVITY OF OUR LORD 2
CHRISTMAS DAWN

DECEMBER 25, 1998

REVISED COMMON	EPISCOPAL (BCP)	ROMAN CATHOLIC
Isa. 62:6-12	Isa. 62:6-7, 10-12	Isa. 62:11-12
Psalm 97	Ps. 97 or 97:1-4, 11-12	Ps. 97:1, 6, 11-12
Titus 3:4-7	Titus 3:4-7	Titus 3:4-7
Luke 2:(1-7), 8-20	Luke 2:(1-14), 15-20	Luke 2:15-20

PARADOX PERMEATES THESE PASSAGES. Isaiah reminds us of how God faithfully keeps the divine promises and what that means for God's people. Psalm 97 penetrates behind faithfulness to celebrate God's character and the good news it entails for Israel. Titus 3 affirms the divine character described in the psalm but goes further to summarize how the divine act in Christ transforms human existence. The Gospel lesson, however, relates the birth of a tiny baby in an obscure village. The paradox is that this mighty God appears among us in the most unlikely form and fulfills promises in ways we would never expect.

FIRST READING
ISAIAH 62:6-12

Interpreting the Text

God will not forget the divine pledge to Israel. This fragment of Third Isaiah (chapters 56–66) is part of chapters 60–62 focused on the restoration of Jerusalem. Verses 6-9 assure readers that God remembers Jerusalem, and the concluding verses suggest the results of God's remembrance.

The "I" in verses 6-9 is God, who like a king appoints assistants to remind the ruler of programs to be accomplished. The "sentinels" are symbols of the divine memory, constantly keeping God mindful of the promise. God will not forget the vow to make Jerusalem great among the nations (vv. 6-7), for the Lord has taken a solemn oath about the destiny of the people (v. 8a). Farmers will consume their own harvests and no longer have to surrender them to invading armies or the taxation of oppressive regimes (v. 8b). They will be able to present the first fruits to God in the "holy courts" (v. 9).

The tone shifts in verses 10-12, which recall bits of earlier portions of Isaiah (for example, compare v. 10 and 52:11). The "way" refers to the path of obedient living, and the "ensign" to a universal announcement that God has reestablished the city. God has rescued the people and brought about their just "reward" (v. 11). Therefore, Israel receives four new names, each of which result from God's faithfulness to the divine promise (v. 12). A radical change necessitates a new name, since a name represents the essential character of an individual or a people (see 62:2).

Responding to the Text

Names are important. If for whatever reason we should take a new name, it is as if we take on a new identity. On the occasion of their marriage, some couples choose to take new last names, often hyphenating their two last names to produce a new one. They do so because they feel their marriage makes them new people.

What's your name? Who are you? Many of us have wrestled with those questions. In a television drama, a patient in a hospital suffers from severe amnesia. So serious is his loss of memory that he doesn't know his identity. He wanders about the hospital floors, taking on different identities, pretending to be a psychiatrist or a pediatrician. With each new identity he adopts a new name. He would have been comical had his condition not been so tragic. He suggests the loss of identity many of us have experienced, and his change of names reminds us of our own sense of namelessness.

> Christmas renames us! God changes our identity with the birth of the beloved Son in Bethlehem. Rescuing us in Christ from our desolation, God makes new people of us and gives us new names.

In the ancient biblical world, people's names were thought to identify their essential character. Isaiah declares that the people of Israel are given new names to indicate that God had rescued them from their desolation. "They shall be called, 'The Holy People, The Redeemed of the Lord.'" God reestablishes them in their homeland, changing their identity; hence, they receive new names.

A young woman struggled through the process of finding her true identity after a painful divorce. As she began to realize who she really was apart from the oppression of a destructive marriage, she took a new name that symbolized her new life. Her name, she believed, represented who she had become.

Christmas renames us! God changes our identity with the birth of the beloved

Son in Bethlehem. Rescuing us in Christ from our desolation, God makes new people of us and gives us new names. We are no longer called "lonely," but "befriended of God"; no longer "desolate," but "embraced"; no longer "loveless," but "beloved." In Christ's birth God keeps faith with us and opens new possibilities for our lives. Christmas renames us God's beloved children!

Responsive Reading
PSALM 97

Interpreting the Text

This song of praise celebrates God's universal reign through describing the character of the divine ruler in terms of power (vv. 2-5), singularity (vv. 6-9), and righteousness (vv. 10-12).

Successive images of mystery, consuming fire, lightning, and heat picture God's power. The true God illumines the meaninglessness of all other objects of worship, and cherishes, protects, and "rescues" those committed to the good. The divine rule is the first light of dawn for such people and is the cause of their joy.

Responding to the Text

I like stories in which the good triumphs over evil. Evil seems so powerful that many of us hunger for assurance that goodness will reign.

Our psalm voices a dimension of Christ's nativity that offers us an antidote for cynicism and hopelessness. God's reign begun in Christ's birth promises us who will have the last word in the cosmos. It is, as the psalm says, the dawning of new light. A dawn is at first unobtrusive. Before the sun appears on the horizon, it begins to lighten the sky. Those slivers of light promise a new day. The light emitted from the stable signals the reign of a righteous King and invites us to trust the daylight that follows.

Second Reading
TITUS 3:4-7

Interpreting the Text

This portion of the epistle is a bit of the author's suggestions to Titus for his ministry and sounds like a mini-creed. The reading has two parts: God's rescue in Christ (vv. 4-5) and the gift of the Spirit (vv. 6-7).

In spite of humanity's foolish disobedience and immorality (see v. 3), God's compassion and generosity emerged in Christ. "Loving kindness" translates a Greek word which might literally be rendered "love of humans." Out of those divine features, God extricates us from our predicament. That act arose from God's merciful nature alone and not from any human endeavor to achieve merit. "Works of righteousness" identify deeds done out of a natural human capacity for the purpose of achieving some acceptance in God's eyes (see Rom. 3:28). God's compassion is channeled through a washing with "the water of rebirth" (doubtless an allusion to baptism—see John 3:3-8). "Renewal by the Holy Spirit" is associated with that revitalizing (see, for example, the link between the Spirit and baptism in Acts 9:17-18).

But the Spirit's renewing power came from Christ (v. 6; see also Acts 2:14-18). "So that" (Greek, *hina*) attaches the Spirit to the inheritance of hope (see 2 Cor. 5:5). Justification is God's gracious acceptance of us into a relationship, and "faith" our trustful reception of that gift. To become "heirs according to the hope of eternal life" is to be promised a life unbound by death.

As a whole, the passage states basic Christian beliefs in a nutshell.

Responding to the Text

In Jon Hassler's novel *Rookery Blues*, Victor Dash is a loud, foul-spoken, cynical, argumentative, and intimidating professor of English. He is notorious for his quick temper and sharp criticism of the college where he teaches. Generally his colleagues tolerate him but treat him gingerly so as not to arouse his caustic side. Then one day a group of them see Victor with his three children. Lovingly and tenderly he guides them across the college campus. Suddenly he appears to his associates in a different role, not the rough, tough critic but a caring and compassionate parent.

BUT THEN IN THE BIRTH OF GOD'S BELOVED SON A NEW SIDE OF GOD APPEARS: LOVING, COMPASSIONATE, AND GRACIOUS. AND OUR RELATIONSHIP WITH GOD IS NEVER THE SAME.

Many of us have had the experience of seeing another side to a person we thought we knew, and our new insight changes our relationship with that individual. The author of the epistle to Titus seems to suggest something like that happens when God appears in Christ: "But when the goodness and loving kindness of God our Savior appeared, he saved us . . . " God had seemed a demanding judge and a stern ruler. But then in the birth of God's beloved Son a new side of God appears: loving, compassionate, and gracious. And our relationship with God is never the same. In the divine appearance in Christ we come to know God's merciful acceptance of us. In spite of who we are, God loves and forgives us and invites us into the divine family.

Christmas is the appearance of God's love—a love so boundless that it embraces us even though we are often unlovable. In another scene in Hassler's novel, the ten-year-old Laura speaks of her mother's loss of patience with her alcoholic father. She recounts her mother's words: "I've had all I can take, I've reached my limit, I'm worn out!" Then Laura asks, "How could you possibly reach your limit with somebody you loved?"[10]

Christmas celebrates God's limitless love for us—a love that does not give up on us but continues without reserve in spite of our addiction to sin. In the divine love found in that Bethlehem babe we at last understand the extent of God's commitment to us.

Gospel
LUKE 2:1-20

See "Nativity of Our Lord 1/Christmas Eve" above, pp. 38–40.

NATIVITY OF OUR LORD 3 CHRISTMAS DAY

DECEMBER 25, 1998

REVISED COMMON	EPISCOPAL (BCP)	ROMAN CATHOLIC
Isa. 52:7-10	Isa. 52:7-10	Isa. 52:7-10
Ps. 98	Ps. 98 or 98:1-6	Ps. 98:1-6
Heb. 1:1-4, (5-12)	Heb. 1:1-12	Heb. 1:1-6
John 1:1-14	John 1:1-14	John 1:1-18 or 1:1-5, 9-14

THE LESSONS REVOLVE AROUND God's victory. Both Isaiah 52 and Psalm 98 celebrate that victory and what it solicits from God's people. The Hebrews reading continues the theme by speaking of the character of Christ ("the reflection of God's own glory") and the essence of divine being through whom God's victory is accomplished. John 1 names the agent of the divine victory as the Word who came to dwell among us as a human. While our Christmas celebration is a victorious occasion, the prologue of John keeps us aware of the reality of the rejection of the Word.

FIRST READING
ISAIAH 52:7-10

Interpreting the Text

This portion of Third Isaiah is a song of praise for what God is about to do in defeating Babylon. The first verse announces the good news, and verses 8-10 invite praise for what God has done.

The messenger of the news bulletin is welcomed as "beautiful" for Jerusalem's inhabitants. The message is described in four parallel expressions, climaxing in "Your God reigns." "Peace" means the wholeness of harmony and is "salvation" in the sense of rescue or victory (v. 7). The imagery of verse 8 is drawn from the scene of the sentries posted on the city wall who are the first to spot the king returning after defeating the enemy.

The word of God's triumphant return produces singing in the streets of the devastated city (v. 9). "For" introduces the reasons for song, stated in four consecutive declarations of what God has done: comforted, redeemed, bared his holy arm, and saved (vv. 9b–10). "Comfort" names the assurance brought by God's victory, and "redeemed" here means reclaimed or recovered. God's "arm" is a standard metaphor for power, and to bare the arm pictures the warrior throwing back his garment to draw his sword. The prophet declares that the defeat of Israel's enemies will inform all the nations of God's faithfulness to the people.

Responding to the Text

Imagine the scene that day many years ago when the news bulletin announced the end of World War II. There was dancing in the streets that "V-Day." Our troops were returning, triumphant in a war that had taken thousands upon thousands of lives. How beautiful that news was! Victory at last!

But how strange that image is this day. Compare it to the silent night on which our Lord was born in a stable. What dissonance there is between these scenes: Isaiah's picture of God's triumphant and victorious return to Jerusalem after defeating Israel's enemies, and God's quiet appearance in a baby wrapped in birth cloths in a manger in Bethlehem. The comparison of these scenes captures the mystery of our Lord's nativity. How does God reign? Through an infant child, born to common people in a tiny village in Palestine. Is this any way for the King of the universe to reign?

HOW DOES GOD REIGN? THROUGH AN INFANT CHILD, BORN TO COMMON PEOPLE IN A TINY VILLAGE IN PALESTINE. IS THIS ANY WAY FOR THE KING OF THE UNIVERSE TO REIGN?

God often claims us as children in the most inconspicuous ways. A mother led her two young daughters to the communion table to receive the bread and wine. One of the little girls was restless, so her mom picked her up. There she stood holding one child with in one arm and the second in her other arm. The communion assistant came to her with the plate containing the Eucharistic wafers, but both her hands were filled! The little girl she was holding looked at the wafers then at her mother and promptly reached down, picked up a wafer, and put it in her mother's mouth. Inconspicuously a child fed her mother with the body of Christ, and inconspicuously God claimed them all as members of the divine family.

So there is a sense in which the reading of Isaiah is appropriate this day, for the infant Jesus is our King whose rule in our lives rescues us from enemies who would do us in. "Your God reigns!" through that One who will go to the cross for us. Today is a V-Day! Because today the news bulletin is issued: God has defeated the forces that imprisoned us. But, my, look at how God has done it!

RESPONSIVE READING
PSALM 98

Interpreting the Text

This song to solicit songs begins with the invitation to voice "a new song," then proceeds to specify why the occasion is one for rejoicing (vv. 1b-3). God is victorious in redressing wrong, and faithful in keeping the promise to Israel. Verses 4-6 bid the people to use all their musical instruments in the service of praise, and the natural order will join in with its own brand of music (vv. 7-8). Like humans, it too yearns for righteousness (v. 9).

Responding to the Text

Have you ever felt the joy of learning that someone remembered you, perhaps on a holiday or a birthday? It is a pleasure to know another has not forgotten you.

This psalm celebrates the joy of having God remember Israel. But sometimes we think surely God has forgotten us—we who regard ourselves as insignificant specks in the cosmos. We feel like the child left at a service station restroom by her parents. But Christ's birth informs us that God has not forgotten us or abandoned us along the roadside. Instead, God comes in the infant Jesus to be among us as one of us and thereby to embrace us in loving arms.

SECOND READING
HEBREWS 1:1-12

Interpreting the Text

Hebrews begins with a creedlike statement about Christ (vv. 1-3) followed by an argument for Christ's superiority to angels (vv. 4-14).

The author claims that God's speaking through Christ climaxes a history of divine communication with humans (vv. 1-2a). "Prophets" is used in a general way here to include all God's agents throughout Israel's history. Christ is God's pure and untainted voice, since his relationship with God is unique ("Son," which is contrasted to "prophets"—see John 1:1-2). As God's child, Christ inherits all that belongs to God and is the medium through which everything is created and held up (vv. 2b and 3a). Christ's divine nature is portrayed in two images in verse 3: "reflection of God's glory" (the radiance of the divine presence) and "imprint of God's very being" (the representation of divine essence). The author summarizes Christ's death as a cleansing of sin, and with the snapshot of Christ's position at the place of highest honor next to God condenses his resurrection-ascension (v. 3).

Tagged onto this compressed confession of Christ's identity is the introduction to the author's argument that Christ is superior to the angels (v. 4). That argument consists of the citation of a number of psalms. In the first set of three passages God speaks to or about the divine Son (vv. 5-6). The next pair contrasts the angels' temporary nature (they are like "wind" and "fire") with Christ's eternal character (vv. 7-12).

Responding to the Text

To whom should we listen? It's hard to know these days. There are so many voices pleading for our attention and so many different messages that all claim to be important. Advertisers would have us believe that even our choice of deodorants is crucial to our well-being. To whom do we listen? Whose voice is really important?

God has a history of communicating messages to humans, but there is one voice that stands out as the pure Word of God. The second lesson begins with just that claim: "Long ago God spoke to our ancestors . . . by the prophets, but in these last days he has spoken to us by a Son . . ." This last voice speaks to us with clarity and authority, for the Son is the very heart of God. His voice is a reflection of God's will and is imprinted with the divine mind.

That voice first spoke in an infant's cry years ago in a meager manger. An infant's cry that was later to speak the words of good news for us. His voice seems sometimes to be drowned out in the torrents of messages we hear today, but if we listen carefully we can still hear his purifying message of love and forgiveness.

Not long ago there was an African American teenager (let's call him William) who lived in a subsidized housing project in an urban area. William heard the voices of many saying that he would never amount to anything, that he was an inferior and deprived youth. But in another setting he heard other voices that spoke to him about God's love and how very precious he was to his Creator. To whom should he listen? To which of the voices should he attend? William chose to hear Christ's voice speaking through Scripture, the sacraments, and the community of faith. Listening to it, he went on to college and is now a teacher.

Listen now!
Hear the infant's first cries.
Listen now!
Hear God's heart speaking words of love.

Gospel

JOHN 1:1-18

Interpreting the Text

The introduction to the Fourth Gospel is a hymn that sings of who Christ is. It has these parts: vv. 1-4—the relation of the Word to God; vv. 5 and 9—the Word as light; vv. 6-8—the Baptizer as a witness to that light; vv. 10-13—the Word's rejection and the gift he gives to those who accept him. Verse 14—the Word became a human; v. 15—the Baptizer's witness to him; and vv. 16-18—the benefits of his appearance.

The hymn begins in a time before all time with both the Word's identity with and distinction from God ("was with . . . was"). "Word" translates *logos* which implies both the Hebraic "Word of the Lord" and the Greek concept of the mind of the cosmos. This mysterious Word was the agent of creation and the source of "life" (that is, true human existence). That life is then pictured as "light," meaning the universal illumination of reality. Even the powerful absence of light (that is, false human existence) could not subdue this true light (vv. 1-5).

Lifting Christ out of his humanness does violence to the starkness of John's message: He became flesh!

An aside distinguishes the Baptizer from this light and defines his role as one who points to the light. He is later quoted performing that role (vv. 6 and 9).

Now this divine illumination enters the world he has created, but is rejected. In spite of the fact that the world is "his own" possession, the people who in fact belong to him refuse to welcome him. On the other hand, those who do welcome and trust him receive a power to be reborn as God's children (vv. 9-13).

This Christ-Word came into the world by becoming a human himself and dwelling temporarily (camping out) among humans. In the Word-become-human, people of faith perceive God's very own presence ("glory") among them, as only a child could represent her or his parents' presence. "Grace and truth" are attributes of God's own self turned toward humanity (v. 14).

Since Christ is the embodiment of God, who is the whole of all reality, through him one gift after another is piled on believers—benefits that are distinct from those of the Old Testament. God's commands are known through "Moses," but the gracious side of God and its importance for life are known only through Christ. Even though no one is privileged to look on God, in the divine Son we glimpse the heart of God, for he comes from that divine heart (vv. 16-17).

Responding to the Text

It is almost embarrassing! To claim that this newborn infant, wrapped in rags to protect him from the cold of the night, is actually God's own Son come among us as a human! A scandalous and even ridiculous claim! But it is the message with which John begins the Gospel. "The Word became flesh and lived among us!" This One who is God and was the means by which all reality was created is now a squalling baby in a makeshift crib. What are we to do with this offensive message of Christmas?

Well, we could soften it with sentimental and imaginative additions to the birth story. We often see pictures of the scene in the stable in which the infant wears a halo or is already preaching to those around him. We could pretend that he never wet himself or took nourishment from his mother's breast. We seem naturally to want to compromise Christ's fleshly reality. In a sense, a Christ who is never human and purely divine is safer, for he is more distant and less likely to impinge on our lives. But lifting Christ out of his humanness does violence to the starkness of John's message: He became flesh!

We do better to take Martin Luther's advice: ". . . let Christ be a natural human being, in every respect exactly as we are . . . [For t]he more we draw Christ down into nature and into the flesh, the more consolation accrues for us."[11]

That consolation is the simple fact that God has identified with us in all our suffering and pain, our joys and sorrows, our dreams and weaknesses. The only way God could let us know the extent of the divine love is by becoming one with us and walking in our shoes! The only way God could free us from bondage to death is to go to the cross in the Son and there suffer our deaths.

EACH TIME WE FEEL OSTRACIZED AND REJECTED WE CAN BE ASSURED THAT CHRIST WALKED THIS ROAD BEFORE WE CAME TO IT. WE CAN BE CONFIDENT THAT GOD KNOWS OUR EXPERIENCE BECAUSE THE DIVINE WORD BECAME FLESH AND LIVED AMONG US.

So, each time we suffer and feel alone we know that God has been there ahead of us. Each time we feel ostracized and rejected we can be assured that Christ walked this road before we came to it. We can be confident that God knows our experience because the divine Word became flesh and lived among us.

A counselor was trying to convince her client that she understood the experience of addiction, but the client resisted. "You can never know how it feels to *have* to have another drink!" But the counselor did know and proceeded to tell her own story of alcoholism and the pain she went through in recovery. Suddenly the client knew his counselor could understand, for she had journeyed through that torment. So too do we know that God's love is understanding, for Christ has traveled the human experience.

When we take John's words seriously and allow Christ to be truly human, the light of love illumines our lives. One of Andy Rooney's writings complains about pictures of Christ. They all seem simply to portray the artist's own image of Christ. He concludes his reflections by quoting Carl Sandburg who suggested that such a face would "cry and laugh with every face born human. And how can you crowd all the tragic and comic faces of [hu]mankind into one face?"[12] How indeed could all our experiences be crowded into one solitary person? Such is the marvel of this day we celebrate! And such is the good news we hear today. God stands beside us in all our experiences because the Word became flesh and lived among us.

FIRST SUNDAY AFTER CHRISTMAS

THE HOLY FAMILY

DECEMBER 27, 1998

Revised Common	Episcopal (BCP)	Roman Catholic
Isa. 63:7-9	Isa. 61:10—62:3	Sir. 3:2-6, 12-14
Ps. 140	Ps. 147 or 147:13-21 or 147:13-21	Ps. 128:1-5
Heb. 2:10-18	Gal. 3:23-25; 4:4-7	Col. 3:12-21
Matt. 2:13-23	John 1:1-18	Matt. 2:13-15, 19-23

Like life itself, the season of Christmas leads us into somber reflection on human evil. The two Gospel lessons stimulate such reflection with the reality of Christ's rejection (John) and a narrative of an effort to kill the Christ child (Matthew). The two Isaiah lessons, joined by Psalms 147 and 148, keep praise of God's works before us. The lessons from Hebrews and Galatians speak of God's accomplishments in Christ. Matthew's story, an exhortation to honor one's parents (Sirach), the results of goodness within a family (Psalm 128), and the insistence that Christian morality influences family life (Colossians) intersect around the holy family.

First Reading
ISAIAH 63:7-9 (RCL)

Interpreting the Text

The reading introduces a long community lament (63:7—64:12), but lament begins with praise. The reasons for such adoration are in the community's experience of God throughout its history.

Isaiah draws attention to "deeds of the Lord" that have rescued the people. Those deeds express a kindness ("gracious") and evoke praise from their beneficiaries. "Because" introduces a recitation of phrases that describe the Lord's nature as seen in deeds. The first ("favor") captures the sense that God has given beyond what the people have merited. The second ("mercy") loads God's deeds with forgiveness and reconciliation, and the third ("steadfast love") evokes the ancient agreement God made with the people and to which the divine actions have been stubbornly faithful (v. 7).

In verse 8 God first expresses the divine perception of the people. They are the Lord's own community who deal truthfully with one another and others. Then the prophet continues the report of what God has done, this time in deliverance ("savior") from misfortune and affliction. But God's rescue was worked not through agents or representatives but through the divine "presence" itself. Where God is present, there is salvation and restoration because divine presence is the experience of "love" and compassion. Redemption in this case is parallel to salvation and being lifted up; it has to do with liberation from actual physical difficulty. The phrase "all the days of old" suggests that the prophet's perspective is the people's whole history (v. 9).

Responding to the Text

Christmas does not exist in a vacuum, sealed off from the past. The celebration of Christ's nativity has a history and a future. Think of the Christmas season as a joyous and pivotal point in your individual life. Such an event doesn't just pop up. It is planted in the soil of what has come before. In a similar way Jesus' birth is the apex of a long history of God's dealings with humankind.

As a church celebrating the good news of Jesus' birth, we need to remember who we are—not to wallow nostalgically in it but to employ it to lead us into the future.

That is the perspective our first lesson takes. The prophet scans the landscape of Israel's history and etches the people's experience of God through "all the days of old." The etching has one continuous theme: God's unrelenting kindness and love expressed through what has been done for the people.

But such a historical perspective is harder to achieve these days. Tradition is being challenged on all fronts as the new and novel sweep over our culture. We are so hurried in our efforts to deal with change and innovation that it may be hard for us to remember the past.

As a church celebrating the good news of Jesus' birth, we need to remember who we are—not to wallow nostalgically in it but to employ it to lead us into the future. Isaiah's words in our lesson introduce the people's plea to God to help them in a difficult situation. The prophet recalls the past to equip the people for dealing with the present.

In the Disney movie *The Lion King,* Simba, the princely young lion, escapes to a carefree life away from his family. But in the story's pivotal scene, he is forced to remember his deceased father and hears his father's voice saying, "Remember who you are!" Simba is then empowered to return to his land and rescue them from the oppressive rule of his uncle who has usurped the monarchy.

"Remember who you are!" Remember who God has called us to be. Remember the unfailing love and devotion God poured out on this congregation to make us part of the divine family. And let that remembrance empower us for the days that lie beyond this Christmas season.

ISAIAH 61:10—62:3 (BCP)

Interpreting the Text

With the theme of Jerusalem's restoration the lesson laces the final words of the announcement of that event (chap. 61) together with the beginnings of another section that anticipates it (chap. 62). Throughout the reading the prophet scatters graphic images of the divine bounty. God's kindness is pictured as new clothing like that of a couple about to be wed (61:10). Then gardening spawns the scene of the plants of "righteousness and praise" growing out of seeds God implants in the soil of the community (61:11). Naming a new reality is still another snapshot of what God will do for the city (62:2). Finally Jerusalem is imagined as a royal "crown" God proudly displays to the world (62:3). The prophet's commitment to the renaissance of the holy city bubbles over in the lesson's language (62:1).

Responding to the Text

New clothes are a fun way of celebrating something special in our lives. Wearing a new shirt or blouse, clothing ourselves with simply a new scarf or tie—they all are expressions of something new in our lives. And we need the new to replace the old.

Christmas is like being given the gift of new clothing, because in Jesus' birth God has given us new love and identity. Isaiah describes God's restoration of Jerusalem from its shambles as "garments of salvation," "the robe of righteousness," the bridegroom's lapel flower, and the bride's jewelry. What God gives us in Christ is a jewel of love, a flower of peace, and clothing of a new people.

In 1996, when Robert Dole left the Senate to campaign for the presidency, he shed his dark blue suit, white shirt, and tie. He began appearing in public for the first time clad in a running jacket with his shirt collar open. The new garments suggested his new role as a common citizen and the end of his political role in the Senate.

God dresses us in the garments of divine love. We are common people given a new role as God's people in a loveless and love-hungry world. Put on the raiment of Christ and let the world know our faith.

SIRACH 3:2-6, 12-14 (RC)

Interpreting the Text

Ben Sira wrote in troubled times for the Jewish people (perhaps between 200 and 180 B.C.E.), when their nation was threatened and its cultural heritage was vulnerable to decay. In this passage he combines ancient injunctions with the realities of his time to interpret the commandment to honor one's parents.

Verses 2-6 promise reward to those who practice the commandment. The promise is premised on the divinely instituted role of parenting; God "honors" and "confirms" parents (v. 2). If God is so disposed to parenting, then enacting that divine disposition removes our guilt, invests our lives in lasting values, and turns God's attention to our petitions. Honoring our parents spills over into our own role as father or mother, producing delight in our own children. Obedience and longevity are the fruits of faithfulness to our parents.

Verses 12-14 then instruct readers on how to honor an aged father. "Help" is a loaded word in biblical language, since God has been our "helper" in times of distress (for instance, Ps. 54:4). Sirach urges us to do for parents what God does for us! Verse 13 appeals to us to understand one whose capacities have failed. God remembers kindness done to our parents and weighs it against all our failures to be kind to others.

Responding to the Text

The family has gone through radical changes in recent decades, and we have often heard pleas to restore "family values." For that reason the reading from Sirach has a remarkably contemporary ring about it, for the author urges us to value both parenting and our own parents. But his "family values" have a peculiar basis. He claims that God "honors a father" and "confirms a mother." Our Creator has assigned a special role to those who are entrusted with the parental role (whether of their own children or those of others), a ministry, if you will, that is at the heart of society.

Perhaps the value that family life needs so desperately today is one rooted in God's design for humans to care for those closest to them. God gives us our lives through parents, and our growth is entrusted to those who act as nurturers in our lives. Dan Fogelberg wrote a song titled "Leader of the Band" that expresses his gratitude to a father who nurtured him and allowed him his freedom to go when that time had come. Most of us have had a "leader of the band" in our lives, someone (whether a biological parent or another) who has helped us find ourselves in the swirling chaos of our world.

Simply put, our calling is to practice our experience of God's help in our relationships with others, including those whom we call "mom" and "dad." As God has helped us, we are asked to be helpers of others.

Responsive Reading
PSALM 148 (RCL)

Interpreting the Text

This psalm calls the whole creation to acknowledge its divine source. First, it beckons every corner of the heavenly realm and its inhabitants (vv. 1-6). Then it turns toward the created order, including all creatures evil or benign, the elements, vegetation, and animals (vv. 7-10). Last the psalmist invites humans of all rank and age (vv. 11-12).

Such praise is appropriate because the Lord is the apex of all reality and has posted a notice of the divine love for Israel (vv. 13-14).

Responding to the Text

Public notices invite participation. The psalm uses the word *horn* for God's public notice because the sound of the horn invited people to a public event.

The birth of the divine Son is God's newest public notice, inviting humans to gather around that manger. Christmas is not restricted to a few but announces God's love for all the world, as the old African American spiritual says:

> Go, tell it on the mountain,
> That Jesus Christ is born![13]

The blast of God's horn beckons us to fix our lives on that expression of divine love and drives us out to share the public notice with others who may not know its meaning.

PSALM 147 (BCP)

Interpreting the Text

This psalm praises God for the divine care of Jerusalem. In three stanzas (vv. 1-6, 7-11, and 12-20) it recites God's deeds on behalf of the city and alternates between the divine concern for humans and the Lord's accomplishments in creation. The concluding stanza takes up God's "word." It is sent out and does its work. The divine breath "melts" snow and ice as well as conveys God's will to the chosen people (vv. 15-20).

Responding to the Text

God's word "runs swiftly" to do its work. We know words are powerful, don't we? We know words can transform our lives. But God's words are different from the many words that try to corner us into buying or believing something. A television commercial exploited a charming fellow's words, "I love you, man!" in order to sell beer.

The divine Word of which the psalmist speaks, however, is God's powerfully utterance that transfigures all it reaches. Such a Word as this is whispered in the Bethlehem manger, but it then shouts in our hearts, for that simple infant-Word makes children of God out of ordinary creatures like you and me.

PSALM 128 (RC)

Interpreting the Text

In the context of the conviction that righteous living produces material rewards, this psalm affirms the repercussions of faithfulness (vv. 1-2). The word *happy* catches the sense of the consequences of living in a right relationship with God. In a patriarchal society where children are one's life after death, a fertile wife ("fruitful vine") is a special gift. Young sprouts spawned from the mature tree evoke the children of such a marriage (vv. 3-4).

Responding to the Text

Many of us may not agree with the psalmist that righteousness assures material success, that a wife's fertility is of prime importance, or that the number of children we have measures God's presence. But the psalm confronts us with a deeper truth. The family—or any intimate relationship with others—needs a center outside itself. Without it they become ingrown and fixated on themselves. Reinhold Niebuhr observed, "it is not possible to divorce the meaning of life from the vocation of parenthood."[14]

The psalmist invites us to ground our intimate relationships (especially the family) on God's caring compassion for the whole world. With a purpose beyond ourselves we become means of serving our Creator.

Second Reading
HEBREWS 2:10-18 (RCL)

Interpreting the Text

Christ suffered in solidarity with humanity. The lesson's first segment (vv. 10-13) stresses that Christians are Christ's siblings and the second (vv. 14-18) that his bond with humanity enabled Christ to defeat evil.

Christ was made one with humanity through his "suffering," a bond that is part of his perfection as God's sacrifice for us. This process of identification with humans puts Christ on the frontier of humanity's renewal (see 2:12). Humans and Christ share the common parenthood of God, so we are Christ's sisters and brothers as the references to Psalm 22:22 and Isaiah 8:17b and 18 attest (vv. 10-13).

If Christ is our sibling, then he shares our "flesh and blood." That commonality with humans enables him to overcome the power of death, which the author identifies with evil's source ("the devil"). By defusing death's potential, Christ liberates us from our enslavement to the dread of death that casts its shadow over the whole of human existence. Otherwise Christ's life might have aided angels but would be of little value to us (vv. 14-16).The only way in which Christ could effect our rescue from death is through becoming one of us in every way. That identification with us qualifies Christ to represent us (as "high priest") before God, for in Jewish sacrificial worship only the priest can offer God that which takes away human transgression. Having shared with us the experience of being put to the test, he is able to deliver us from our plight (vv. 17-18).

Responding to the Text

Siblings share a special bond. After my parents died, I came to a new appreciation of my brothers, for they share a common background with me. There is something healing about relationships with others who know our experience. Support groups of all kinds use the healing miracle of simply knowing that we are not alone, that another has gone through the pain we feel.

In Christ's birth we all received a new brother. Our second lesson today claims Christ became "like his brothers and sisters in every respect." In every respect! That eliminates our suspicion that Christ was in some way shielded from some of the difficulties we experience.

But most important, Christ shared our experience of death. The fear of death hangs over us like a dark cloud blocking the light and warmth of the sun. A public figure was asked what plans he had for the future. He replied that he didn't make plans for the future any longer. In recent years two of his friends had been killed in accidents and a third had committed suicide. Consequently, he said he just lives each day without goals for the future. Such is the power of death! It blocks our path to the future!

This brother of ours went through death but with a difference. He did so in order that through his death God might break death's grip on you and me. In Christ, God seem to say, "The only way I can destroy death is by myself entering it." So, in Christ God experienced death in order to defuse it of its power. Christ went into the darkness of nothingness so that God could raise him and together they could laugh at the remains of death's power.

CHRIST WENT INTO THE DARKNESS OF NOTHINGNESS SO THAT GOD COULD RAISE HIM AND TOGETHER THEY COULD LAUGH AT THE REMAINS OF DEATH'S POWER.

What a brother this Christ child is! One destined to share all our experiences, even death and dying itself. With a brother like this, we can be a family of those liberated from death's hold on us.

GALATIANS 3:23-25; 4:4-7 (BCP)

Interpreting the Text

The lesson combines two fragments of Paul's effort to distinguish between life under the law and life under grace. The first fragment explains the role of the law before faith, and the second how in Christ we are freed of law to become God's children.

The law was our tutor or instructor before Christ, but it bound us like those who cannot act on their own. When Christ came, "faith"—and not obedience to law—became our defining principle. Then our relationship with God was transformed from one of frightened student to one who had received a gift of love. Hence, we were freed from bondage to an instructor (3:23-25).

That bondage existed until the time was ripe for God to act in Christ, who himself was "born" as a human under law's tutorage. He shared bondage to the law in order to free us from our own enslavement. That liberation is a form of "adoption"—meaning that God becomes our new parent through Christ's earning us our freedom. As God's children we receive the divine presence in our lives that enables us to call God our parent. Slavery to law is ended when we become God's children; and when we are made divine children we are entitled to inherit what belongs to our new parent (4:4-7).

Responding to the Text

Sometimes we feel like we are only God's slaves, forced to obey rules and regulations we don't understand. In those times we don't feel very good about ourselves or about God! God is the heartless master who imposes all these requirements on us without consideration of our weakness and limitations. And we are worthless servants, good for nothing but filling our master's every wish.

But Paul insists that Christ has changed all this. When God sent the divine Son, our slavery ended, and God adopted us as children. We, who feel like orphans forced to obey One who has no feelings for us, are embraced as daughters and sons of God. "So you are no longer a slave but a child" with a loving parent. The birth of the Christ child is our birth as children of our Creator.

COLOSSIANS 3:12-20

Interpreting the Text

Paul describes here the lifestyle of those who have found new existence in Christ. He first speaks of the quality of that style of life as garments in which we "clothe" ourselves (vv. 12, 14). The virtues he commends climax in love that knits us together in a single unity. Such a lifestyle arises from allowing Christ's "peace" (wholeness) and message ("word") to rule our lives, and bursts forth in gratitude. Above all, everything we do or say needs to be consistent with the identity ("name") of the one who has given us the possibility of such new life (vv. 12-17).

Verses 18-21 are the first part of the "household duties" (which continue through 4:1), a description of the relationships that ought to be nurtured within the family unit. First, the relationship between wives and husbands is pictured in a manner consistent with the patriarchal system of the author's culture. But the wife's subjection to her husband is qualified with the quality of his love for her. Next children are urged to be obedient to their parents since such compliance is their divine obligation. But the harshness of that subjection is conditioned by the injunction that fathers should not arouse their children's disheartening resentment.

Responding to the Text

The old adage that charity begins at home has some truth to it. The virtues of the Christian life begin at home! Too many of us know the experience of practicing love in our relationships beyond the home without living them in our dealings with those who are closest to us. In a sense, it may be easier to love those more distant from us than it is to care for those with whom we are more intimate. The parents of a personal friend are known in the community as the most giving Christians you could ever ask for. But as their child, my friend experienced more harshness and control than love and care from her parents.

Paul brings the virtues of the Christian life into the living room and the kitchen, claiming that there too everything we say and do should be done "in the name of the Lord Jesus." But how do we do that? Where do we gain the power to love and care for those with whom we live on a daily basis? Paul makes it sound easier than it is.

Paul's response would be that we have been chosen, made righteous, and loved by God in Christ and that the divine love we have received is the source of our power to love others, even those closest to us. We are in a sense like mirrors that reflect back to others what we have seen. When we look into ourselves, we reflect only our own confusion and brokenness; but when we look into Christ's face, we reflect the love we see there.

God's love and care in Christ evoke and empower our love and care for others. We know that a child who is loved is inclined to become a loving person. In Christ we have been loved, and hence made loving.

Gospel
MATTHEW 2:13-23 (RCL, RC)

Interpreting the Text

A violent reaction from the political establishment immediately sobers Christ's wondrous birth and alerts us that Jesus will evoke such responses from the powers that be! The reading narrates the family's escape to Egypt (vv. 13-15), then the danger they fled (vv. 16-18), and finally their return to Nazareth (vv. 19-23). Matthew concludes each segment with a citation from Hebrew Scriptures.

Joseph's life is once again interrupted by an angelic visit (see 1:20-21), this time warning him of Herod's intent and instructing him to flee to Egypt (outside Herod's jurisdiction). And again Joseph is obedient. The family steals away and becomes aliens until Herod's death removes the danger. Matthew quotes Hosea 11:1 to suggest that the family repeat Israel's migration to Egypt and then its call back out of that land. As Son of God, Jesus relives Israel's history and shares God's protective custody with the Hebrew people (vv. 13-15).

This story is consistent with Herod's notoriety as a heartless and cruel ruler. The "wise men" had not been fooled by Herod's pretense of wanting to honor the infant (see 2:8 and 12), and so the ruler resorts to more drastic actions to eliminate any threat to his station posed by one "born to be king of the Jews" (2:2). Without knowing the identity of the child, he simply orders the slaughter of all baby boys under the age of two. The evangelist interprets this atrocity in terms of Jeremiah 31:15, which was first spoken about the exile of the Northern Kingdom at the hands of the Assyrians (vv. 16-18).

The watchful angel informs Joseph the coast is clear and the family is safe to return to their homeland. Joseph obeys but becomes fearful. Now a "dream" (see 1:20) directs him to take his family and settle in Nazareth, outside the jurisdiction of Herod's son, Archelaus. Upon the death of Herod the Great, his kingdom was divided into three parts with one of his sons assigned to rule each parcel. Galilee was noted for its relative peace, as compared to Judea under the rule of Archelaus who soon proved himself as ruthless as his father. In contrast to Luke, Matthew explains that Bethlehem and not Nazareth was the family's original home. Matthew views this fact in the light of Scripture, although the exact words cannot be found in the Old Testament. The word "Nazorean" could mean "one from Nazareth," "branch," or "one devoted to God," each appropriate to Jesus (vv. 19-23).

Responding to the Text

Power is dangerous! And the more power the greater the danger. Yet our society is constructed on the value of power, and the most powerful are honored and admired while the powerless are disregarded and even disdained. Our culture is enamored with influential celebrities whose books are best sellers and whose presence on television talk shows attracts viewers. Celebrities themselves are hounded by the news media and swarms of admirers. All the while, incidents of the corruption of power fill the daily news.

Not accidentally Matthew concludes the stories of Jesus' birth with the account of King Herod's slaughter of innocent children in his effort to rub out the baby who has been hailed as "king of the Jews." Herod's brute power and the atrocity he perpetrates to ensure his position sharply contrast with the Christmas birth story—a helpless infant and a mighty ruler, the embodiment of love and peace and the enactment of ruthless power.

We celebrate Christmas as a time of joy and peace. But we are never far from the reality of powers turned evil and violent in our world. Simon and Garfunkel, in one of their early recordings, performed a song called "The 7 O'Clock News/Silent Night." As they quietly sing the Christmas carol, you hear the voice of the radio news announcer reading a report of the day's events. Racial conflict, a narcotically induced death, murder, war, and corruption are narrated over the peaceful music and gradually increase in volume as the music fades into the background. It is a vivid portrayal of our world even in the midst of a season of peace and goodwill.

The somber side of the season forces us to ask questions of power and its use. Worshipers of the Christ child are compelled to be on their guard against power gone sour. Like the holy family, we watch the horizon for signs of injustice clothed in respectability. In the beginnings of the movement to free African Americans from the oppressive powers of segregation, Martin Luther King Jr. wrote, "It has always been the responsibility of the church to broaden horizons, challenge the status quo, and break the mores when necessary."[15] We Christians still bear that responsibility, all the more in a day when power seems more and more concentrated in a few at the expense of the many.

LIKE THE HOLY FAMILY, WE WATCH THE HORIZON FOR SIGNS OF INJUSTICE CLOTHED IN RESPECTABILITY.

But the intrusion of power's heinous presence into our Christmas celebration also raises the question of the nature of true power. Herod and Jesus offer us our options. Is power defined by the authority to command others' lives? Or, is it defined by sacrificial love that is willing to lose life to gain it?

In *A Tale of Two Cities* Charles Dickens portrays the love that defines power. In this classic tale Charles Darnay wins the heart of Lucie Manette, in spite of the efforts of his look-alike, Sydney Carton. But Carton continues to love Lucie even after she and Darnay have married. The power of the revolutionary movement finally succeeds in convicting Darnay of treason and sentences him to the guillotine. Carton, however, steals his way into the prison, drugs Darnay, has him smuggled out of the prison, and takes his place in the prison cell. Because of his resemblance to the prisoner, Carton goes to his death, while Lucie and Darnay escape to England.

Resembling us in every way, Christ goes to the death we deserve. In doing so, he saves us from powers too great for us and invites us to find real power in his love.

JOHN 1:1-18 (BCP)

See the Gospel for "Nativity of Our Lord 3/Christmas Day" pp. 50–52.

ST. JOHN, APOSTLE AND EVANGELIST

DECEMBER 27, 1998

REVISED COMMON	EPISCOPAL (BCP)	ROMAN CATHOLIC
Gen. 1:1-5, 26-31	Exod. 33:18-23	
Ps. 116:12-19	Ps. 92 or 92:1-4, 11-14	
1 John 1:1—2:2	1 John 1:1-9	1 John 1:1-4
John 21:20-25	John 21:19b-24	John 20:2-8

THIS FESTIVAL CELEBRATES THE FIGURE that tradition has named the author of the Gospel of John, 1, 2, and 3 John, and Revelation. Early church writers also identified this John with John, son of Zebedee, one of the intimate circle of disciples in the other Gospels (for instance, Mark 9:2). Irenaeus (ca. 180–200) named John "the disciple whom Jesus loved" in the Gospel of John (21:20). It was also Irenaeus who first said John lived and wrote in Ephesus.

Modern scholarship has questioned each of these assumptions. But the tradition remains strong. The festival is above all a celebration of the beloved disciple who is mentioned six times in the Fourth Gospel. His name and identity remain a mystery. But the Gospel's portrayal of his relationship with Jesus models discipleship especially in its intimacy with and affection for his master. On this occasion we may appropriately focus on how relationships comprise the essence of Christian discipleship.

As the following discussion will show, each of the readings connects with some portion of or theme in the Gospel of John. The Genesis reading has to do with light and darkness, and Exodus with seeing God's glory. Psalm 116 suggests that service and thanksgiving are our proper response to God's gifts. Psalm 92 speaks of seeing God's work in the world, and 97 of God's kingship. First John refers to the "word of life" and "eternal life." John 21 includes Jesus' promise that "the disciple whom Jesus loved" would "remain." John 20 tells how that disciple entered Jesus' empty tomb, "saw and believed."

FIRST READING

GENESIS 1:1-5, 26-31 (RCL)

Interpreting the Text

This reading focuses on two parts of the creation story: God's formation of light (vv. 1-5) and the origin of humanity (vv. 26-31).

"In the beginning" is that mysterious time before time when the watery chaos ("the deep") was without pattern or shape. "Wind" represents God's spirit moving over the waters, since the Hebrew word means both spirit and "wind" (vv. 1-2). Simply by speaking, God creates "light," separates illumination from the pre-creation darkness, and declares it "good"—acceptable to God (v. 4; see also verse 31a). Since naming constitutes being, God gives separate names to the light and the darkness (v. 5a). "Day" refers to an indefinite period of time in the timelessness of creation and originates the Sabbath (see 2:2).

In verse 26 God speaks in the royal plural ("let us") as kings did. Humans are in God's "image" and "likeness," two parallel ways of saying the same thing. Humanity's similarity to God is our rule over other beings. Humans "have dominion" over other creatures as God has dominion over all creation. God then creates a domain for human rule—creatures in the three realms of nature (sky, sea, and earth).

Humans are created "male and female," because God comprises both genders (v. 27). They are then "blessed" and commanded to procreate (v. 28). To "subdue" the earth means to bring order and control and to be accountable for our own livelihood (vv. 29-30). And God finds pleasure in the whole of creation (v. 31).

Responding to the Text

John, the evangelist, was fond of the images of light and darkness. Our first lesson today describes the origin of light and its separation from darkness. Darkness is part of the formless void—the chaos—before creation. Everything was in shambles, and God brought order by creating light.

We know the chaos that comes with darkness. Remember the times when we experienced a power failure? We were suddenly immersed in darkness. We groped around to find a flashlight. Maybe we found some old candles in the cupboard and some matches in the drawer. We sought light to defeat the darkness.

For John darkness represents the disorder and chaos in human lives, the disarray of our lives when we don't know who we are and what we are for. The Nobel Prize-winning Jewish author Elie Wiesel wrote of his experience as a boy in a

Nazi concentration camp. He recounts the disorder thrust upon his family and neighbors by Hitler's program to purge Europe of Jews. He remembers the horrors of gas chambers, the prisoners' meager existence, and the deterioration of the human spirit. Wiesel chronicles the devastation of his own religious faith in the face of this unimaginable evil. God seemed absent and silent amid such madness. Wiesel entitled his autobiographical book simply *Night*—a period of utter darkness.

Few of us know the experience of darkness in such extremes. But we know our own moments of darkness—times when nothing makes sense, when everything seems to be formless void, moments when God seems distant and silent.

But God created light amid the darkness. God would not allow the darkness to rule. Into that darkness God spoke the divine Word and light came to be. Now "the light shines in the darkness and the darkness did not overcome it" (John 1:5). Into lives that are ever threatened by the darkness, through Christ God sends light. Because of him we have a light to illumine our lives and world when our own power has failed us. By his light we can order our lives and see our way through the world's darkness, even death's darkness.

EXODUS 33:18-23 (BCP)

Interpreting the Text

This is the nearly humorous story of God's response to Moses' plea for a vision of the divine glory. God promises that the people will know God's presence and blessing (v. 17), but Moses wants more. "Glory" translates the Hebrew word that means God's manifest presence (v. 18). God repeats the promise made to the children of Israel, but insists that there are limits to what humans can bear. To see God's "face" entails such awe that the human spirit would melt away (vv. 19-20; see Exod. 3:6).

So God offers a compromise. Moses is placed in a crack in the rock. God will shield Moses' eyes while the divine glory passes by, and then Moses may be permitted a glimpse of God's back (vv. 21-23). Moses will have to be satisfied with such a peek. The passage is obviously filled with metaphorical images of God—face, hands, back.

"Show me your glory," Moses prays. God, let me see you face-to-face. The usually strong Moses is experiencing doubt and weakness. And he pleads with God for a reassuring vision.

"Been there, done that!" At least, many of us have had our times of doubt and weakness, just like Moses. And we have done what Moses did: pleaded with God for a reassuring vision of the divine glory. Maybe it was depression. Maybe terrible grief and loss. Perhaps a series of failures when everything that could go wrong did just that. Whatever the occasion, we have all wanted to see God and be assured of a faith that was nearly exhausted.

Well, Moses gets only a shred of what he requested. He would never survive a face-to-face encounter with the Almighty. But God grants him a quick view of the divine backside. Perhaps we may feel that our own pleas have resulted in little more—only a peek at what might be taken to be God.

But then, again, maybe we were looking in the wrong place. As I age I am becoming increasingly absentminded. Where did I leave my keys? And I go rummaging through my dresser. My dear wife then suggests that I look in my pocket. Sure enough, there they are.

Sometimes when we need that reassuring glimpse of God's presence, we are looking in the wrong place. John, the evangelist, suggests that there is only one place we need look. He claims "No one has ever seen God. It is God the only Son, who is close to the Father's heart, who has made him known" (John 1:18). We aren't going to see God, no matter how we may plead for such vision. But we don't have to. God has already made the divine glory visible to us in a human being named Jesus. When we need to see God's face, we can look at Christ and see God's very heart.

WHEN WE NEED TO SEE GOD'S FACE, WE CAN LOOK AT CHRIST AND SEE GOD'S VERY HEART.

Responsive Reading
PSALM 116:12-19 (RCL)

Interpreting the Text

This is part of a psalm of thanksgiving. The psalmist offers a response to God's graciousness in time of need (v. 15—God's care for the death of the faithful). The grateful recipient asks what possible "return" could be offered to God (v. 12), and then proceeds to make what "vows" are conceivable: worship in the presence of others (vv. 13-14 and 17-19), and service (v. 16). "The child of your serving girl" suggests the lowest of all servant positions.

Responding to the Text

We often think we have to repay a favor. Our psalmist, however, knows there is no way to repay God and vows to worship and serve. And we can do no better.

In the opera *Amahl and the Night Visitors,* little Amahl decides he will give his crutch to Jesus as a gift. With that decision his affliction is healed, and he joins the wise men on their trip to the birthplace. We have only crutches to offer in response to God's love: guilt, selfishness, and pride. Then thankfulness and gratitude can result in healing.

Jesus asks Peter to "Feed my sheep," if Peter loves him (John 21:15-17). Loving service and thanksgiving is all God expects of us.

PSALM 92 (BCP)

Interpreting the Text

This is a psalm of thanksgiving for victory over opponents. The first stanza recites why thanks and praise are good (vv. 1-4). The second claims that the righteous can see God's works, but the "wicked" are destined to perish (vv. 5-9). Verses 10-11 give thanks for the defeat of the psalmist's enemies, and the closing verses declare that the righteous prosper, thereby showing God's justice.

Responding to the Text

In the Gospel of John, Jesus stresses the difference between believers and the world (for instance, 17:25). Our psalmist declares that the righteous know God's work while the "dullard" does not (vv. 5-6). What makes Christ's community distinct in our world is that we claim God is active among us. It is not an arrogance (for there is much we do not know). But it is a faith perception that sets us apart (see John 20 pp. 75-76).

Glasses correct our vision and enable us to see sharply. The church believes that, in Christ, God has graciously provided us with lenses through which to see our world sharply.

PSALM 97:1-2, 5-6, 11-12 (RC)

See Nativity of Our Lord 2/Christmas Dawn, p. 43. On Christ's kingship in the Gospel of John see John 18:28—19:22. Verse 11 declares that "light dawns." On light, see Responding to the Text, pp. 67–68 under Genesis 1:1-5, 26-31.

SECOND READING

1 JOHN 1:1—2:2

Interpreting the Text

The reading includes the epistle's introduction (vv. 1-4) and its discussion of God's light and human sin (1:5—2:2).

"The beginning" probably means the origin of the Christian faith (but see John 1:1). Speaking for the community ("we"), the author claims a firsthand sensory experience of "the word of life" (the gospel embodied in Christ). "Life" is synonymous with "eternal life"—authentic existence as God intended it. This proclamation seeks to include readers in the community's relationship with God and Christ (v. 3).

"God is light," and "darkness" represents chaos. For us that excludes living an unenlightened life. Living in darkness makes us liars, for truth is lived, not simply believed (v. 6). "Walking in the light" is living Christ's model and puts us in the Christian community where we are "cleansed" of sin. "The blood of Jesus" compares Christ's death with the Jewish temple sacrifices (v. 7).

To claim to be sinless is self-deception and evidences alienation from "truth." Truth refers to the revelation of God in Christ (v. 8). Confession of sin brings God's forgiveness and cleansing. God's constant goodness ("faithful and just") eradicates our "unrighteousness" (v. 9). To sin makes God "a liar," and to lie is to stand against God's revelation in Christ (v. 10—see 2:22). Nonetheless, the author writes to enable readers to avoid sin (2:1a). Christ is like our defense attorney ("advocate") in a court of law. "Atoning sacrifice" (2:2) means an offering that wipes away the sin (expiation) "of the whole world" (2:2).

Responding to the Text

At some stage of life, perhaps, like me you have asked this question: What is life all about? It's a dreadful thought: We are given life and we don't know quite how to spend it. Like the child with a nickel in the candy store. How should we spend our precious nickel's worth of life? In my adolescence the question hit me like a sledgehammer. It made me get serious about this life I have.

But the question won't go away. We set out on our lives toward some vision. But obstacles fall across our path—a death, loss of a job, illness. And we have to choose another route.

The author of our epistle speaks of having experienced "the word of life." This life has been revealed to Christians. Through it we come to know "eternal life." Eternal life does not mean simply life beyond death. It surely includes that. But eternal life is a quality of life in the here and now. This kind of life is the sort of existence for which God created us. It is our true life.

So, what makes life true? What is the message of the word of life? The message is that God has come among us to let us know about divine love and forgiveness. Because of that love and care we are tied to our Creator; pulled into a relationship with the one who gives us life. Christ showed us the center of real life.

Gospel

JOHN 21:20-25 (RCL/BCP)

Interpreting the Text

Many scholars believe John 21 is an appendix to the Gospel in which an editor tied together some loose strings from chapters 1–20. One of those untied strings is the destiny of "the disciple whom Jesus loved" and his relationship with the Gospel. The reading contains Jesus' conversation with Peter about this disciple (vv. 20-23) and the Gospel's conclusion (vv. 24-25).

Verses 20-23 continue the conversation between the risen Christ and Peter contained in verses 15-19. In verse 20 the unnamed "disciple whom Jesus loved" is identified as the one "next to Jesus" at Jesus' last meal with the disciples and the one bold enough to ask Jesus to name the betrayer among them (13:23-26; see also 19:25-27). Peter sees this disciple and asks Jesus about him (v. 21).

Jesus' response to Peter's question is simply that it is none of Peter's business. His business is to "follow" Jesus (see v. 19). "If it is my will that he remain until I come" contains two ambiguities. The first is the use of "remain," which translates *menō*, the rich verb used to speak of relationships with God and Christ (for instance, 15:5-10). Does it here mean "remain alive"? The second ambiguity is Jesus' coming. Does that mean Jesus' triumphant return in glory, his coming in the Spirit, or his appearance as the risen Lord? Perhaps Jesus' words here, as elsewhere (for instance, 3:3), convey several meanings at the same time. Verse 23 seems to correct a popular notion in the Johannine church that the beloved disciple would never die. Tradition claims that this disciple lived a long life. Perhaps his death occasioned the writing of this conversation to address the community's grief at the beloved disciple's death. He indeed continues to "remain" (that is, abide) with Christ in death.

Verse 24 appears to connect the beloved disciple with the contents of the whole Gospel. The precise reference of "these things" is unclear but has been interpreted to mean the details of the Gospel's story. "Has written them" has been understood in different ways: (1) direct and actual authorship of the Gospel, (2) indirect authorship (that is, he caused the writing of the Gospel), and (3) the source of the tradition written in the Gospel.

The final verse concludes the Gospel for a second time in words similar to the first conclusion (see 20:30-31). The Gospel does not pretend to present all that Jesus did, for that would entail a gigantic library

Responding to the Text

We tend to idolize our heroes. We even make gods out of them. (Did George Washington really chop down that cherry tree and never lie about it?) Consequently, it's big news when one of our heroes is shown to have human frailties. That is one reason the O. J. Simpson trial captured so much attention. One of our heroes might have fallen from the pedestal on which we had placed him.

The idealizing of a hero is behind our Gospel lesson for today. One Christian community claimed a particular disciple as its hero. In the Gospel of John that disciple is never named. He is, however, consistently referred to as "the disciple whom Jesus loved." The Gospel story suggests that he shared a particularly intimate relationship with Jesus—closer even than Peter's.

Jesus had said this disciple would "remain" until Jesus "came." And this congregation took that to mean that the beloved disciple—their hero—would never die. He was immortal in their imaginations.

Church history identified this unnamed but beloved disciple with John. Early church writers believed he was the one who wrote the Gospel of John. Whether that tradition is true or not, today we celebrate this disciple's life and witness. He is thought to have had a long life, but he did finally die.

His death sent shock waves through the disciple's church. Jesus had not yet returned in glory, at least not as they believed he would. But the disciple whom he loved had died. The passage we read today corrects the church's misunderstanding of Jesus' words. Jesus had said this disciple would *remain* until he came. But Jesus had not said he would not die.

What, then, we wonder, did Jesus mean by saying the disciple would "remain"? The Gospel of John elsewhere uses the word *remain* to speak of the believers' relationship with Christ. In those cases, the same Greek word is translated "abide." "If you abide in me, and my words abide in you, ask for whatever you wish, and it will be done for you" (John 15:7). Did Jesus mean that the beloved disciple would remain in a relationship of love with Jesus?

When a loved one dies, we wonder about his or her relationship with God and Christ. That relationship of love does not mean we do not die. But it does mean that the relationship is sustained through death. Death cannot break the bond of love God has created with us through Christ. Nothing can snatch us from God. Not even death itself (see Rom. 8:38-39).

It is as if divine love is the safety rope that climbers use as they descend a steep and dangerous cliff. We descend into the dark recesses of death. But we are attached to a rope whose end is anchored in the Creator of all. A rope of love that does not let us fall.

The disciple whom Jesus loved remains attached to God through a rope of love around his life. Yes, he has died. But still he "remains" in Christ. When my mother died, I missed her presence. But death never broke the relationship of love I have with her. If death cannot shatter human relationships of love, neither then can it shatter God's bond of love with us.

And who is this mysterious and unnamed disciple whom Jesus loved? Finally it is you and me. For Jesus has loved us and dwells with us. The beloved disciple of the Gospel of John represents all of us who cling to God in Christ. And we too will remain, even in death!

Interpreting the Text

This reading is a portion of the story of Mary Magdalene's discovery of Jesus' empty tomb. It includes one of the references in the Gospel of John to "the disciple whom Jesus loved." Mary finds the tomb empty (v. 1) and races back to tell Peter and the unnamed disciple of her distress. She fears that someone has stolen their master's body (v. 3; see also vv. 13 and 15).

The two other disciples run to the tomb. The beloved disciple outruns his colleague, but does not enter the tomb. Instead, he looks in to see the burial "wrappings" still there (vv. 3-5). Peter boldly goes in and observes what the beloved disciple had seen, but also the large napkin that had covered the corpse's face (vv. 6-7; see 11:44). When the beloved disciple enters, however, "he saw and believed" (v. 8). Two different Greek words are used for Peter's seeing in verse 5 and the beloved disciple's in verse 8. The second word (*thorein*) seems to suggest a penetrating and understanding vision that enables belief. (For other examples of seeing and believing in this Gospel, see 6:40; 11:45; and 12:45.)

The story implies a contrast between Peter and the beloved disciple. The latter not only beats Peter to the tomb but is also granted the kind of seeing that arouses faith. Peter sees the evidence but goes away wondering what it all means.

Responding to the Text

In "The Unicorn Song," Peter, Paul, and Mary sing of a child's belief in what she saw, even though others did not see. Believing in the things we think we see is risky business. Especially when others see things differently.

But love often provides unusual visions. (Remember that poor fellow who had a face only a mother could love?) When we love another, we see them differently than do others. Intimacy brings visions into another's personality. Live with and love another person for years, and you gain a perception of them that others are denied. Some years ago a television drama told the story of a man and woman who were each impaired in their sight. They loved one another and were married. They could not see with their eyes as most of us do. But their love and intimacy allowed them to see each other in another way. And seeing in love nurtured their belief in each other.

The disciple whom Jesus loved entered Jesus' empty tomb and "saw and believed." Peter saw the same things. But he did not believe. He walked away from the empty tomb scratching his head—unsure of what it all meant. Why the difference? Could it be that the unnamed disciple saw differently? His love and intimacy with Jesus opened his eyes to see more deeply. He was so close to Jesus that he saw in the empty tomb something that evaded Peter's perception.

We Christians see differently because of the love God implants in our lives. That divine love opens our eyes to see the world in a distinctive way. We see the horrors of evil with a depth that tears at our hearts. And we see genuine human affection differently because it resonates with our experience of God. We see the world filled with the divine presence, in spite of its brokenness. Where others may see human conduct, we may see divine activity.

John, apostle and evangelist, helps us to see and believe. Yes, it's risky business. Others may laugh. But seeing through the eyes of love makes us go on believing. (See my comments on Psalm 92, p. 70.)

SECOND SUNDAY AFTER CHRISTMAS

January 3, 1999

Revised Common	Episcopal (BCP)	Roman Catholic
Jer. 31:7-14 or Sir. 24:1-12	Jer. 31:7-14	Sir. 24:1-4, 8-12
Ps. 147:12-20 or Wisd. 10:15-21	Ps. 84 or 84:1-8	Ps. 147:12-15, 19-20
Eph. 1:3-14	Eph. 1:3-6, 15-19a	Eph. 1:3-6, 15-18
John 1:(1-9), 10-18	Matt. 2:13-15, 19-23 or Luke 2:41-52 or Matt. 2:1-12	John 1:1-18 or 1:1-5, 9-14

Jeremiah celebrates God's return of Israel to its home, a gift for which Psalm 147 praises God. Israel's home is in God's temple (Psalm 84). Ephesians recites the gifts God gives in Christ, and John features the favor of Christ's revelation. John declares that the Word lives among us, and Sirach speaks of wisdom's resting place among humans. The Wisdom of Solomon describes wisdom's role in God's liberation. The holy family repeats Israel's Egyptian sojourn (Matt. 2:13-15, 19-23); wise men journey to Jesus (Matt. 2:1-12); and Jesus grows in wisdom and favor (Luke). The themes of journey, home, and God's gifts emerge from the lessons.

First Reading
JEREMIAH 31:7-14 (RCL/BCP)

Interpreting the Text

A series of "oracles of salvation" comprise this reading. Within them are God's declaration of the people's rescue interspersed with their joyful reception of God's gift.

Most striking in this passage are the images of God: loving and faithful (v. 3), builder (v. 4), father (v. 9b), shepherd (v. 10b), and redeemer (v. 11). The metaphors for the people's transformation are equally impressive. They shall dance (vv. 4 and 13), be "radiant," and their life shall be like "a watered garden" (v. 12); they are redeemed "from hands too strong" for them (v. 11); and their sorrow shall be consoled and turned to joy (vv. 9 and 13). Together these words form a picture of the divine action by which God reclaims the people (v. 1).

Verses 1-6 promise the restoration of the Northern Kingdom of Israel (for instance, "Samaria," v. 5) and recalls God's gracious behavior toward the people in their desert wanderings ("grace in the wilderness," v. 2). The verses climax in the promise of the reuniting of the kingdoms (v. 6). The remainder of the reading speaks of the people's deliverance from exile. Divine justice caused their scattering, and now divine care for them motivates God to return them to their home (v. 10). God's regathering of the people is widespread and inclusive. This "great company" is brought from "the north" and "from the farthest parts of the earth," including those in every imaginable condition (v. 8).

The passage is a celebratory song of God and God's recovery of the people.

Responding to the Text

It's a homecoming! The prophet Jeremiah announces that God is bringing the people back home. Back from their scattered lives. Freed of oppression. Back home where their lives become like "watered gardens."

Homecomings are often joyous events. Some of us enjoy gathering the family together for Christmas. These days families often scatter, and reunions are all the more precious. Home constitutes for many of us a safe and loving place. Even if we have sour memories of home, we still yearn for an imaginary home with the warmth of love, peace, and security. Our actual homes may not be all of that. But we yearn for such a place and for such relationships.

JEREMIAH DECLARES GOD'S PROMISE THAT THE ORPHANED PEOPLE OF ISRAEL WILL BE BROUGHT HOME—A NEW COMMUNITY OF PEACE AND LOVE, CONSOLATION AND JOY.

The trouble is that often we do not know where to find such a place of peace and love. Our lives are filled with broken relationships. So, where's a home for us? How do we find our way there? Who will take us there?

In the popular movie *Fly Away Home,* a young girl leads a group of orphaned geese to their migratory home. The geese have lost their mother. Without a relationship with others of their species, they have no sense of where they belong. And winter is coming. Through an ingenious plan, the geese follow the girl as she flies a plane from Canada to the South. She leads them home, where they rejoin the family of geese.

Like orphaned geese, we need to be led home. Brought to a place where we are part of a company of God's own people. Jeremiah declares God's promise that the orphaned people of Israel will be brought home—a new community of peace and love, consolation and joy.

But who will lead us home? God surprises us with a homecoming. But the surprise is not that we are taken home. Home is brought to us! In the birth of Christ, God makes the divine home among us. God made this place, this world, this congregation home (John 14:23). So, here we have the opportunity to be at peace in loving relationships. We do not have to fly away home, because home is here!

Welcome home!

SIRACH 24:1-12 (RCL/RC)

Interpreting the Text

The heart of this passage is this: Wisdom seeks and is given a "resting place" (vv. 7 and 11). The poet first introduces Wisdom as the speaker. Then the poem moves through two stanzas, one of searching and one of resolution. The first six verses depict the "glory" and wonder of Wisdom, holding sway "over every people and nation" (v. 6). But they also betray a wandering (for instance, v. 5). In verse 7 the poem turns. In spite of her glory, she seeks a "resting place." Like human wisdom, she seeks a final fulfillment, a peace and wholeness.

God assigns Wisdom such a place among humans (vv. 8-12). Her "tent" is in Zion among God's people (vv. 8b and 10-12). Verse 10 suggests that Wisdom's place was among the priests and not strictly among the learned.

Responding to the Text

Wisdom finds a home among the people. Her glory, her power, even her pervasive presence through the whole cosmos were not fulfilling. Instead, she is sent to dwell among God's people.

What a strange passage this is. We would think that her glory would be Wisdom's fulfillment. What could be more fulfilling? That greatest for which we so naturally yearn was already hers. Yet it was not her "resting place." Instead, she finds that place "in the midst of her people." The passage reverses our own expectations, our own assumptions about greatness.

Indeed, Christmas does just that. It blows our minds that God would make the divine resting place amid us. Christ, the divine Word from the beginning, rests in a manger in Bethlehem. Christ himself is not content being with God and being God. Instead, the divine fulfillment comes in dwelling here with you and me. In Christ's birth God honors our lives and our world. We think God would not want to dirty the divine hands in our world. But God comes to be one of us. And all of our assumptions about glory and greatness get turned upside down.

A story is told of a janitor who meets a magical mouse in the boiler room of the building he cleans. Fearing for its life, the mouse promises the janitor his every wish. He wishes for promotions but is dissatisfied with each of them. Finally, he wishes that he could inhabit God's own office, and this wish too is granted. He finds himself back in the boiler room!

Christ finds his resting place among us. Here among God's people is his place. And here among one another we find our resting place—our fulfillment.

Responsive Reading

PSALM 147 (RCL/RC)

See the First Sunday after Christmas/The Holy Family, p. 58.

PSALM 84 (BCP)

Interpreting the Text

Pilgrims sing this psalm as they approach the Temple. It begins and reaches its climax by speaking of the temple as God's house. The Temple is the place God's presence dwells (v. 1), the worshipers' home (vv. 4 and 10), and even a home for birds (v. 3). Between these affirmations of the Temple as the believers' home, the psalmist describes the richness of the lives of those who find their belonging there (vv. 4-9).

Responding to the Text

For the psalmist the Temple is a home for the homeless. Like birds without nests, all of us who seek a home find it in God's house. But God has now taken a new home. Home is where the heart is. And Christ is God's heart (John 1:18). In Christ's birth the world has become God's dwelling place. Our home is with God in the world, among the community of faith. (See also Responding to the Text under Jeremiah 31:7-14, p. 78.)

WISDOM OF SOLOMON 10:15-21 (RCL)

Interpreting the Text

The reading is the final stanza of the author's ode to wisdom (vv. 1-21). It attributes to wisdom God's liberation of Israel from Egypt through Moses. Wisdom guided the people in their wilderness trek (v. 17), led them through the sea (v. 18), defeated their "oppressors" (vv. 15-16 and 19-20a), and opened their mouths to praise God (vv. 20-21). Wisdom is pictured here as the divine presence that empowered Moses (v. 16) and the people.

Responding to the Text

Through wisdom God led the people out of their oppression in Egypt. Wisdom—God's very own presence—broke the bonds of Israel's slavery and freed them to become God's children.

God has now acted for our liberation. Wisdom became flesh and blood in Jesus to break the bonds that hold us in oppression—the "dread kings" of our own sin and brokenness. In Christ God repeats the Exodus experience of Israel for our benefit. The liberator God will not rest until all humans are free and embraced by divine care.

SECOND READING
EPHESIANS 1:3-19

Interpreting the Text

After a salutation (vv. 1-2), the epistle to the Ephesians begins with a prayer in typical Jewish form ("Blessed be the God," v. 3). Some of the features of a Pauline thanksgiving are evident in the prayer. The passage has two components. The first is the rich theological statement in verses 3-14, and the second the author's further petitions for readers in verses 15-19 (which continue through v. 23).

Verses 3-14 capture the benefits of God's act in Christ for humans. The author speaks of that act first as part of the divine plan for humanity from the beginning (vv. 3-6). The next verses explore the "mystery" of the divine will, including redemption, forgiveness, and grace (vv. 7-9). Christ revealed the divine destiny "to gather all things" and to bestow an inheritance of hope (vv. 10-12). The first section comes to a conclusion by speaking of God's "pledge" to us in the Holy Spirit (vv. 13-14).

The second part of the reading begins with the author's statement of gratitude for the readers (vv. 15-16). It then turns to petitions on their behalf (vv. 17-19a). In summary, those include knowing "the hope to which he has called you" (v. 18) and the divine power put at our disposal (v. 19a). The themes of "inheritance" and "hope" are repeated in this closing part of the reading. Christians are said to be chosen (v. 4) and "called" (v. 18).

The reading gathers a vast array of theological themes in only sixteen verses.

Responding to the Text

Many of us love a good mystery. There is nothing like watching the events unfold. Trying to find the decisive clue to the story. Puzzling out the solution to the mystery. Look at the list of best-selling novels. Scan the television dramas. Mysteries intrigue us!

The season of Christmas intrigues us, in part, because it entails a mystery. The author of Ephesians begins the letter with reference to the "mystery" of God's will. Why has the divine Son been born in this world? What is God up to?

The mystery begins with the birth of a baby. Mystery stories often begin with seemingly insignificant events. Agatha Christie loved to intrigue us with a gathering of people drawn from a variety of places. My favorite mystery for several years was the television series *Murder, She Wrote.* The hero of that series, Jessica Fletcher, would most often travel somewhere to visit friends. In both cases an innocent-enough beginning led to complications and eventually to a solution.

A seemingly innocuous birth begins the Christmas mystery. But you will have to hear the rest of the story to discover what was to unfold from that birth. The author of Ephesians claims there is a design to it all. A divine plan being worked out in Christ. Reading this passage in the Christmas season is like turning to the final chapter of a mystery novel.

The purpose of Christ's birth is to lavish us humans with God's love, kindness, forgiveness, and recovery. It is to pull us together as adopted children into God's community. Christmas leads us on in God's mystery. On to the ministry, the death, and finally the resurrection of the one born in Bethlehem.

The Christmas mystery is really only a door into a greater mystery: the mystery of God's love for us, the puzzle of how our Creator's good pleasure should name us beloved children. For that reason the author of Ephesians offers this prayer for us: May God "give you a spirit of wisdom and revelation as you come to know him."

And we go on trying to comprehend the mystery of God.

GOSPEL

JOHN 1:1-18 (RCL/RC)

Interpreting the Text

See Nativity of Our Lord 3 Christmas Day, pp. 50–52.

Responding to the Text

In the recent movie *City Hall*, the young vice-mayor thinks he knows his boss, the mayor of the city. He watches with amazement as the mayor manages the great city of New York. He admires his mentor's courage, persistence, and wisdom. Here is a politician who is making a difference! But then events take a puzzling turn. A six-year-old girl is killed in a shootout between police and a paroled convict. Why was the convict paroled so early? The young vice-mayor finally discovers that his hero had sold out to a powerful criminal organization. His mentor was responsible for the convict's parole. He didn't really know his boss after all.

Sometimes we wonder if we really know another. And sometimes we wonder if we really know God. Our world is filled with evil, and we wonder why God allows it. Some believe with confidence that God causes the death of innocent people, because it is God's will. Others claim God never causes pain and suffering. There are so many conflicting views of God. So many claim to know God, but their gods are so very different. In every war, the opposing sides always believe that God is on their side. Athletic teams sometimes even pray that God will be on their side in the competition. Do we really know God?

And the ways by which people say they have come to know God are so vastly different. We are rightly suspicious of some who say that God speaks to them. One deranged man recently entered a bank and shot and killed three people in cold blood. They say that the whole time he was doing it he was reciting the Lord's Prayer. Others find the God they know in the majesty and beauty of nature. Some discern God's will and strength for them through crystals or astrology. By what means do we come to know God?

The Gospel lesson for today ends with a clear and certain declaration of how it is we know God. The author writes: "No one has ever seen God. It is God the only Son, who is close to the Father's heart, who has made him known" (v. 18). God's very heart becomes a human being and lives among us. That is the way we know God. Through one man, grown from a baby born in an obscure village, we know our Creator. It may seem scandalous to make such a claim. But Christians have always taken this as the core of our faith. We do not come to know God through our own search. Not through the power of reason. Not through mysterious means. Not even through nature alone. God comes to us as a human being to reveal the divine heart.

The young vice-mayor in *City Hall* was looking for someone who made a difference in our world. In the one whose birth we celebrate this season we find a person who made a real difference. In Christ, God's true light and life has come into our world. We know God when we know Christ.

GOSPEL

MATTHEW 2:13-15, 19-23 (BCP)

See the First Sunday after Christmas/The Holy Family, pp. 63–65.

LUKE 2:41-52 (BCP)

Interpreting the Text

This story is found only in Luke and is the only story in the Gospels concerning Jesus' life prior to his ministry. The tale follows a simple pattern: setting (vv. 41-42), problem (vv. 43-45), resolution (vv. 46-49), and implications (vv. 50-52).

As good Jews who live outside of Jerusalem, the holy family makes the pilgrimage to the city for Passover. Passover celebrates Israel's exodus from Egypt (see Exod. 12:1-27; 23:15; Num. 9:2-14; Deut. 16:16). At twelve years, Jesus was old enough to begin formal religious training. The parents' loss of their son is a realistic scene; Jesus, they first think, is somewhere in the crowd of pilgrims. But they find Jesus engaged in learning from the teachers in the Temple (v. 47). His precocious participation in dialogue with the teachers points forward to his "wisdom" in verse 52.

His parents' distress is another touch of realism (v. 48). Jesus' response in verse 49, however, is the heart of the story. It alludes to that special relationship he has with God. His reference to God as "Father" contrasts with "father" used of Joseph. Jesus' parentage is not simply human.

Verse 50 foreshadows the human failure to understand Jesus' prediction of his passion (for instance, Luke 9:45 and 18:34). Jesus was an obedient child of his earthly parents as he was of his heavenly parent (v. 51a). The words used of Mary in verse 51 echo 2:19, and in both cases the Greek word can be translated either "things" or "words." The concluding verse summarizes Jesus' maturation in three categories. "Years" has often been translated "stature" (see Luke 19:3). "Wisdom" is the gift that was to enable his teaching. "Favor" may also be translated "grace," and refers to the love Jesus received from both humans and God. With verse 52 the author brackets this story with Jesus growth in wisdom and favor (see 2:40).

Responding to the Text

Have you ever said to another person, "Grow up!"? Has someone at some time ordered you to "grow up"? To grow up is to mature; it is to move from one stage of life to another. Growing up involves a process. It suggests that we are never done changing until the day we die.

My wife and I enjoyed a friendship with a couple through a period during which all four of us were making important vocational decisions. We shared a standing joke each time we were together: "Well, what do you want to be when you grow up?" In a sense it is no joke. It is a serious question about the process of maturing, growing, and becoming.

Luke shares with us a story of Jesus' process of growth. This fascinating glimpse into Jesus' childhood is filled with meaning. But one thing it surely suggests is that Jesus went through stages of growth. The verse in Luke 2 that immediately precedes our Gospel lesson for today reads: "The child [Jesus] grew and became strong, filled with wisdom; and the favor of God was upon him" (2:40). It sounds very much like the concluding verse of our reading. The evangelist seems to want to stress that Jesus grew up. Even this special child was subject to growth.

God invites us on an adventure in this season of Christmas. It is an adventure in discovering who we might become when we are empowered by God's grace. It is an adventure in discerning the gifts God may yet give us.

Human life is comprised of a process of becoming. When that process is halted, something dreadful happens. Psychologists speak even about people stagnating, stalled at one stage in maturation. Such tragedies abound today. Adults who have temper tantrums. People who have never resolved childhood conflicts with their parents. Each of us has probably experienced something about ourselves that betrays a failure to grow up.

Luke's attention to Jesus' growth is important. The process of our own growth is part of our calling as Christians. Christian discipleship is a process of becoming—one that entails wisdom and favor as well as physical growth. Too often we may want to freeze at one stage. Growing in favor with humans and with God entails always stretching ourselves with new ideas. Jesus allowed himself to be stretched that day in the temple.

We venture to grow because we don't know what we might yet become. God invites us on an adventure in this season of Christmas. It is an adventure in discovering who we might become when we are empowered by God's grace. It is an adventure in discerning the gifts God may yet give us.

Gospel

MATTHEW 2:1-12 (BCP)

Interpreting the Text

This well-known story is found only in Matthew. The narrative develops through three stages. Verses 1-2 introduce the wise men and their quest; verses 3-8 involve Herod; and verses 9-12 recount the wise men's discovery of Jesus, their actions there, and their return to their home. (See Matt. 2:13-23 in the First Sunday after Christmas, pp. 63–65, for a related exegesis.)

The "wise men" were probably court priests in an eastern country (perhaps Syria). Their task was the interpretation of dreams and the study of the heavenly planets (that is, astrology). They are important in the Gospel because they represent Gentiles who seek Jesus out. Verse 2 summarizes their quest and its purpose. Because the wise men themselves are from the east and see the star in the western sky, "star at its rising" is a preferable translation here of the ambiguous Greek phrase that can also mean "star of the east." "King of the Jews" is Herod's official title and suggests Jesus is his competitor.

Herod and "all Jerusalem" are appropriately "frightened," since they correctly understand that this birth threatens the security of the status quo (v. 3). Matthew's second Old Testament citation (v. 6) is on the lips of Herod's advisors and is a mixture of Micah 5:2 and 2 Samuel 5:2. Under the guise of piety Herod then attempts to deceive the wise men into aiding his plan to eliminate this rival to his office (vv. 7-8).

The wise men follow the star to the house where the holy family dwells. There they pay "homage" to Jesus and present their gifts (vv. 10-11). The tradition that there were three wise men arose from the fact that they present three gifts. "Gold" is an appropriate gift for any king. "Frankincense and myrrh" were aromatic substances, sometimes thought to have medicinal as well as religious value (see Isa. 60:6). The wise men present gifts that were valued in their own culture. These interpreters of dreams have received their own dream that warned them of Herod's intent. So, they do not report their discovery to him but return to "their own country" (v. 12).

Responding to the Text

(This story is interwoven with the succeeding one in 2:13-23, so readers may want to consult Responding to the Text connected with it in the First Sunday after Christmas/The Holy Family, pp. 63–65.)

The wise men followed a star in their quest. "Following a star" is precarious at best. Who knows where it will lead you? But these men were willing to risk it. So, they became "star followers." And it paid off! Their efforts led them to Jesus where they worshiped him and presented their gifts.

We hear lots of less successful people who follow stars but remain only wannabes. But these wise men are different. They do not follow a star in hope of fame and fortune. They risk the long journey in order to worship and present gifts to one they have heard is a new king. Their star following seeks to honor another, not to gain honor for themselves.

Christmas makes all of us Christians star followers. The Gospel message invites us to undertake a journey, a risky trek into the unknown. Stars are not very specific. Matthew's story never makes clear how exactly the star's location led the wise men to that one house in Bethlehem. Disciples who follow stars need all the wisdom they can muster. And where the star leads us may not be where we had hoped we would go.

The movie *A Family Thing* is the story of an apparently Caucasian man who finds out his birth mother was an African American. He sets out to find his brother, who unlike him is clearly African American. But finding his brother only moves him out on another journey to reconcile himself with his parentage. Every fiber of his racist being aches. But to his surprise he discovers love and dignity in his new family. He wins a new brother, aunt, and nephew. His journey leads him where he did not want to go, but at journey's end he is a new man.

CHRISTMAS MAKES ALL OF US CHRISTIANS STAR FOLLOWERS. THE GOSPEL MESSAGE INVITES US TO UNDERTAKE A JOURNEY, A RISKY TREK INTO THE UNKNOWN.

Star following for us Christians is no less predictable. It leads us to find a new family. The disciples who followed Jesus were surprised by the journey, surprised by the startling things they learned along the way, and even more surprised by the empty tomb at the journey's end.

But star followers never go it alone. Tradition tells us there were three wise men. Matthew actually never tells us how many of them there were. What we know is that they were not loners. They undertook their quest together. So, we Christian star followers travel in groups called congregations. We need one another for the journey. The community's support, wisdom, and companionship make the journey possible.

Christmas invites us as a community of faith to follow the star of God's promise in Christ. The star of that promise may take us along difficult paths, and we may not end up where we thought we would. But we can depend on one another when the going gets tough. And, after all, the joy is in the journey itself.

Notes

1. Samuel Beckett, *Waiting for Godot: A Tragicomedy in Two Acts* (New York: Grove Press, 1954), 59.

2. Joseph A. Fitzmyer, *Romans: A New Translation with Introduction and Commentary,* The Anchor Bible, William Foxwell Albright and David Noel Freedman, general eds. Vol. 33. (New York: Doubleday, 1993), 706.

3. Martin Luther, "Lectures on Romans. Glosses and Scholia." Hilton C. Oswald, ed. *Luther's Works.* Jaroslav Pelikan and Helmut Lehmann, general eds. Vol. 25. (Saint Louis: Concordia Publishing House, 1972), 518.

4. Isaac Bashevis Singer, *Shosha.* Hilda Rosner, trans. (New York: Farrar, Straus and Giroux, 1978), 277.

5. Herman Hesse, *Siddhartha* (New York: New Directions, 1951), 118.

6. Dietrich Bonhoeffer, *Act and Being*, Bernard Noble, trans. (New York: Harper and Row, 1961), 89.

7. Amos Niven Wilder, *Grace Confounding: Poems by Amos Niven Wilder* (Philadelphia: Fortress Press, 1972), 1.

8. Arthur Miller, *Death of a Salesman* (New York: Penguin Books, 1976), 138.

9. Allen Oliver, "A Night at the Inn." *The 11 O'Clock News and Other Experimental Sermons.* John Killinger, ed. (Nashville: Abingdon Press, 1975).

10. Jon Hassler, *Rookery Blues* (New York: Ballantine Books, 1995), 82.

11. Luther, Martin. "Sermons II." Hans J. Hillerbrand, ed. *Luther's Works.* Helmut T. Lehmann, general ed. Vol. 52. (Philadelphia: Fortress Press, 1974), 12.

12. Andrew A. Rooney, *A Few Minutes with Andy Rooney* (New York: Warner Books, 1981), 322.

13. *Lutheran Book of Worship* (Minneapolis: Augsburg Fortress Publishers, 1978), number 70.

14. Reinhold Niebuhr, *The Nature and Destiny of Man: A Christian Interpretation* (New York: Charles Scribner's Sons, 1955). One volume edition, 313.

15. Martin Luther King Jr., *Stride Toward Freedom* (New York: Ballantine Books, 1958), 167.

Recommended Works

Boring, M. Eugene. "The Gospel of Matthew: Introduction, Commentary and Reflections." *The New Interpreter's Bible.* Leander E. Keck, general ed. Vol. VIII. Nashville: Abingdon Press, 1995. Pages 87–505.

Brueggemann, Walter. *The Message of the Psalms: A Theological Commentary.* Augsburg Old Testament Studies. Minneapolis: Augsburg Publishing House, 1984.

Clements, R. E. *Isaiah 1–39.* New Century Bible Commentary. Ronald E. Clements and Matthew Black, general eds. Grand Rapids and London: Wm. B. Eerdmans Publishing Co. and Marshall, Morgan and Scott Publishers, Ltd., 1980.

Davies, Margaret. *Matthew.* Readings: A New Biblical Commentary. David Clines, general ed. Sheffield, England: Sheffield Academic Press, 1993.

Fitzmyer, Joseph A. *The Gospel According to Luke I–IX: A New Translation with Introduction and Commentary.* The Anchor Bible. William Foxwell Albright and David Noel Freedman, general eds. Vol. 28. New York: Doubleday, 1981.

Garland, David E. *Reading Matthew: A Literary and Theology Commentary on the First Gospel.* New York: Crossroad, 1995.

The HarperCollins Study Bible. New Revised Standard Version with the Apocryphal/Deuterocanonical Books. Wayne A. Meeks, general ed. New York: HarperCollins Publishers, 1993.

Harrington, Daniel J. *The Gospel of Matthew.* Sacra Pagina. Daniel J. Harrington, S.J., ed. Collegeville: The Liturgical Press, 1991.

O'Day, Gail R. "The Gospel of John: Introduction, Commentary and Reflections." *The New Interpreter's Bible.* Leander E. Keck, general ed. Vol. IX. Nashville: Abingdon Press, 1995. Pages 491–865.

Whybray, R. N. *Isaiah 40–66.* New Century Bible Commentary. Ronald E. Clements and Matthew Black, general eds. Grand Rapids and London: Wm. B. Eerdmans Publishing Co. and Marshall, Morgan and Scott Publishers, Ltd., 1975.

THE SEASON OF EPIPHANY

ROBERT H. SMITH

To call Epiphany "the Season of Light" is to speak the truth and nothing but the truth, but it is not the whole truth. Epiphany is the season not of light alone but of light and kingship. Or since "kingship" is a word burdened with heavy negative baggage in much current discussion, we might better call Epiphany the season of starburst and sovereignty.

If ever there is a time for massing candles in church, it is during the season of Epiphany. Kings come to the brightness of his rising, led by a splendid star shining nova-like in the night sky, guiding the Magi on their long, difficult journey through many dark valleys. What star was that? What is any star? Large dictionaries have a way of overdoing it. One defines a star, any star, as "a self-luminous, gaseous celestial body of great mass whose own gravitation produces high internal pressure and temperature resulting in atomic and nuclear processes that cause the star to emit electromagnetic radiation."[1] Readers may be excused for scratching their heads in wonder and deciding to consult poets instead of scientific entries in dictionaries. The poets do seem more helpful. They celebrate the "Star of wonder, star of night, star with royal beauty bright."[2] That familiar hymn correctly notes the connection between "star" and "royalty."

The star bursting out of the East led the Magi by a crooked path to Bethlehem, where the Magi came to understand that Israel and all humanity had a really new King. And wasn't it the same star that burst through the clouds on the Mount of Transfiguration, when Peter, James, and John heard the voice of God greeting Jesus with the words, "This is my Son"? That echoing of the old royal psalm at the end of Epiphany means that God has indeed designated Jesus to be the "prince" of a bright and peaceable "kingdom," just as the Magi thought.

And the light of that star keeps bursting forth in reading after reading all through Epiphany. The bright sky split wide open to reveal the still brighter light of heaven when the Spirit came down like a dove onto the head of Jesus standing knee-deep in Jordan's water (Matt. 3:13-17). The disciples saw his shining glory when he provisioned the wedding at Cana with great quantities of new wine, and while the chief steward may have been unclear on the concept, the disciples took a significant step on their journey from darkness to light (John 2:1-11). The psalmist extols God as "my light and my salvation" (Psalm 27), but Jesus surprises his followers by telling them that they themselves are "the light of the world" (Matt. 5:13). And before Jesus begins his descent into the dark pathways leading him to the cross and us to Lent, his face shines like the noonday sun atop the Mount of Transfiguration (Matt. 17:1-9).

So the mysterious star ruling the sky above the Magi did not burn itself out on Christmas Night in Bethlehem long ago. Nor was Transfiguration the last of it. It leads us today along a path through all the Sundays of this season, casting light in many directions but insisting especially that we examine kings and kingship in the sometimes harsh light of the Star of Bethlehem. Epiphany's light in fact exposes the spectacular failings of ordinary human sovereignties, calls them into question, and leads us to "Another King." Light and kingship, or starburst and sovereignty, are twin themes of the readings for these days.

THE EPIPHANY OF OUR LORD

JANUARY 6, 1999

REVISED COMMON	EPISCOPAL (BCP)	ROMAN CATHOLIC
Isa. 60:1-6	Isa. 60:1-6, 9	Isa. 60:1-6
Ps. 72:1-7, 10-14	Ps. 72 or 72:1-2, 10-17	Ps. 72:1-2, 7-8, 10-13
Eph. 3:2-12	Eph. 3:1-12	Eph. 3:2-3a, 5-6
Matt. 2:1-12	Matt. 2:1-12	Matt. 2:1-12

"WHERE IS THE NEW KING?"

ISAIAH FORESAW KINGS OF THE NATIONS coming in caravan and festal procession, bearing precious gifts for the beautification of Zion-Jerusalem, and he rejoiced at the prospect of the birth of a new king calling him "Prince of Peace" and honoring him with other high titles. Partly because of Isaiah's far-seeing prophecy and partly because they bear gifts "fit for a king," the pilgrims whom Matthew calls "Magi" have become "three kings" in the Christian imagination. Far from claiming kingship for themselves, they came to surrender their gifts and their very selves to the service of the newborn king. They met two kings on the way: Herod and Jesus. The star was responsible for leading them to Jerusalem but then away from Jerusalem to Bethlehem, a mere six miles away. But in those half-dozen miles they discovered a world of difference between Herod's rule and God's fresh sovereignty in Jesus. What an odd "king" this Jesus turns out to be, with his words and his silence, with his action and his passion, his deep powers and his puzzling cross.

WHAT AN ODD "KING" THIS JESUS TURNS OUT TO BE, WITH HIS WORDS AND HIS SILENCE, WITH HIS ACTION AND HIS PASSION, HIS DEEP POWERS AND HIS PUZZLING CROSS.

First Reading

ISAIAH 60:1-6, 9

"Endless Dominion or New Politics?"

Since the end of the nineteenth century, Isaiah 56–66 has been widely regarded as a separate section of the great prophetic book and has been called "Third Isaiah." "First Isaiah" (chaps. 1–39) was composed by Isaiah of Jerusalem in the latter half of the eighth century B.C.E. during the crisis precipitated by a cruel and expansionist Assyria. "Second Isaiah" (chaps. 40–55) consists of oracles addressed by disciples of Isaiah to exiles in Babylon almost two hundred years later (ca. 550 B.C.E.). "Third Isaiah" (chaps. 56–66) addressed not Israelites languishing in exile but returnees back in Judea.

The returnees had regained their beloved city of Jerusalem, repaired its fallen walls, built a new Temple (515 B.C.E.), and developed a civic and religious life centered on the Temple. From the point of view of this Third Isaiah, however, the rebuilt Temple was a problem. The leaders promoted a temple-oriented spirituality, insisted on prescribed ritual at prescribed times in the prescribed place, and enforced a strict separation from the Gentiles. When not condemning the narrow outlook of the appointed leaders, or otherwise lamenting the sad spiritual state of the returnees, Third Isaiah waxes eloquent about the future glory of Zion beyond the present Jerusalem and about the wonder of a new Temple beyond Zerubbabel's poor substitute for Solomon's lost original.

Isaiah 60 opens with a vision of God's coming theophany. In a time when "darkness shall cover the earth and thick darkness the peoples," precisely then "the glory of the Lord will arise upon you" (60:2). "Nations shall come to your light and kings to the brightness of your dawn" (60:3). God will suddenly burst upon the world more brilliantly than the sun exploding on the world at each day's dawning, scattering the deep darkness of night.

What does the prophet see in that light? All the children of Zion wending their way home from the nations where they have been scattered (60:4). Moving in concert with that stream of humanity, the prophet sees caravans laden with the wealth of the nations flowing to Jerusalem (60:5-7). That great river of wealth will finance the reconstruction and beautification of Jerusalem in most glorious fashion (60:13, 17). Foreign peoples, including even their kings, will labor to rebuild her walls and minister to her (61:10-11). In the words of the prophet, "You [Zion] shall suck the milk of nations; you shall suck the breasts of kings" (60:16).

The problem with this vision so far is that it sounds all too much as though one system of domination simply replaces another. Maybe the new system is bigger, more powerful, more splendid, but is it still a great pyramid with a king and courtiers at the apex supported by a vast faceless populace at the bottom? The prophet struggles to find images that will show how the coming theophany issues not only in a new polis but also in a new politics. He announces that the walls of that city have the name "Salvation," and its gates are called "Praise." It has overseers and taskmasters named "Peace" and "Righteousness" (vv. 17-18). In that bright future day, Jerusalem, blessed so abundantly and in such astonishing fashion, will finally become what Yahweh always intended: a light to the nations (60:3). This is no ordinary city. It is the inspiration behind John's vision of the New Jerusalem in Revelation 21–22. But it is easy to misread Isaiah and Revelation in triumphalistic fashion, as if God is promising that those now oppressed will some day turn the tables and, having seized power, will begin to oppress their former oppressors.

Women, long excluded from the corridors of power, are in the vanguard of those calling into question our continued churchly use of the words *king* and *lord* to describe God and the Christ. Those titles are freighted with the baggage of patriarchy, hierarchy, and domineering ways. And yet most American Christians exhibit a nearly boundless capacity to tolerate the language of kingship. Our patience with that language arises in part from the fact that it is biblical. But other reasons can be found. One of my students raised the possibility that our tolerance for such language may be due in part to the fact that we have had no personal experience of kings and other royalty. Our necks have not felt the sole of a king's boot bearing down on us. To us the language of kingship is all sanitized and grand. Feminists insist that we may not have literal kings, but we do live in systems of domination, and the biblical language of kingship lends its prestige to those systems to the detriment of women and children, to the terrible hurt of all the poor and the powerless in our society. We must find better language, we are told.

CHRIST IN HIS TERRIBLE WEAKNESS, WITH HIS CROSS AND WITH HIS HABIT OF CRITICIZING DOMINATION, IS A MOST POWERFUL FIGURE, SENDING SHIVERS DOWN THE SPINES OF ALL GUARDIANS OF OLD-FASHIONED PATRIARCHY AND ENTRENCHED PRIVILEGE.

But isn't the whole point of Isaiah and all the readings of Epiphany to convince us that Christ is our long-awaited king and lord? Isn't he King and Lord with a capital *K* and a capital *L*? The answer has to be "Yes, but!" Jesus is something like a king and yet far different. He is something like a lord or boss or owner, but he is no ordinary "lord."

Of course, many (not men alone) say that we are obliged to continue speaking of God and Jesus as Lord and King. If we shun the language of kingship, on the grounds that attendant images of domination have long been used to legitimate oppression, will we not be in danger of falling into a saccharine sentimentality? The latter has been lampooned by Dorothy Sayers, herself a feminist and certainly sensitive to the issues involved, in these words: "We have very efficiently pared the claws of the Lion of Judah, certified him meek and mild, and recommended him as a fitting household pet for pale curates and pious old ladies."[3] In actual fact, as Dorothy Sayers knew quite well, Christ in his terrible weakness, with his cross and with his habit of criticizing domination, is a most powerful figure, sending shivers down the spines of all guardians of old-fashioned patriarchy and entrenched privilege.

So is he "king" or not? Which nouns and verbs are adequate to the task of naming God and Christ? And which are inadequate? It is far easier to define the problem than it is to offer practicable solutions with any broad base of acceptance. Poet and hymn writer Brian Wren works on these issues steadily and with great imagination. He offers these guidelines for re-imaging God in a way that is innovative and yet faithful to Scripture: Use strong images that clash with one another and yet together offer a balanced picture; follow the liberating lead of divine love that always moves in the direction of embracing the oppressed; experience God as Trinity, which is to say, experience God "not as a single, isolated being, the mon-arch, but as a complex, coequal unity in relatedness."[4]

The lectionary itself offers us multiple readings each Sunday morning, from more than one moment in the history of God's dealings with humankind, and the readings are far richer in imagery and suggestion than the more sanitized language of philosophical theology or the carelessly repeated images of popular piety.

Responsive Reading
PSALM 72

"A Song for a King"

Psalm 72 is a "royal psalm" composed on the occasion of the king's coronation. John F. Kennedy revived the ancient custom by inviting Robert Frost to read a freshly composed poem on the occasion of his inauguration in 1961. Maya Angelou and then Miller Williams were invited to write a poem on the occasion of Bill Clinton's first and second inaugurations.

The inauguration of the American president always comes in the season of Epiphany. Newspapers editorialize about "the orderly succession or transfer of power" in the U.S.A., unlike some other systems. It is that, but it is also a time when people listen hard to the new president to hear whether he has anything significant to say about the use to which he proposes to put the powers transferred to him in such peaceful and orderly fashion. What is the program? How does he identify the ills of the nation and his own response to those ills? Does he have a vision for the nation?

After Bill Clinton's second inaugural one reporter listed words used for the first time in any inauguration speech. Among them was the name "Martin Luther King Jr." Many recalled King's memorable speech with its stirring refrain, "I have a dream." Many in the land today think of their elected leaders not as dreaming great dreams but only as scheming low schemes.

The royal psalmist (Psalm 72) has a dream of long life for the king. He lays it on thick. He hopes that the king may live as long as sun and moon rise in the sky day by day and night after night through all generations (vv. 5-7). No term limits for this king! And he envisions not only length of days but breadth of reign, from sea to sea (Mediterranean to Persian Gulf), "from the River to the ends of the earth" (Euphrates to the islands of the Mediterranean). The psalmist envisions powerful rulers becoming clients of the new king of Jerusalem, rendering him rich tribute (vv. 8-11). With further flattering phrases the ancient poet prays that the king's name and fame might endure until the sun burns itself out like a cinder (v. 17).

But the real business of this psalmist and the fundamental hope of people deserving of the name "biblical" comes in the descriptions of the program set for the new king in this royal psalm: justice, righteousness, and peace. And those great words are defined in terms of defense of the poor, deliverance for the needy, liberation of the oppressed, and the crushing of the oppressor (vv. 1-4), and pity on the weak and rescue for the needy (vv. 13-14). Under such a royal rule the people will "blossom in the cities like the grass of the field" (v. 16). Then the promise of blessing to the nations through Abraham will be realized (v. 17). When king and people live in such justice and peace, then God's glory (not theirs) will fill the whole earth (v. 19).

Miller Williams on January 20, 1997, read his poem "Of History and Hope." In it he spoke of "believing ourselves toward all we have tried to become: just and compassionate, equal, able and free." What gives Williams hope, he says, in spite of our repeated failures, is "the children, the children." The gospel for the festival of Epiphany pins hopes on "the Child, the Child."

Second Reading

EPHESIANS 3:1-12

"Teaching Wisdom to the Rulers"

The opening of the third chapter of Ephesians should come as a shock. In the earlier chapters Paul is pictured as spilling out a torrent of phrases blessing God, "the Father of glory" (1:17), who deliberated and made a plan even before the foundation of the world (1:4), and who in the fullness of time enacted that mystery of his will, gathering up everything in heaven and on earth in Jesus Christ (1:9-10), who now sits at God's right hand, exalted high above all angelic powers (1:20-21).

Ephesians 3 goes on to picture Paul, the agent and envoy of this world-creating, powerfully active God, as a prisoner of the Roman Empire! Writing to the churches from behind bars (3:1; 4:1), he is an "ambassador in chains" (6:20). He became Christ's agent, not as one of the original Twelve summoned by Jesus from fishing or from the toll collector's booth but by a sudden incursion into his life on the part of the resurrected and glorified Jesus (Gal. 1:11-17). Because he was faithful to that glorious Jesus, Paul wound up behind bars in one of Rome's dingy prison cells!

Paul may be in chains (6:20), but his vision is unfettered. He claims to know "the mystery of God's will" (1:9), which is the "mystery of Christ" (3:4). This long-hidden plan of God, now at last made known and set in motion through the death and resurrection of Jesus Christ, is God's decision to seize the Gentiles and include them together with the commonwealth of Israel, the people of the ancient covenant (2:12), in one new people.

This mystery of the inclusion of the Gentiles is the mystery of the divine generosity, God's boundless riches in Christ (3:8). It is a stunning and humbling mystery, the mystery of God whose ways and thoughts are not our own. God is a deep wellspring of continuous surprises, and God is more giving than we deserve or even desire. "God is greater than our hearts" (1 John 3:20). *Deus semper maior:* God is always and in all ways simply greater.

At first it looks as though Paul is using fresh images but essentially repeating what he has already said in chapter 2. There he talks of God's work in breaking down the dividing wall of hostility between Jew and Gentile and of the way God the Creator and Redeemer has taken the two disparate masses of humankind and made out of them one new human being in Christ (2:11-22). In chapter 3 Paul offers three new images hard to reproduce in idiomatic English: Gentiles are coheirs, co-members, co-participants in the promise (3:6).

But Paul goes beyond even that when he utters fresh and astonishing words about how God plans to use the church to make something new known. Making known, of course, is the theme of Epiphany. But what is made known, and to whom? God's plan, says Ephesians, is to make known "the wisdom of God in its rich variety" not simply to the nations but "to the rulers and authorities in the heavenly places" (3:10).

Like other ancients Paul believed that tribes and peoples and nations not only have different histories and traditions, different languages and customs, different perspectives and energies; they have different angels. And the evil angels are organized by "the ruler of the course of this world," a.k.a. the devil (2:1-2). But now in the fullness of time God is acting to create one new humanity, liberated from the oppressions and distortions of the evil one.

In Ephesians Paul celebrates in singing words the inclusion of Gentiles into the commonwealth of Israel, God's gracious embracing of Gentiles together with Jews. Elsewhere Paul offers an even more comprehensive vision, saying that in Christ "there is no longer Jew or Greek, there is no longer slave or free, there is no longer male and female; for all of you are one in Christ Jesus" (Gal. 3:28).

Jew and Gentile, slave and free, male and female are racial, cultural, economic, and gender categories that have exerted tremendous power over the human imagination through the millennia. Through much of Western history it has been assumed that Jews and slaves and women must defer to the free Christian men who happen to have the power. And "defer" is a very mild word to describe the submissiveness that has been demanded.

But when human beings who deeply differ from one another manage to live together and rejoice together in the grace or wealth of God, they teach the demons an elementary lesson about whose universe this is and whose name shall be hallowed and whose will shall be done. God is the Creator (3:9), the source and ground of all peoples and in fact of all that is, visible and invisible, material and spiritual. And God, the source of all and lover of all, wants to teach the demons of division a severe yet glorious lesson. What kind of teachers are we in our churches?

WHEN HUMAN BEINGS WHO DEEPLY DIFFER FROM ONE ANOTHER MANAGE TO LIVE TOGETHER AND REJOICE TOGETHER IN THE GRACE OR WEALTH OF GOD, THEY TEACH THE DEMONS AN ELEMENTARY LESSON ABOUT WHOSE UNIVERSE THIS IS AND WHOSE NAME SHALL BE HALLOWED AND WHOSE WILL SHALL BE DONE.

Epiphany is, of course, a time of worship, of giving glory to the Lord of the universe. But what does it mean to glorify, to worship? Jesus is not exalted and glorified when we praise his name with proper titles and at the same time refuse to practice love. What a tortured history burdens relations between "Jew and Gentile." And how terribly the American nation is burdened still today because of its history of slavery. And glass ceilings in corporations and crimes of violence on American streets and in American homes offer grim testimony to the continuing warfare of the sexes even in our enlightened time. All this is neither easy nor pleasant to contemplate. The history of relations between male and female, Jew and Greek, rich and poor has been bedeviled by demonic powers from the beginning and not just by demons floating in the air high above the human scene. Demons inside the church, inside the Christian heart, inside the human heart have worked terrible wrongs, in deepest contradiction of Paul's expansive vision.

When once-alienated people live reconciled lives, practicing love for those who are "other," then they not only talk about but enact the new situation: demons are dethroned, and the crucified and resurrected Christ is exalted.

Gospel

MATTHEW 2:1-12

"Three Kings or Two?"

In the old hymn, the Magi say of themselves, "We Three Kings of Orient Are." The number three derives of course from the fact of three gifts. That they were kings is nowhere stated by Matthew, but it is a deduction drawn by pious people from the first lesson (Isaiah 60) and the psalm (Psalm 72). Justin Martyr (d. ca. 165) thought they came from Arabia but the view of Clement of Alexandria (d. ca. 215) has prevailed. He said they arrived from Persia, and artists have clothed them in Persian garb ever since. From sometime in the sixth century they have had their now-familiar names: Balthasar, Caspar, and Melchior.

Many feel that their story has been hopelessly sentimentalized. They would like relief from Sunday School kids dressed in bathrobes, wearing paper crowns on their heads, marching down the center aisle bearing brightly wrapped packages in their small hands. And yet it would be an unimaginable loss to give up the story. Opera companies and repertory theaters repeat the same old stories season after season, and audiences keep returning. The story all by itself is as necessary as earth, as air, as fire, as water. Theater has been described as the "temple of story."[5] That label fits the church even better than the theater and in fact looks like it was borrowed from the church.

But what's going on here? Karl Rahner says that when the Magi laid their gifts before the child, they did not do a new thing but did what they had actually been doing all along in their lives, what they had been doing throughout their search and journey: "They brought before the face of the invisible God now made visible the gold of their love, the incense of their reverence, and the myrrh of their suffering."[6]

Rahner is hardly the first to contemplate the meaning of those gifts. Gold is a gift fit for a king, incense is an offering to a god, and myrrh is a necessity of every human funeral. That's an ancient christological interpretation. But the gifts have also spawned many other edifying interpretations. Johann Bengel, for example, thought of the gold of a believing heart, the incense of prayer, and the myrrh of self-denial.

It is worth mulling over those gifts time and again. In one of her books, Barbara Kingsolver tells how one day she walked into her kitchen and was startled to find three strangers burglarizing her house. "What a bizarre tableau of anti-Magi they made, these three unwise men, bearing a camera, an electric guitar, and a Singer sewing machine." Somehow, she writes, she persuaded them to put down the things they were holding and flee from her house.[7] Think of the "treasures" they were about to carry off. These "gifts" of the "anti-Magi" reveal something of the character of the Kingsolver household. They tell a story of the family and its interests and habits.

We will never finish unwrapping the gifts of the original Magi. We can always find something new in them. We are following Matthew's lead when we examine the gifts in line with Matthew's interest in the kingship of Jesus as a total contrast with the kingship of Herod. The Magi laid gold and frankincense and myrrh at the feet of the new "king." Gold means they give up the old economics. Frankincense means letting go of old patterns of worship and ever-new forms of propaganda. Myrrh means the renunciation of death and violence, bloodshed and slaughter, arms and warfare as means of settling our disputes.

In the advent and adoration of the Magi, Matthew sees the fulfillment of scripture, of God's purpose, of a design written in the cosmos ages ago. The universe had been groaning in anticipation, straining forward, full of good hope. But anticipating what, hoping for what? Not just one more king, perhaps incrementally superior to all other kings. Both Isaiah and the psalmist lifted eyes beyond the newly crowned king to the full epiphany of God's sovereignty. What did they behold in their ecstatic visions? They saw nothing less than old kingships overthrown, old systems of domination undone, old politics deconstructed.

Herod the Great was a seasoned practitioner of the old politics. He had become king through bribery (gold) and bloodshed (myrrh), and he longed for the people's adoration (incense). Josephus, in his histories of the ancient Jewish people, fills page after page with stories about Herod and his intrigues. Josephus says nothing of the "slaughter of the innocents" at Bethlehem (Matt. 2:16-18), but what he does tell us agrees with the impression of a cruel tyrant painted by Matthew. Herod murdered his wife Mariamme, her mother Alexandra, and three of his own children, prompting the Emperor Augustus to exclaim, "I would rather be Herod's pig than Herod's son."

The Gospel for Epiphany is of course a story not only of Magi and their gifts but of Herod and Jesus, of the old king and the very new king. We have come to call the Magi "kings," but Matthew does not. He wants to focus our minds not on "three kings" but on two and two alone: King Herod and King Jesus. These are two different royal majesties with competing sovereignties, one with a very old politics and one with a quite new politics.

THE BAPTISM OF OUR LORD

JANUARY 10, 1999

FIRST SUNDAY AFTER THE EPIPHANY

REVISED COMMON	EPISCOPAL (BCP)	ROMAN CATHOLIC
Isa. 42:1-9	Isa. 42:1-9	Isa. 42:1-4, 6-7
Psalm 29	Ps. 89:1-29 or 89:20-29	Ps. 29:1-4, 9-11
Acts 10:34-43	Acts 10:34-38	Acts 10:34-38
Matt. 3:13-17	Matt. 3:13-17	Matt. 3:13-17

"PAX ROMANA, PAX HEBRAICA, PAX AMERICANA"

ISRAELI WRITER JACOBO TIMMERMAN, surveying the destruction wrought by Israel's bombardment of Tyre and Sidon and Beirut during the war in Lebanon, spoke bitterly of a "Pax Hebraica." He was of course echoing ancient propaganda of the Caesars who boasted of establishing a "Pax Romana." A conquered British chieftain is quoted by Tacitus as saying, "The Romans create a desert and call it 'peace.'" Today some critics of American policies in the world speak sneeringly or sadly of a "Pax Americana," as the United States continues to insist on sanctions against Iraq and Cuba in spite of the crippling effects on those nation's infrastructures and the hurt inflicted on the weakest members of those societies.

> WHAT "PEACE" AND WHAT "KINGDOM" DO CHRISTIANS SEEK AS THEY FOLLOW JESUS, INSTALLED AS "KING" AT HIS BAPTISM IN THE JORDAN RIVER?

The record of the developed nations is one of enlightenment and generosity mingled with gloomy clouds of industrial pollution and factories pumping out military hardware destined for sale to countries too poor to support their own military-industrial complex. What "peace" and what "kingdom" do Christians seek as they follow Jesus, installed as "king" at his baptism in the Jordan River?

First Reading

ISAIAH 42:1-9

"The Power of the Servant"

This first of the "Servant Songs" opens with none other than the Lord pointing to Israel. God solemnly declares that this poor people, on the verge of return but still in exile, holds a special place in God's affections and intentions. God is Creator of the whole vast universe (v. 5a) and has given breath and spirit to every living creature (v. 5b). But this servant-people is uniquely "my chosen, bearer of my spirit, my life, my energy, my purpose" (v. 1). The whole scene is played out again at Jesus' baptism (Matt. 3:16-17).

The servant is both blessed and burdened. Servant-Israel is entrusted with the hard task of bringing forth justice to the nations. That means more than talking about God's justice or advertising God as a God of justice. It means causing the righteousness of God to become a reality all the way to the ends of the earth. It means exporting God's sovereign rule of justice to distant peoples, just as the sun rises in the east and spreads light upon all nations (v. 6).

Can this really be the task of God's puny servant? This job description is so astonishing that the prophet fears we may not hear it, and so the phrase echoes three times in four verses: "Bring forth justice to the nations" (v. 1), "faithfully bring forth justice" (v. 3), "establish justice in the earth" (v. 4). And the coastlands, distant peoples, are pictured as anxiously waiting for this "teaching" (v. 4). Could that be true? All serious persons and not prophets alone are convinced that the deepest yearning of all peoples is for a world that is whole, with all wounds healed, all brokenness mended. And what is that but a world that is "all right," a world of righteousness or justice? This note of justice is also sounded at Jesus' baptism (Matt. 3:15). In fact, justice or righteousness is a persistent theme in Matthew's whole portrait of Jesus.

In establishing righteousness, the servant is not to swing a rod of iron and smash the nations like so much fragile pottery. The servant will not snap bruised reeds or quench dimly burning wicks (vv. 2-3; see Matt. 12:15-21). In the eyes of many, the servant's gentleness will be misread and mocked as miserable and maddening weakness. But Matthew sees the prophet's words coming to fulfillment in Jesus' journey to the cross. For Matthew the cross is a moment of powerful healing and mending and quickening. With Jesus' blood there springs forth a river of forgiveness (26:28), and at his dying, dead saints come alive (27:51-53). And the crucified Jesus rises up to summon "all nations" to submit to his sovereign rule of righteousness (28:18-20).

The alternative to the cross is and always has been the sword. Swords seem so efficient and effective, but can they establish justice among the nations? Brian Wren writes about G. A. Studdert-Kennedy, a British army chaplain in World War I. In the midst of mud and bloodshed on Europe's battlefields he became convinced that the traditional idea of God as "Almighty" is a terrible idol, leading us to value domination and to worship conquest and control. "I want to kill the Almighty God and tear him from his throne," he wrote.[8] Caesar and czars and kaisers worship gods of power and lead us to war.

To establish justice means first of all to remove blindfolds from people's eyes so that they face up to their idolatries. Our modern idols are not likely to be crude images carved in wood or stone. They are more likely to be listed on "the big board" or fashioned from gold or printed on paper by treasury department presses. Or they are made of case-hardened steel and fashioned in the shape of guns and tanks and fighter-bombers. Can all these make our lives secure? It is possible that someone might answer that question with a "yes." But can they heal us and make us whole? No!

Giving birth to God's justice requires the willingness to endure the birth pangs. Matthew declares that Jesus was willing. In fact Jesus prayed, "Abba, your will be done" (Matt. 26:42), and then he went to the cross, and through the cross he traveled to new life. He now invites all the rest of us to pray exactly as he prayed, saying, "Your will be done on earth [by us] as in heaven [by all the saints and angels]" (see Matt. 6:10). And he calls us to living that accords with our praying.

Responsive Reading
PSALM 29 (RCL/RC)

"All Shout, 'Glory!'"

At the heart of Psalm 29 is a poetic description of a powerful thunderstorm rising out of the west, at first brooding over the Mediterranean, finally reaching the eastern horizon. It fills the sky and the poet's imagination. In the booming of thunder the poet hears the "voice of the Lord, full of majesty," the same divine voice that conquered the waters at creation (vv. 3-4). The psalmist watches awestruck as the storm, blowing in across the water, begins to lash Sirion (Mount Hermon), breaking great cedars of Lebanon and making them jump (vv. 5-6). Lightning flashes across the sky to the east as far as eye can see (vv. 7-8). The storm in its fury strips the bark from the trees (v. 9).

When such a God speaks, what can angels do? The psalmist calls to the members of God's heavenly court of gods and angels, "Give God glory" (vv. 1-2), and in God's heavenly temple all shout, "Glory!" (v. 9). The Lord is enthroned above the flood, over all the unruly powers of chaos, ordering all of life anew (v. 10).

When God speaks, what can we humans do? We have no choice but to join the heavenly chorus, adding our shout of "Glory!" to theirs. To glorify God means turning from idols and trusting God. Trusting God who conquered chaos in the beginning means trusting God to conquer not only our personal confusions but our social and political chaos as well, trusting the glorious God to give us "peace" (v. 11). Angels at the Messiah's birth shouted, "Glory!" and "Peace!" (Luke 2:14). "Glory!" means "God is the victor!," and "Peace!" means "God gives us wholeness!"

At his baptism the sky was split, but no lightning flashed, no thunder sounded. No preternatural rumbling in the bowels of the earth stirred the waters of Jordan. All that happened (!) is that the Spirit of the living God settled on Jesus, gentle as a dove. And in the voice from heaven, God did not shout. At times God comes in hurricane or quaking earth or devouring fire. But as Elijah learned (1 Kings 19:11-12), sometimes God moves so quietly that we miss the presence, miss the action, miss the blessing, can't hear the sound. We need an eye for the invisible and an ear for silence. At the Jordan God spoke in a whisper, "This—of all people—is my beloved Son, your new sovereign" (Matt. 3:16-17).

PSALM 89 (BCP)

"Highest of the Kings"

The psalmist begins (vv. 1-14) and ends (v. 49) by praising God's faithfulness to the house of David. Apparently trust in that faithfulness was shaken by some military or political setback, but the psalmist declares that God is still worthy of our trust. God rules high above all heavenly beings (vv. 5-8) and is in fact the one who created the universe, crushing Rahab to pieces (vv. 9-12). Rahab is a primeval chaos monster and sometimes a poetic code word for Egypt, so the psalmist is evoking old images of creation and exodus. The Lord who chose David is none other than the world's creator and Israel's redeemer. "Steadfast Love" and "Faithfulness" are the names of God's acolytes, moving before God in festal procession (v. 14).

After this beginning, the psalmist reports words of God heard in a vision (vv. 19-37). The heart of the speech is God's pledge: "I [God] have found my servant David; with my holy oil I have anointed him [as king]; my hand shall always remain with him" (v. 20). Or God's promise can be summed up in the adoption formula: "I will make him [the Davidic king] the firstborn, the highest of the kings of the earth" (vv. 27-28). The psalm echoes events narrated in 2 Samuel 7 and foreshadows Jesus' baptism in the waters of the Jordan.

Both Psalm 29 and Psalm 89 celebrate God's power, and yet here is a paradox. Our powerful God, smashing and subduing and setting free, sometimes speaks in silence and acts like a dove descending. And we are moved to cry, "Glory!"

Second Reading
ACTS 10:34-43

"Lord of All"

I suppose this story was selected for reading on this Sunday for two reasons. First, it offers another perspective on the baptism of Jesus, which is featured in the Gospel for this day. Second, this story prepares for the baptism of a Gentile, and so it has connectors attaching it not only to Jesus' baptism but also to the prophecy of Isaiah. In fulfillment of prophecy, light really comes to the nations (Isa. 42:6) when Cornelius and his household are baptized.

The story has even more riches. Not only is Cornelius a Gentile; he is an officer in the Roman army, and so he has sworn his soldier's oath of allegiance to "Lord Caesar." From Peter's mouth he is reminded (and we with him) how God has shared a "word" with the world, proclaiming "good news of peace" through the life and death and resurrection of Jesus who is "Lord of all" (v. 36; cf. Acts 2:34-36).

What does Luke mean by that "word" that God sent? Is it the message about Jesus? Is Luke here speaking in Johannine fashion of Jesus as the word of God, the Logos? In any case, back there in the fullness of time, after all those centuries and generations of waiting and hoping for light to dawn, God most certainly did not share a sword or gun with the world. God shared a word. Instead of sending twelve legions (twelve divisions or two army groups) of angels (Matt. 26:53), God sent Jesus. What a strange way for "almighty" God to move into the midst of the nations to bridge their moats, to deconstruct their walls, to storm their barricades, to disarm them, to take them captive and so set them free.

When they stood face-to-face in the doorway that day in Caesarea ("Caesar's City"), Peter and Cornelius represented two different lords, two different sovereignties. Peter brought to the house of Cornelius everything that the Roman propaganda promised to bestow on subject peoples: liberating power, benefactions of all kinds, comprehensive healing, and protection from evils (v. 38). Here are some of blessings the Caesars promised on their coins: *Abundantia* (abundance or plenty), *aequitas* (equity or fair dealing), *clementia* (clemency or mercy), *concordia* (harmony), *fecunditas* (fertility), *felicitas* (happiness or prosperity), *fortuna* (good fortune), *hilaritas* (mirth or rejoicing), *indulgentia* (indulgence or mercy), *justitia* (justice), *laetitia* (joy), *libertas* (freedom), *pax* (peace), and, of course, *victoria* or *nike* (victory).

The Pax Romana was achieved and maintained by violence and bloodshed. And if the blessing of peace was supposed to stream from Rome to the farthest province, it was even more obvious that the wealth of the provinces was flowing in a steady stream to Rome.

Peter describes both Jesus' baptism (vv. 37-38) and his crucifixion: death by "hanging on a tree" (v. 39). And then he speaks of Jesus' surprising manifestation after three days, and how he was seen and known (vv. 40-41). Peter names water and cruel wood, bread and wine as the media chosen by God to conquer all the provinces.

Peter begins by saying that "God shows no partiality" (v. 34) and ends by saying that amnesty or "forgiveness" (v. 43) is the gift of this Jesus, newly enthroned as Lord of the Universe. Luke here shares his vision of a great alternative to Caesar's cruel empire. Luke sees a new human community under the gracious lordship of Jesus, and he calls us to celebrate Christ's lordship by sharing his vision of a peaceable kingdom.

LUKE HERE SHARES HIS VISION OF A GREAT ALTERNATIVE TO CAESAR'S CRUEL EMPIRE. LUKE SEES A NEW HUMAN COMMUNITY UNDER THE GRACIOUS LORDSHIP OF JESUS, AND HE CALLS US TO CELEBRATE CHRIST'S LORDSHIP BY SHARING HIS VISION OF A PEACEABLE KINGDOM.

Luke's is a countercultural vision, and yet, as far as we know, Cornelius went right on being a centurion in a Roman legion. This same evangelist reports that when tax collectors and soldiers inquired of John the Baptist what they should do, now that they had heeded John's proclamation and had been baptized, he did not tell the tax collectors to get into another line of work but told them to "collect no more than the amount prescribed for you." He did not counsel soldiers to go AWOL but said to them, "Do not extort money from anyone by threats or false accusation, and be satisfied with your wages" (Luke 3:10-14). In both cases Luke calls attention to John's critique of his culture's idolization of money. If we try to excuse ourselves by saying that it is a struggle to know how to mount an appropriate resistance to the status quo in our time, we should be shamed by John's words to tax collectors and soldiers and to those ordinary auditors of John whose only "defect" is that they had two coats.

To call Jesus "Lord" and to recall his story should disturb our slumbering, stimulate our moral imagination, and entice us to work for something better than the same tired old personal, social, and political arrangements.

GOSPEL

MATTHEW 3:13-17

"With Liberty and Justice for All"

It pays to contemplate the first utterance of the chief character in any story. And that is no less true of the Gospels. Each of our four Gospels reports something different as Jesus' first utterance, and in each Gospel what Jesus says first of all is an extraordinary clue to his work and import as seen by each evangelist. In Mark's Gospel, Jesus announces the end of empty times of waiting and hoping, and he proclaims the fullness of time and the approach of God's own sovereignty (Mark 1:14-15). In Luke, Jesus focuses on his anointing with the Holy Spirit and his work of liberation for captives and the oppressed and his good news for the poor (Luke 4:18-19). In John, Jesus asks a very leading question, "What are you looking for?" (John 1:38).

Matthew has, of course, already introduced Jesus in the first verse of the Gospel, naming him "Jesus Christ, Son of David, Son of Abraham" and equipping him in the next paragraphs with a grand genealogy (1:1-17). We learn much from Jesus' family history, extraordinary in the unusual inclusion of four women, the provocative reference to David's kingship, and the poignant reminder of Babylonian captivity. The message of the genealogy is clear. Jesus comes as fulfiller, at the end of long years of waiting, as the climax of deep sighs and yearnings.

His conception and birth are a wonder (1:18-25), and his early days and years are marked by angelic voices and visions in the night (2:1-23). But all those generations and interventions are prelude to the main act, namely his sudden, brilliant bursting onto the scene as an active adult. And when he volunteers for baptism as described in Matthew's Gospel, and in Matthew alone, he has an arresting conversation with his baptizer.

Jesus and John could have talked about many things: their parents and families, the faltering economy, the state of the nation, the quality of the priesthood, the program of the Pharisees, the intrusiveness and offensiveness of Roman rule. But they didn't. Whatever the precise nature of the movement spearheaded by John, Jesus had arrived, ready to sign on. And John protested. Does John recognize some intrinsic superiority in Jesus, so that he wishes to reverse roles and subordinate himself to his younger cousin? Did John really see in Jesus the long-awaited "stronger one" who would winnow Israel like newly cut grain? Or are we perhaps overhearing a concern of Matthew's community about the sinlessness of the one born of a virgin, who needed no washing in Jordan's water?

Usually John is the witness to Jesus, but here the usual order is turned on its head as Jesus bears witness to John and his ritual: It is the finger of God that is stirring John's heart and Jordan's water (see 21:25). By his appearing at the Jordan, Jesus affirms that God has raised up John. God has sent John as the forerunner in the business of reforming and rebirthing the people (3:9). God will lead the people in a new crossing of the water from desert place to promised land. Indeed Jesus-Joshua (both are "Iesous" in Greek) has come to claim his own leadership of God's people and to bring them to surprising freedoms and perplexing victories.

So Jesus tells John to get on with the baptizing, because, he says, in a first and most significant word: "It is proper for us in this way to fulfill all righteousness" (3:15). That is the way Jesus' saying is worded in NRSV. Here is my paraphrase of the saying: "It is fitting for us in this way to begin bringing righteousness to fullest expression." Whether the "us" is "you and me, John" or Jesus speaking in a kind of royal plural or even "us readers together with Jesus" hardly matters. Central to the "us" is Jesus himself. He is articulating the core of his program as Matthew understands it. He brings "the righteous rule of God" (see 6:33) first as gift but then also as calling.

> MATTHEW CLAIMS THAT GOD IN JESUS LAYS HEALING HANDS ON OUR UNIVERSES AND BEGINS TO MAKE US AND OUR WORLDS "ALL RIGHT."

Here is the key that unlocks everything in Matthew! Jesus begins to fulfill the age-old hopes for a new genesis (1:1; 19:28). "We look," says another New Testament writer, "for new heavens and a new earth in which righteousness is perfectly at home" (2 Peter 3:13, my paraphrase). That new cosmos of righteousness is what begins to emerge out of Jesus' teachings and silences, out of his actions and sufferings.

The narrative of Jesus' baptism closes with the divine declaration, "This is my Son, the Beloved" (Matt. 3:17). And that means that Jesus is the promised sovereign of the last times. But Matthew has carefully nuanced his sovereignty with that initial saying of Jesus about righteousness. Jesus' governance will be marked not by oppression but by peace ("Blessed are the peacemakers!" 5:9), not by violence but by meekness or nonviolence ("Blessed are the meek!" 5:5; the same Greek word translated as "meek" in 5:5 is "gentle" at 11:29 and "humble" at 21:5). His rule will be marked not by colossal victories of arms in which thousands are killed but by healings with justice (12:15-21), not by crushing the enemy but loving them (5:43-44) and enlightening them, as he is himself "great light" (4:16). He proclaims "righteousness," both as "victory over evil" and as "the establishment of justice." As king of righteousness, he gives the gift of righteousness (healing and wholeness), and he summons us citizens of his realm to live lives of righteousness.

What in our world is not all right? In our personal and social worlds, in our cultural and spiritual worlds, in our economic and political worlds? Matthew claims that God in Jesus lays healing hands on our universes and begins to make us and our worlds "all right."

Jesus in Matthew has a passion for righteousness. And he disturbs the hearts of those whom he heals, so that they too are unsettled and begin to share his hunger and thirst, and that is good, and those who feel it will not be disappointed (5:6).

SECOND SUNDAY AFTER THE EPIPHANY

JANUARY 17, 1999

SECOND SUNDAY IN ORDINARY TIME

REVISED COMMON	EPISCOPAL (BCP)	ROMAN CATHOLIC
Isa. 49:1-7	Isa. 49:1-7	Isa. 49:3, 5-6
Ps. 40:1-11	Ps. 40:1-10	Ps. 40:2, 4, 7-10
1 Cor. 1:1-9	1 Cor. 1:1-9	1 Cor. 1:1-3
John 1:29-42	John 1:29-41	John 1:29-34

"THE CITY OF GOD"

EVERY EMPIRE HAS ITS CAPITAL CITY: Jerusalem, Athens, Rome, Moscow, Tokyo, Beijing, Berlin, London, Washington. Nations lavish wealth on their capitals, putting on display their might and their culture. The character of the people defines their city, and the capital city reveals the people. What is the government of Jesus? What is the seat of his government and the character of his governing? Where is it that he dwells? And is it a place of darkness or of light?

FIRST READING
ISAIAH 49:1-7

"Princes Fall Prostrate"

The second of the "Servant Songs" opens by articulating once more the servant's sense of vocation. He was destined for his servant's role from the moment of his conception in his mother's womb (see Jer. 1:5; Gal. 1:15). He was "named" by God, and that means both claimed as God's own and given his life's work, even before he was born (see Matt. 1:21).

His is a prophet's calling. God made his mouth like a sharp sword, so that his word cuts to the heart of things. He imagines himself to be an arrow in God's quiver, always at hand when God spies a target. He and his words are weapons in God's armory (Heb. 4:12; Eph. 6:17).

God has weapons and a battle plan, and God's strategy will not be frustrated. Nevertheless the servant Israel feels that his sharp word is falling on deaf ears. He is at times crushed and weary, fearful that he labors in vain, but God again promises, "You are my servant, Israel, in whom I will be glorified" (v. 3).

But what is the glory or victory that God seeks? And what exactly is the servant's mission? The song speaks of God's gathering the scattered people of Jacob-Israel. But this ingathering, absolutely astonishing as it may be, is not great enough. The restoration of the captives to their old homeland is not the end but a beginning. Their liberation from exile and return to the land to be a new community is not the capstone and climax but the laying of a foundation. It is preparation for something new. It appears that it is "too light a thing" that God should be concerned about Israel alone, that God should "raise up the tribes of Jacob and restore the survivors of Israel" (v. 6a). Instead of simply restoring the exiles to their land, an event which has already occurred, God now promises to make Israel "a light to the nations so that salvation may reach to the end of the earth" (v. 6b).

Now we see why the song begins with a call for the attention of the "coastlands" and "peoples far away" (v. 1). Servant-Israel has a mission to perform in the midst of all nations. But it seems so preposterous. Even though some exiles had returned to their ancestral land, they occupied a tiny tract of land and were still "deeply despised, abhorred by the nations, the slave of rulers" (v. 7a). But God makes a colossal commitment to the servant: Kings and princes, who by long custom sit in their courts while all others stand, will stand up when they see you. Kings and princes are accustomed to having petitioners fall on their faces in front of them, but they will prostrate themselves before you (v. 7b).

IT IS THE WILL OF GOD THAT ALL NATIONS SHOULD SEE THE LIGHT AND LIVE TOGETHER IN PEACE AND JUSTICE. THIS WIDE POLITICAL VISION IS NEVER RENOUNCED IN SCRIPTURE. IN FACT IT HOLDS SWAY ALL THE WAY TO THE FINAL CHAPTERS OF REVELATION.

Here again the prophet uses political language, and yet there is nothing narrowly nationalistic or chauvinistic about the vision. In fact, narrowness is here rejected in favor of a stunning ecumenism. It is the will of God that all nations should see the light and live together in peace and justice. This wide political vision is never renounced in Scripture. In fact, it holds sway all the way to the final chapters of Revelation.

RESPONSIVE READING

PSALM 40

"Lips That Tell"

The psalmist was delivered from some unnamed trouble, like a person who escaped alive after nearly drowning in the dark waters of a turbulent river. God drew him back from the "pit," which in Psalm 16:10 is a synonym for Sheol. He had been on the brink of death, but now once more he is alive and his feet rest secure as on a rock.

His rescue has put a song on his lips. It is a "new" song (Rev. 5:9; 14:3), because he has received a new lease on life, and his mouth is no longer full of complaints. Filled with relief, the psalmist tries to recite all of God's wondrous deeds, but the task is too large, for the deeds of God on behalf of those who trust in the Lord are beyond numbering (vv. 4-5).

Rejoicing in God's mercy, the psalmist contemplates the appropriate acts to accompany his praise. How should he show thanks? With sacrifice and offering? No, what God really desires is an "open ear," a spirit of ready obedience (1 Sam. 15:22; Heb. 10:5-7), and a heart that delights in the law of God (vv. 6-8). Ear and heart are important, but so are lips that tell "the glad news of deliverance in the great congregation" (v. 9).

CONTEMPLATING GOD'S INTERVENTIONS IN OUR LIVES AND BEARING WITNESS TO GOD'S HELP IS A CENTRAL THEME OF EPIPHANY AND IS IN FACT A NECESSITY OF HEALTHY LIVING.

Open acknowledgment of the saving deeds of God is an essential element in genuine thanksgiving. So the psalmist has not restrained his lips, has not concealed God's help deep in his heart, but has proclaimed, told, and spoken of God's "steadfast love and faithfulness" (three times in three verses). He has in fact composed his psalm as testimony.

Contemplating God's interventions in our lives and bearing witness to God's help is a central theme of Epiphany and is in fact a necessity of healthy living. Prayer cells and study groups meeting in congregations and homes permit the kind of grateful testimony that the psalmist celebrates. Such celebrative, commemorative testimony not only happens in the community but builds the community.

SECOND READING

1 CORINTHIANS 1:1-9

"At His Great Epiphany"

The salutation (1:1-3) is followed by Paul's customary thanksgiving section (1:4-9), which here as so often serves as a table of contents for the letter. Both salutation and thanksgiving seem heavily ironic.

Paul addresses the Corinthians as "sanctified" people, set apart as "saints" (v. 2). Those are the words he chooses in spite of the fact that he will go on in the letter to detail serious and deep defects in their thinking and behavior. Paul thanks God for them, declaring that they "are not lacking in any spiritual gift" (v. 7), singling out for special mention how by God's grace they have been "enriched in speech and knowledge" (v. 5).

It does not take long to learn that speech and knowledge are two of the areas where Paul is at odds with the Corinthians. They glory in their knowledge. They have a slogan, "All of us possess knowledge" (8:1). This slogan expresses their conviction that they have been initiated into deep spiritual understanding and enlightenment, freeing them from old taboos and outdated doctrines concerning sex and food offered to idols.

As for riches of speech, it soon becomes obvious that the Corinthians place a premium on one kind of speech: speaking in tongues, apparently regarded as a heavenly language spoken by angels (13:1) and so a sure sign of spiritual power.

When Paul begins to discuss their gifts of knowledge and speech in earnest, he introduces a criterion. Do they use their gifts to build up the body of Christ or not?

From Paul's perspective their knowledge was leading them to boasting and to insisting on their individual personal liberty. Paul responded, "Knowledge (*gnosis*) puffs up, but love (*agape*) builds up" (8:1). As for speech, Paul was led to the judgment that "prophecy" is superior to "speaking in a tongue." Tongues may build up the speaker but such speaking yields zero benefits to hearers, who can't understand any of it. Prophecy, on the other hand, builds up the church (1 Cor. 14).

"Agape" and "building up" or "edification" (*oikodomia*) are key words in Paul's spiritual lexicon and receive extended treatment in his letter to the Corinthians. Edification of the body is one of Paul's highest values and functions as a criterion as he deals with all the varied issues in the congregation. What builds up is good. What does not edify and what may even divide Christians is of lesser value or no value at all.

Throughout the sixteen chapters of 1 Corinthians, Paul struggles against anything that tends to split or divide the community into factions. Strange to say, not lack of spiritual gifts but their rich abundance contributed to factionalism. So Paul concludes the opening thanksgiving section by introducing one more significant term in alongside the words *gift* and *speech* and *knowledge*. And that is the word *fellowship*. Paul climaxes his introduction by reminding the Corinthians that their high vocation as they live their lives toward "the day of Jesus Christ" is to be "the fellowship" or *koinonia* of God's Son (v. 9).

A crucial test is whether people can take their own advice. If agape and edification are high values for Paul, does he himself live by them as he deals with the Corinthians? The truthful answer is "yes." Paul builds them up. He is, in these opening paragraphs of his letter, reminding them of their identity in Christ. He shows them who they really are, reveals it to them, preaches it to them once more, proclaiming it both as present reality and as promise.

Even in the body of the letter, when Paul wrestles more directly with the issues of speech and knowledge, he does not shame or scold or harangue. Nor does he simply demand their obedience to himself as an authority figure. He "argues" in the best sense of the word. He sets out reasons, offers some history lessons, brings in scripture, reminds them of pros and cons. He is the pastor and out of pastoral concern works with them and pleads with them in these days of waiting for the "revealing" (the apocalypse or epiphany) of our Lord Jesus Christ (v. 7).

In one of her essays, Barbara Kingsolver comments that human beings have the wonderful capacity "to reach beyond the self and encompass the common good." But having celebrated that "inspiring thought," she laments, "In mortal fact, here in the U.S. we are blazing a bold downhill path from the high ground of 'human collective' toward the tight little den of 'self.'"[9] Paul's letter to Corinth is of more than antiquarian interest, as we confront issues of community in our contemporary culture and in our congregations.

Robert Bellah, sociologist at the University of California at Berkeley and an active Episcopalian layman, led a team of researchers in producing a book called *Habits of the Heart*. The book was based in part on thousands of interviews of American citizens across the length and breadth of the land. And the book has another foundation, namely the conviction that our nation owes its greatness to two groups of founders: religious communities arriving on these shores in the sixteenth and seventeenth centuries and then the great political giants who wrote the Declaration of Independence and the Constitution in the late eighteenth century. Both groups of founders agreed that on these shores there would be a new community of people enjoying unprecedented freedom. Bellah and his associates conclude that dedication to freedom, especially individual freedom, is alive and well. We celebrate freedom, flaunt it, insist on it. But community has fallen on bad times. The citizens of this vast land have by and large lost the vision of community, lack a commitment to community, do not even have a very well-developed language for speaking about community when they want to. Bellah fears that we are becoming a more selfish people, committed to the pursuit of private pleasures, and in some ways his book is a call to churches to help citizens recapture the vision of being one nation, one new community, under God, with liberty and justice not merely for me and mine, but for all.[10]

Gospel

JOHN 1:29-42

"Jesus, Where Do You Dwell?"

The miraculous provision of wine out of water at Cana has been associated with Epiphany for more than a millennium and a half. However, the lectionary now confines the account of events at that wedding to Year C. In Years A and B, the sections of the Gospel of John immediately preceding Cana are appointed for reading (A: John 1:29-42; B: John 1:43-51; C: John 2:1-11).

In the Fourth Gospel, John the forerunner is not so much the "baptizer" as he is a "witness" to Jesus. The Father, the Spirit, Jesus' own deeds or "works," and the Samaritan woman (4:39) are other witnesses, unveiling Jesus' identity. John has already spoken negatively about himself (John 1:19-28). Now he begins to speak (to priests and Levites, to the crowds, to his disciples, to us?) in extravagant terms about Jesus.

In a word of witness that serves as a general introduction to the significance of Jesus' work, John calls him "the Lamb of God" who "takes away," or destroys, the sin of the cosmos (v. 29). According to John 9 (the healing of a man born blind) the meaning of "sin" is unbelief, the failure to trust God and enter into communion with God as revealed in Jesus.

The Fourth Gospel shows hardly a glimmer of interest in any sin except unbelief. It has nothing about murder, theft, adultery, greed, or envy. It has nothing on rules and regulations for the inner life of the new community (as in Matthew 18) and nothing about prayer or fasting or almsgiving (as in the Sermon on the Mount). It lacks anything like the Golden Rule or the saying about rendering tax money to Caesar and oneself to God. So when the Baptist says that Jesus removes sin, he does not mean that Jesus has come to deal with infractions of divine law in these ethical and moral areas, no matter how important they may be.

Sin in John's Gospel is unbelief, and getting rid of that one "sin" is the highest priority of the Jesus of the Gospel of John. Faith, the opposite of sin, is a spiritual knowledge: knowing God and Jesus whom God has sent into the world (17:3). Those who know God are set apart from the world's blindness and hatred of God, and they enter into oneness with God (chap. 17). Indeed, the Gospel was written that people might get rid of their sin of unbelief and come to faith and so have real life, eternal life an unobstructed and deathless union with God (20:31).

Jesus, coming from above, from realms of glory, always held a rank infinitely higher than John (v. 30). John did not recognize the worth of Jesus immediately, but he had been told by the one who commissioned him to baptize: The one on whom you see the Spirit descend and "remain" is the one who will pour out into human life the Spirit of God, the life of God, oneness with God (vv. 32-33).

The Spirit "remains" on him. "Remain" or "abide" (*meno*) is a loaded word in the Fourth Gospel. John 14 is an extensive commentary on the meaning of "abide" as it speaks of abiding or remaining or dwelling (depending on which translation you are using) and then also uses the cognate noun, "places of abiding" ("mansions" in the King James Version, "rooms" in the RSV, "dwelling places" in the NRSV).

The imagery of dwelling and indwelling occurs with other vocabulary besides *meno* and its cognates. The Logos became human, and in doing so the Logos "tented" or "tabernacled" among us like the presence of God (the *shekinah*) in the tabernacle of ancient Israel or in the temple more recently (1:14). Jesus is Bethel, the House of God, the place where angels ascend and descend, connecting earth and heaven (1:51; cf. Genesis 28). His crucified and resurrected body fulfills the functions of temple (2:19-22).

When John said a second time on a second day, "Look! The Lamb of God," two of John's disciples began to follow Jesus (1:35-37). Jesus turns and sees them and asks them (and us readers) a surprising question. This now is the first time that Jesus himself speaks in the Fourth Gospel. The evangelist has spoken (1:1-18), priests and Levites have spoken (1:19-25), and John the Baptist has spoken (1:20-36). Now for the first time Jesus opens his mouth to speak. And the first word he speaks is a question. He asks John's two disciples, "What are you looking for?" (1:38).

This first word of Jesus is a highly charged question. Jesus is asking, "What are you seeking? What is it you want to gain by all your striving and working and thinking? What is the goal of all your living? What do you wish to achieve or gain or be?"

Curiously, John's two disciples answer Jesus' question with a question of their own, "Where are you staying?" Is this question simple, nonsensical, a piece of stuttering on the part of people taken off guard? Or is it profound and important? The word translated "staying" is that same word *meno*, which means stay, abide, dwell. They are not simply asking Jesus for his address. They are not asking, "What town are you from? Which house do you live in? What's the name of your street? Who are your neighbors?" As far as the evangelist is concerned, they have asked the perfect question. These disciples and the readers of the Gospel should above all else desire to know where it is that Jesus really dwells (in God and God in him), and how they might dwell there also, at one with God and Christ.

It may very well be that we want less than that. Maybe we want simply to have more historical information about Jesus. Or perhaps we desire some gift or favor that Jesus in his power might offer us (a better job, greater success in our personal relationships, enlightenment or fulfillment, healing for our ills). Jesus might even give us any or all of that out of his deep and abundant grace, but we will not have arrived at the goal of "eternal life" or oneness with God which the Fourth Evangelist says is the purpose of the appearing of Jesus. Abiding with Jesus or oneness with Jesus involves a fundamental shift in our way of seeing the world and being in the world. Psalm 27, next Sunday's psalm, with its talk about seeking God's face (Ps. 27:8), would be a perfect companion to John 1:29-42.

ABIDING WITH JESUS OR ONENESS WITH JESUS INVOLVES A FUNDAMENTAL SHIFT IN OUR WAY OF SEEING THE WORLD AND BEING IN THE WORLD.

All kinds of organizations, sacred and secular, commit themselves to periodic self-study and commit time and energy to goal-setting and to producing a mission statement. The evangelist would not mind at all if congregations and subgroups within congregations would meditate on this first chapter of the Gospel and these first words of Jesus.

THIRD SUNDAY AFTER THE EPIPHANY

JANUARY 24, 1999

THIRD SUNDAY IN ORDINARY TIME

Revised Common	Episcopal (BCP)	Roman Catholic
Isa. 9:1-4	Amos 3:1-8	Isa. 8:23—9:3
Ps. 27:1, 4-9	Ps. 139:1-17 or 139:1-11	Ps. 27:1, 4, 13-14
1 Cor. 1:10-18	1 Cor. 1:10-17	1 Cor. 1:10-13, 17
Matt. 4:12-23	Matt. 4:12-23	Matt. 4:12-23 or 4:12-17

"Empires of Darkness, Empire of Light"

Every political revolution promises a cornucopia of blessings for the people, and yet history teaches that all too often a new tyranny replaces the old. Our readings this Sunday speak of Assyrians and Chaldeans, Persians and Romans, of Damascus and Tyre, Bethel and Jerusalem. They raise questions about the "empires" of China and Russia and France and the U.S.A. And they call us to reflect on our ecclesiastical or denominational "empires" bearing such names as "Catholicism" and "Lutheranism" and "Episcopalianism." Is the "Lord Jesus" an empire builder? If so, what "empire" would this Jesus, "born a king on Bethlehem's plain," bequeath to us? And what blessings does he promise?

First Reading

ISAIAH 9:1-4 (RCL/RC)

"Born a King"

This text (which in Hebrew is 8:23—9:3, as listed in the Roman Catholic lectionary) is the first part of an oracle originally spoken at the coronation of a new king or at the birth of a royal child. The king or royal child will rule in the Southern Kingdom, Judah, but the focus of the action in the first part of the oracle is the conquered North. The Assyrian emperor Tiglath-pileser III had taken Samaria and annexed the territories of the Northern Kingdom in the campaigns of 733-732 B.C.E. "The land of Zebulun and the land of Naphtali," "the way of the sea" (the coastal strip south of Mount Carmel), and "the land beyond the Jordan" were reorganized as three Assyrian provinces. They were simply swallowed up by the voracious appetite of the Assyrian empire.

Abraham Joshua Heschel writes of Assyria, "Her greed is reckless, her weapons devastating, her armies formidable, crushing all resistance, sweeping to victories. No one seems to question her invincibility except Isaiah, who foresees the doom of the oppressor, the collapse of the monster."[11] The time of Assyrian expansion was a time of gloom and anguish (9.1), but Isaiah sees a new day dawning with the accession of the new king, probably Hezekiah (715–687 B.C.E.), successor to Ahaz. Surely this new king will embody the full promise of the house of David. Conquered territories will be restored to Israel, and both Israel and Judah will be reunited under the new Davidic king.

The vision is glorious. Instead of stumbling in darkness, the people will walk in the light shining from the royal presence. Hezekiah's rule will bring the kind of rejoicing that marks harvesting. It will be like the joy felt by victors after a battle dividing the spoils among them. A frankly militaristic image, good news to winners, bad news for the losers.

THE PROPHECY CELEBRATES THE BREAKING OF THE YOKE AND STAFF AND ROD OF THE OPPRESSORS, AS THOUGH THAT DIVINE SMASHING WERE ALREADY A PRESENT REALITY.

This new king, as God's "son" (9:6), will break the yoke of oppression which has lain heavily on the shoulders of the people (9:4). The prophecy celebrates the breaking of the yoke and staff and rod of the oppressors, as though that divine smashing were already a present reality.

The rule of this new king will bring unending peace, symbolized by the burning of warriors' boots and uniforms. No more need for an army! No more triumphant warriors returning in bloodied cloaks! Throw those old uniforms into the oven and bake the bread of tranquillity!

Five throne names were solemnly bestowed on the Pharaohs of Egypt upon their accession, and perhaps there once was a fifth name to go with the four preserved here. It is worth comparing these four titles or coronation names in various translations. Here they are, as given in the NRSV: (1) "Wonderful Counselor"—a sovereign full of social and political wisdom; (2) "Mighty God"—divinely empowered leader in the nation's battles (also in the war on poverty, war on crime, war on drugs?); (3) "Everlasting Father"—compassionate and concerned about the needs of the people, like the father of a family and not a tyrant with his slaves; (4) "Prince of Peace"—dedicated to the pruning hook and plowshare and not always seeking to make his name great with sword and spear (Isa. 2:4; see also 11:6-9).

Who is this royal child or new king seen by Isaiah's far-seeing eye? The new king is very strange. He is one who rode into life as an unknown child of unknown parents in the bypassed hamlet of Bethlehem, who rode into Jerusalem on an ass and a colt (the foal of an ass), who rode to the stars on a cross of hard wood fashioned by cruel and unfeeling hands.

Lowly, lowly, lowly, and yet thrice holy, he is the one whose sovereignty, if that is the right word for it, is celebrated in the unforgettable line sung repeatedly in Handel's *Messiah*, "And the government shall be upon his shoulders" (Isa. 9:6). When the king of England first heard the Hallelujah Chorus of Handel's *Messiah*, he stood up. No one could remain sitting while the king stood, so the entire audience leaped to its feet. So should all, both rulers and the ruled and everyone in between, honor the one who was "born a King on Bethlehem's plain."

AMOS 3:1-8 (BCP)

"God Says, 'You Are My Family'"

Amos is the earliest of the literary prophets, the first whose words have been preserved for us in writing. He was active around the middle of the long and glorious reign of Jeroboam II (786-746 B.C.E.). From Tekoa in Judah (1:1; 7:12), a few miles south of Bethlehem in the hill country of Judea, he prophesied at Bethel, the spiritual center of the Northern Kingdom (7:10), where he was by no means welcomed.

Isaiah's prophecy of a new king (9:1-4) was spoken after the fall of the Northern Kingdom and announced good news for the conquered territories. Amos, speaking before that calamity, predicted it would come upon the chosen people, as punishment for their iniquities. He stresses that they were the Lord's own "family." Twice he uses that wonderful word (vv. 1-2). Of all the "families of the earth" they were uniquely God's own, uniquely blessed and beloved ever since God rescued them from the land of Egypt. Especially dear, the Lord will hold them especially accountable (3:1-2).

It was a tough time to be a prophet. The mood of the people was complacent. They slumbered and dreamed their dreams of upward mobility. They enjoyed both summer and winter houses, expensively decorated with ivory carvings and inlays (3:15; 6:4). They planted pleasant vineyards (5:11), drank their wine, and anointed themselves with oil (4:1; 6:6). They were generally "at ease in Zion" (6:1).

To these smug and comfortable citizens Amos brought bad news, a word of judgment on Israelite society. It was perfectly acceptable for prophets to wander up and down the land uttering denunciations against Damascus (far away!), and against Gaza, Tyre, Edom, the Ammonites, Moab (1:3—2:3). They were all foreigners! Closer to home, an oracle against Judah might be bearable (2:4-5). But how can this upstart prophet announce judgment on Israel? (2:5-16; 3:1-2)

Amos must defend his daring proclamation of bad news for these good people, and he does so in four images: (1) If two men walk the same path together, it means they made an appointment. (2) If a lion roars, we all know it means the beast is about to leap on its prey. (3) If a bird falls from the sky in midflight, of course it has been snared in the fowler's net. (4) If the trumpet blows, war is upon us.

These images have an ominous overtone, especially the last three of the four. Amos is saying, "I would not be prophesying if God did not compel me, and, make no mistake about it, God has not send me to comfort you comfortable citizens." In fact the first oracle of them all announces, "The Lord roars from Zion!" (1:2). The Lord is a lion ready to pounce on the Lord's own family.

Amos makes for very uncomfortable reading. One way to deal with the unease evoked by his sharp condemnations is to study Amos historically and then stop. That way we may be able to confine the fire and the terror in his pronouncements to the distant past. Modern firefighters do not always pour water on a blaze. Sometimes they just let it burn itself out. Forest rangers actually set fires to produce controlled burns with the aim of ridding the forest floor of the dangerous buildup of combustible materials. So interpreters try to maintain some historical distance from the roar of this prophet, from the searing heat of his denunciations, by letting all the fire of his oracles burn itself out against ancient Israel. They examine the political and economic institutions of Israel, describing in excruciating detail the historical meaning behind such wrenching phrases as "selling the righteous for silver and the needy for a pair of sandals" (2:6; 8:6). Archaeology has given us physical evidence of the ivory ornamentation of which the prophet speaks (3:15; 6:4) and so helps us to paint a lurid picture of an ancient heartless society of conspicuous consumers.

AMOS IS SAYING, "I WOULD NOT BE PROPHESYING IF GOD DID NOT COMPEL ME, AND, MAKE NO MISTAKE ABOUT IT, GOD HAS NOT SENT ME TO COMFORT YOU COMFORTABLE CITIZENS."

But the prophet would be better used if we asked about the practices of the Lord's "family" today, and that means all of us who lay claim to being God's family: our personal family, our church family, and our national family. Across the street from San Francisco's Museum of Modern Art is a plaza containing Yerba Buena Gardens. In the midst of the plaza and garden area is a large, marvelously sculpted waterfall dedicated to the memory of Martin Luther King Jr. Water descends in a continuous roaring flow over great stone slabs on which are carved portions of Dr. King's speech, "I Have a Dream," and the words he quoted from Amos 5:24, "Let justice roll down like waters, and righteousness like an ever-flowing stream."

For ancient Israelites and for us it is a far easier thing to erect monuments and design liturgies and compose poetry than it is to be a family embodying the Lord's will for justice and righteousness. But the composing and remembering are important beginnings.

Responsive Reading

PSALM 27 (RCL/RC)

"The Land of the Living"

The psalmist begins by praising God as "my light and my salvation" (v. 1) and ends with the confident credo, "I believe that I shall see the goodness of the Lord in the land of the living" (v. 13).

Psalm 27 is oriented to meeting God in the temple. The psalmist speaks directly and literally of the temple, when he speaks of his desire to live "in the house of the Lord" and behold the beauty or favor of the Lord "in his temple" (v. 4), and when he speaks of God's "tent" (vv. 5-6). The temple was God's earthly "palace," and people came there to be seen by God, just as petitioners came to the tent of a chieftain or the court of a king. They hoped that king or chief in his daily audience with his subjects would lift up his face toward them, set his eyes on them, and nod to them to come forward and present their request.

The old portable tent or tabernacle and the solid temple were places of meeting, holy places where God pledged to be present and attentive to the pleas of worshipers. And like all sanctuaries, tabernacle and temple were places of refuge. Even if an entire army of adversaries would attack him to devour his flesh, the psalmist retains confidence in God's protection (vv. 2-3). The psalmist trusts that he will be hidden by God "in his shelter" and protected "under the cover of his tent" (v. 5).

Falsely accused, the psalmist's heart urges him to "seek the face" of the Lord, seek the Lord's presence and attention. And he cries out, "Hide not your face from me!" (vv. 7-9).

The psalmist calls God "the stronghold or refuge of my life" (v. 1), and then in an arresting phrase, he says that he hopes to see the Lord's goodness in "the land of the living." What is this "land of the living"? It appears to be a code word for the temple (see Ps. 114:9 LXX; 116:9 in English). But the name has an intriguing afterlife. An old fourteenth-century church with the name "Chora Church" stands in Constantinople-Istanbul today. Its name "Chora Church" is derived from the fact that one of its interior walls bears a mosaic of Christ enthroned in glory, holding a Gospel book in his left hand while raising his right hand in blessing. In the gold field surrounding Christ are the words "Jesus Christ, the land of the living" (*chora ton zonton*). The mosaic bears witness to the ancient tradition which sees in Christ all the blessings long ago associated with the temple of God.

The Psalm Prayer summarizes:

> God, you are the protector of all those who hope in you. Grant refuge to your servants who in times of trouble seek your face and your blessing. May we see the depth of your goodness in him who is himself the land of the living, Jesus Christ, your Son our Lord. Amen.[12]

PSALM 139(BCP)

"You Are There, Lord"

"The inescapable God" is a title that fits this psalm perfectly. The psalmist revels in God's knowledge and meditates on it in image after arresting image.

The Lord knows when we sit or stand, where we walk and work, and where we lie down to rest (vv. 2-3). The Lord knows our words before they are formed in our mouths (v. 4). The Lord is not only with us but before and behind, hemming us in (v. 5). If we would travel up to heaven or down to Sheol, we could not escape the presence of the Lord (v. 7-8). At the rising of the sun and at its setting, in brightest light or deepest darkness, there is the Lord (vv. 9-12). The Lord formed us in our mother's womb and before we were born the Lord could see our whole life stretching out before us (vv. 13-16). The psalmist is nearly overwhelmed at the length and breadth and height and depth of the knowledge of the Lord (v. 17).

Of course the Lord's knowledge of us and our condition can be a terrible threat as in the prophecies of Amos, or the fact that the Lord sees us and knows us can be the answer to prayer, as in Psalm 27. A prayer written on the psalm builds on Jesus' descent into hell and ascent into heaven as fulfillments of the images in the psalm:

Lord Jesus Christ, when you descended among the dead, you brought them the light of day; when you ascended into heaven, you brought it new radiance. Remain with us and lead us along the paths of life until we come to rest with your saints in the holy dwelling-place. . . .[13]

Second Reading
1 CORINTHIANS 1:10-18

"Divisions Among You"

It has been said that Roman Catholics are Petrine Christians, Eastern Orthodox are Johannine, and the Churches of the Reformation are Pauline. That old saw may have some educational and even ecumenical value. It offers us a way of asserting that, whatever our divisions and quarrels (words Paul uses in our lection), we are after all brothers and sisters in one large and messy family. We all trace our genealogy back to the same apostles and through them to the same Lord Jesus Christ, who chose and commissioned not just Peter or John or Paul but all of them and many more besides. Therefore we should just accept the fact that we differ and not fall into the trap of reading one another out of the family.

Of course we once found the divisions among denominations to be entirely offensive. Many still see them that way, even in this age which celebrates diversity and pluralism. Paul celebrated diversity of gifts at Corinth, but begged the Corinthians to use their varied gifts for the common good, for building up the health and integrity of the Body of Christ (12:4-7). He appeals ("begs, beseeches, *parakletes*") the Corinthians to overcome their divisions (*schismata*) and find their way back to a single mind (1:10). The Corinthian "fellowship" (1:9) had dissolved into competing factions, at odds with one another in a way that disabled and crippled the body. They all had their slogans: "I belong to Paul, I to Apollos, I to Cephas, I to Christ" (1:12).

Christians met in private homes, and a wealthy home might be able to accommodate thirty people. We do not know the size of the total community, but it is reasonable to imagine that several groups met simultaneously in different homes. The Christian church in the Roman Empire had no public architecture for another two hundred years. The lack of larger space for meeting and worship hindered the effort to build community in Corinth and contributed to the sharpness of their divisions. But what did their slogans mean?

It is easier to see the fact that Corinthians had slogans and divisions than it is to say precisely what was going on. Apparently they revered the person who had converted and baptized them, the way novices revered their sponsoring gurus in pagan mystery religions. Paul is happy that he did not baptize more than one or two. Some in Corinth were claiming him as their spiritual guide. But he did not even want to give the appearance of founding a "Pauline movement." Through the opening four chapters of 1 Corinthians Paul speaks of himself, Cephas, and Apollos not as great spiritual mentors, not as competing gurus, nor as religious stars lighting up the sky, intent on drawing disciples after them. He says that he and his fellow missionaries are servants of Christ and stewards of the mysteries of God. To make more of them is to think in pitifully human fashion (3:4). Paul labors to attach the Corinthians to Jesus Christ, to the paradoxical power of Christ's cross, and to one another in the solid bond of agape. Their divisions, he says, empty the cross of its power.

Few of us today have the largeness of heart to be equally reverent, not just toward the apostles, but toward Martin Luther, John Calvin, Ignatius of Loyola, Menno Simons, John Knox, and John Wesley. A few figures, if they come from the "early undivided church" like St. Augustine, or if they are pious enough or mystical enough like St. Francis or Johann Arndt, or a martyr to a universally despised evil regime, like Dietrich Bonhoeffer, may have some chance to succeed as a genuinely ecumenical figure. Many Christians exhibit a high level of attachment only to figures associated with the founding of their own particular Christian community.

And Christians are divided not only into denominations but into groups reflecting different perspectives on political issues and different spiritual experiences. So we have, for example, the Christian Coalition and feminists and charismatics as well as groupings like Bread for the World and Habitat for Humanity and Focus on the Family and many more. They all organize and maintain membership lists across the old denominational or theological lines, raise money, publish magazines, and have their own Web page.

In Paul's day the sum total of Christians in the world amounted to a very few thousand. Today with many millions of Christians spread over the whole globe, inhabiting diverse cultures, speaking many tongues, claimed by hundreds of denominations, the task of seeing common ground and building community is far more difficult than in Paul's time but no less pressing. I recall Huston Smith in a lecture years ago quoting Northrop Frye as saying that the twentieth century will be remembered as the time when East and West met together for the first time as equals. It was on Eastern mission fields of divided Western churches that the modern ecumenical movement was born. Sensitive missionaries discovered the awkwardness and offensiveness of speaking on behalf of a "prince of peace" when the varied churches seemed often to be at war. Frye's prediction will be more true of the twenty-first century than of the twentieth. Confucianism, Buddhism, and Islam will be the confident conversation partners with the more traditional Western religions of Judaism and Christianity. That coming conversation all by itself will provide a wider context for some of the quarrels within Christendom. They may come to seem less important, or the larger context may help Christians see more clearly and celebrate more joyfully the core beliefs they hold in common, emboldening them for the adventure of the coming interfaith conversations.

Gospel

MATTHEW 4:12-23

"God's Own Mega-Light"

In the opening chapters of his Gospel, Matthew has most artfully noted Jesus' geography: Bethlehem, Jerusalem, Egypt, Nazareth. After narrating the birth and infancy, Matthew follows the adult Jesus to the banks of Jordan for baptism and then out into the wilderness of Judea for hard testing.

Now in our text Jesus moves to Galilee, but he does not return home to Nazareth. The Son of Man has no place to lay his head (8:20), does not seek the security of home with Mary and Joseph, with brothers and sisters. Jesus cuts family ties, ceases his old occupation as craftsman, and arrives at Capernaum, making it his temporary headquarters.

Capernaum at the north end of the sea of Galilee is visited by thousands of pilgrims and tourists each year. They gape at the magnificent remains of a fourth-century synagogue, erected on the site of a predecessor synagogue of the first century (Mark 1:21-28). A mere hundred yards away is a first-century house, now surmounted by a chapel on stilts that looks like a flying saucer. Pilgrims stare. Can this really be Peter's house, where Jesus healed Peter's mother-in-law (Mark 1:29-31; Matt 8:14-17)?

Matthew views the geography and the stones differently. He reads them in the light of prophecy. This place, "Capernaum," he tells us, is "by the sea, in the territory of Zebulun and Naphtali" (4:13). Zebulun and Naphtali were the first chunks of territory to be swallowed up by the Assyrians in 732 B.C.E. Isaiah (chap. 9) prophesied that these first territories to feel God's wrath would in the days of the Messiah be the first to enjoy salvation.

That promise of Isaiah comes true, says Matthew, with the arrival of Jesus at Capernaum. He is not just one more in a long line of sages or prophets, lifting up his voice in testimony to God's distant triumphs. He is no mere forerunner like John the Baptist.

Jesus' birth was heralded by the rising of the great star (2:2), and he himself is light, God's own mega-light in the flesh (4:16). He has risen like the sun and shines upon people who were sitting in dark prison cells, in the region and shadow of death. Jesus is light and will give light, by his words and silences, by his actions and sufferings, and by his rising from death.

So from that time Jesus began to proclaim the nearness of "the kingdom of heaven," the sovereignty of God holding sway throughout the length and breadth of the universe. Through Jesus, God begins to mount a great counterattack against all evil forces, against the darkness, against death and unbelief, against all unrighteousness infecting human life.

And Jesus calls disciples. This is different from the narration in the Gospel of John (last Sunday), where the first disciples come to Jesus from John the Baptist. Here Jesus himself summons disciples, calls them to follow him, to join their lives and destinies to his, to become apprenticed to him.

The call to discipleship stands exactly here for two reasons. First, Matthew wishes to emphasize that Jesus is light and brings light, great light, not only by his individual, personal efforts but through his community of disciples. He builds community and will not work alone. He called them and he still calls women and men to abandon old securities and old allegiances. He summons them to break free of old routine and join him as light-bearers (5:13) and as wooers of human beings into new dignity as children of the living God. The new community is part of God's counterattack against evil. Matthew has regularly and rightly been called "the ecclesiastical Gospel."

Second, the material is preparation for the Sermon on the Mount. Prophecy is fulfilled, disciples are called and begin to follow him, and Jesus has attracted a great international crowd (4:24-25). It is not only Capernaum that is stirred, but "all Syria" together with Galilee, the Decapolis, Jerusalem, Judea, and the regions "beyond the Jordan" (Isa. 9:1). And who comes from all these regions and territories? Jews alone? Or is Jesus already crossing boundaries and attracting Gentiles? Syria and the Decapolis were by definition Gentile territory. It is a great mixed throng that wends its way toward Jesus, seeking life and light and liberty.

Matthew makes it crystal clear that Jesus' campaign of liberation has nothing to do with swords. He will not even use the sword to save his own life (26:52-53). He comes armed with words of teaching, and his words (as also his deeds and sufferings) are brimming with healing power. Matthew's report of Jesus' moving to Capernaum and calling of the first disciples and the swarming of the peoples to him for light and health and teaching sets the stage for that great burst of light with which Jesus opens his public ministry: the Sermon on the Mount.

FOURTH SUNDAY AFTER THE EPIPHANY

January 31, 1999

Fourth Sunday in Ordinary Time

Revised Common	Episcopal (BCP)	Roman Catholic
Micah 6:1-8	Micah 6:1-8	Zeph. 2:3; 3:12-13
Ps. 15	Ps. 37:1-18 or 37:1-6	Ps. 146:6-10
1 Cor. 1:18-31	1 Cor. 1:(18-25), 26-31	1 Cor. 1:26-31
Matt. 5:1-12	Matt. 5:1-12	Matt. 5:1-12a

"The Cross and Power, The Cross and Blessing"

The oratory of powerful politicians from Alexander and Augustus to Adolf Hitler and Winston Churchill, to Ronald Reagan and Helmut Kohl, has moved nations to war and to peace, to build walls and to tear them down. And Wall Street is sensitive to every word whispered by the CEOs of IBM, General Motors, and Microsoft. But why listen to the speech of one who never led an army, never commanded a nation, never won an election, never stirred a senate, never established a business or commercial empire, never owned an oil well or so much as a single share of AT&T, never made a billion dollars? By what right or what power does this crucified man speak to us the Sermon on the Mount, daring to pronounce us "blessed," and insisting that if we do not heed his words we are building a house on sand?

First Reading

MICAH 6:1-8 (RCL/BCP)

"These Three Things"

Micah was a contemporary of Isaiah, Hosea, and Amos in the eighth century B.C.E. Here Micah acts as God's attorney. The Lord cries out, "I am suing, I am suing, I am suing; I am going to court against my people. I, God, appeal to the mountains, to the hills, and to the deep foundations of the world to hear my complaint and testify that I speak the truth" (6:1-2).

The prophet voices God's complaint. Israel is behaving like a rebellious child, and God cries out, "How can you do that? After all that I [God] have done for you! Did I hurt you, neglect you, not take care of you? Tell me!" (6:3).

The prophet then launches into a description of God's past relations with the people. This brief "history of God and the people" serves as the basis for asserting God's rights, and it undergirds God's claims in the case.

The Lord supplied Israel with great leaders in the persons of Moses and Aaron and Miriam and redeemed the people from their sad life as slaves in Egypt. Then the Lord reminds the people of the way King Balak of Moab hired Balaam to put a curse on the people to keep them from passing through his territory. But remember how Balaam blessed the people instead of cursing them (Numbers 22-24). Who do you think inspired Balaam to stand against Balak? Setting out from Shittim the Israelites under Joshua passed dryshod over the Jordan and set up a memorial to God's powerful intervention at Gilgal (Joshua 3-5). In fact the Lord has done nothing but bless this people, defeating every opposing power with saving acts (6:3-5).

The questions in vv. 6-8 look like rhetorical questions, uttered by God. What do you people think I want from you? When have I ever demanded burnt offerings, delicate and tender calves a year old? Have I ever asked for that? Or did I demand burnt offerings of astronomical proportions? The sacrifice of a thousand rams and the offering of ten thousands of rivers of oil? Solomon departed from the statutes of his father David by sacrificing at the high places. He went to Gibeon and used to offer a thousand burnt offerings on that altar (1 Kings 3:3-4). At the dedication of the temple Solomon offered 22,000 oxen and 120,000 sheep (1 Kings 8:63). But God says, "I don't want all that."

What then? Does God perhaps desire human sacrifice in the form of offering up one's firstborn on a bloody altar? No. God explicitly forbade Israel to imitate the terrible practices of the Canaanites (Lev. 20:2-3). Yet such dreadful sacrifices were practiced in the days of King Ahaz and King Manasseh as people tried to gain or regain God's favor by giving what was most precious of all (6:6-7; 2 Kings 16:3; 21:6).

Micah is here raising what Abraham Heschel calls "The most urgent question of religious existence: What is the way of true worship?"[14] The Israelites were answering as the neighboring nations also answered: Multiply gifts on the altar! But why? Are we trying to bribe God? Are we organizing ourselves like PACs (political action committees), attempting to gain God's favor? Juan Alfaro has said that it is a bad religion in which "people commit sins and animals pay the price."[15]

But we must bring gifts. What could be worse than coming to the sanctuary empty-handed? The prophet's answer is simple and clear: coming with dirty hands, empty hearts, no justice. God does not need animal and grain sacrifices in order to stay alive (Ps. 50:2). So, "What does the Lord require?" The Lord asks three things: that the people do justice, love kindness, and walk humbly with their God (v. 8). These three are the offerings desired by the Lord.

Justice means active defense of the poor. Kindness is solidarity with the needy. Walking humbly means living like Noah. He "was a righteous man, blameless in his generation; Noah walked with God" (Gen. 6:9; cf. 5:2).

Hans Walter Wolff takes these requirements to mean to "execute justice, accomplish deeds of personal kindness, and be attentive to godliness." In fact, Wolff's discussion seems to indicate that he could have written, "execute justice and kindness and in that way be attentive to godliness," because he says that "walking humbly" or being "attentive to godliness" is not a third requirement, something religious in addition to doing justice and kindness. He says that people who imagine that God wants to be served with temple sacrifices fundamentally misunderstand the history of God's saving actions. That history shows that God has always been devoted to human beings, to their lives, their freedom, and their community. So attending to godliness means sharing God's own godly passion for human life, human freedom, and human community of justice and mercy.[16]

So attending to godliness means sharing God's own godly passion for human life, human freedom, and human community of justice and mercy.

Micah's justly famous list of three requirements should remind us of other great summaries of the will of God. Because the numerical value of the letters in the Hebrew word *torah* add up to 613, some ancient rabbis said that there are 613 commandments in the Law: 365 negative and 248 positive commands. Three hundred and sixty-five matches the days of the year, and we have (they thought) 248 bones in our bodies. It seems that this wonderful scheme is intended to say that with all our time (every day of the year) and with all our lively powers of movement (all those bones) we should serve God. Jesus in a memorable saying boiled the whole Law down to two commands: Love God, and love your neighbor (Matt. 22:34-40). And Paul was even more radical: "Love is the fulfilling of the law" (Rom. 13:8-10).

ZEPHANIAH 2:3; 3:12-13 (RC)

"Seek the Lord"

Three times in a single verse (2:3) the prophet cries to the people, "Seek!" "Seek" was originally an exhortation to go to the sanctuary and offer sacrifice, but the cry came to be used, as it is here, as a call to repent and mend one's relationship with God.

The people have apparently lost their grip on God, so that their eyes focus on something or someone else. Something other than God has captured their imaginations and their hearts. So the prophet cries out, "Seek the Lord" and immediately interprets his own cry with the words, "Seek righteousness, seek humility" (2:3). Heschel compares a word of Moses: "Justice [or righteousness] and only justice you shall pursue" (Deut. 16:20). He comments that pursuing righteousness means more than merely respecting it, more than abstaining from unrighteousness. It means to strive for it mightily. The word *pursue,* he says, "carries strong connotations of effort, eagerness, persistence."[17]

This cry of Zephaniah and Moses should be compared with the word of Jesus, "Seek first of all God's kingdom and God's righteousness" (Matt. 6:33). In the Lord's Prayer a few verses earlier in the Sermon on the Mount, Jesus interprets the petition, "Your kingdom come" with the following petition, "Your will be done on earth" (6:10).

In the continuation of the reading, the prophet is talking about the day of the Lord's indignation (3:8). The haughty, the faithless, and the unjust will be cut off (3:1-11). But God will leave a remnant, people marked by humility, trust, and simple righteousness. "They shall do no wrong and utter no lies" (3:13). They are the ones who will "seek" and find refuge in the name of the Lord" (3:12). They will dwell in peace.

Responsive Reading

PSALM 15 (RCL)

"They Will Never Be Moved"

Instead of contrasting ritual and ethics as the prophetic texts for this day do, this Torah psalm combines them in an entrance liturgy. A priest meets the congregation at the doors to the sanctuary and asks who may enter (v. 1). The people respond (vv. 2-5) by reciting a series of statements reminiscent of the second table of the Ten Commandments.

PSALM 37 (BCP)

"Do Not Fret"

Ancients were apparently as agitated as moderns at the prosperity of the wicked and the troubles of the pious. The seeming injustice works as a temptation. Why bother to trust in God? Does it really make any difference whether one is righteous or unrighteous?

The psalmist assures the fretful that nothing escapes the eye of the Lord. And in due time the Lord will act, cutting off the wicked and vindicating the righteous. The psalmist seems to take particular delight in describing the comeuppance of the wicked in juicy and gruesome detail.

PSALM 146 (RC)

"Praise the Lord"

This psalm describes the fall of the wicked in a single unemotional phrase: the Lord will bring them to ruin (v. 9). But then the psalmist lavishes loving attention on describing the positive, loving acts of God: The Lord liberates prisoners, gives sight to the blind, lifts the bowed, loves the righteous, protects strangers (who lack family and friends), and upholds orphans and widows. Without uttering a single complaint or command, the psalmist paints a picture of God and of the life of those who claim to be children of God. Are these acts demands? No, doing these things is simply the nature of God and so of the offspring of God.

SECOND READING

1 CORINTHIANS 1:18-31

"Of the Cross, About the Cross, On the Cross"

Paul might have said that the rivalries and factions in Corinth are petty, or they are personally disappointing to him, or they undermine the church's reputation in the wider community. But he says it is worse than all that. The thinking behind their factionalism empties the cross of its power (1:17). That is an outrageous statement, and Paul knows that he must defend connecting "cross" and "power."

The apostle defines his vocation as proclaiming "the word of the cross" (1:18, RSV) or "the message about the cross" (NRSV). That language reminds me of the way the passion narratives in all four of our Gospels speak of a powerful word "on the cross." John especially takes pains to have readers slow down and reflect on this oddity. The word on the cross declares, "Jesus of Nazareth, King of the Jews," and John (alone of the evangelists) says it was written in three languages, in Hebrew, Latin, and Greek (John 19:20), and everyone was reading it and mulling it over. Alone again of the evangelists, John tells of the priestly protest about that wording and how Pontius Pilate brusquely overruled their protest with his famous word about the word on the cross: "What I have written I have written" (John 19:22).

Can a crucified carpenter really be the king of the Hebrew speakers and of the Latin speakers and of the Greek speakers? Can this crucified man be sovereign over all those cultures and bind them with their diverse populations into one strange new peaceable "kingdom"?

What a foolish thought! But Paul says that if the "word of the cross" or "word on the cross" is nonsense to those who are perishing, it is nevertheless experienced by those who are being saved as the "power of God." And "power of God" means God's being and life powerfully at work in their own lives (cf. Rom. 1:16).

Paul found scriptural backing for God's acting by means of the cross in an ancient word of God recorded by Isaiah: "I [God] will destroy the wisdom of the wise" (Isa. 29:14). God has indeed bypassed the sages and scribes, the philosophers and debaters of the world with all their learning and eloquence.

The Jews, says Paul, see only abject weakness in the cross. What they seek are signs of power as proof of the presence and action of God (v. 22a). "Give us something like the Exodus from Egypt, the crossing of the Red Sea, the destruction of Pharaoh's army, something like the return from Babylonian Exile or the Maccabean liberation from Syrian overlordship!" If they see that, then they might be moved to say, "Ah, now that's God at work in the world to save."

And "the Greeks" (the rest of humankind from the Jewish point of view), says Paul, "seek wisdom" (v. 22b). Messages and teachings have to make sense. Greeks could boast that their philosophers had long ago taught them the vast difference between superstition and truth, and they had stunning achievements in medicine and mathematics and the arts to prove it. To take a crucified man as the foundation for one's life seemed to them to be simply irrational. It cut against the grain of everything they knew.

Yet Paul sums up by saying that Christ crucified is the power of God and the wisdom of God. Jerome Murphy O'Connor, scholar at the École Biblique in Jerusalem, has written several helpful books on 1 Corinthians. In commenting on this statement of Paul, he says that Jesus is the wisdom of God because "his person is the adequate presentation of the divine intention for humanity." By that he means that Jesus embodies and so expresses "the only valid goal" of all human striving toward shalom, toward universal wholeness. Furthermore, Jesus is not merely a sage commenting wisely on what the human condition is, nor is he adequately described as a pattern or model, showing what humanity must become. Jesus is power. He is the enabler. He incarnates and "radiates a transforming love which shows him to be 'the power of God.'"[18]

Can we really say that the absence of the crucified is what plunges families and churches and whole nations into confusion and worse? It may seem foolish to answer that question in the affirmative. It seems so simplistic, and it makes us think of all the old jokes about children in Sunday School finally learning to answer every question put to them with the one word, "Jesus." Question: "Who invented the printing press?" Answer: "Jesus." We need to avoid that kind of thinking. And yet something of the truth enunciated by Paul has worked its way into our common vocabulary. We all know that any unity or community built on one person or one party or one nation "outsmarting" or "overpowering" another is doomed. But how tempting it is to use our wisdom and our power to compel unity and community on our terms, and how often we humans yield to the voice of temptation.

Martin Buber tells a story about addressing a group of industrial workers on "Religion and Reality." When Buber finished speaking, one worker rose to say, "I have had the experience that I do not need this hypothesis 'God' in order to be quite at home in the world." Buber then says that he felt challenged by this worker and tried to get the worker to examine what kind of a "world" that might be in which he felt so much at home. And he asked the worker what gave his world its foundation. He really shattered the worker's security. At the end the worker said slowly and impressively, "You are right," and sat down. Buber tells the story because he was not at all proud of himself. Upon reflection, he says, what he had done was to lead the worker to "the God of the philosophers." What he should have done was lead him to the "God of Abraham and Isaac and Jacob." He should have tried to share with the worker an experience of the living God and not just talk to him about God in the abstract language of the learned.[19]

PAUL SUMMONS "CORINTHIANS," ANCIENT AND MODERN, TO APPROACH THE CROSS AND TO TRUST THE WORD OF THE CROSS TO LEAD TO LIFE AND COMMUNITY.

Buber alludes to the mystic experience of Blaise Pascal in 1654. Pascal wrote the following, among other words, describing his experience: "From about half-past ten in the evening until about half-past twelve: FIRE. God of Abraham, God of Isaac, God of Jacob; not of the philosophers and scientists. Certainty, certainty. Feeling. Joy. Peace. God of Jesus Christ." These, with about fifty other words describing his experience, Pascal wrote on a piece of parchment and carried them with him until the day of his death, sewn into the lining of his coat. He had stood like Moses at the bush and seen its burning. He had with Paul contemplated the cross and seen it shining forth "in mystic glow," knowing in his bones its power and its attraction. In his own words, he had been overwhelmed by the "extraordinary assistance" of God in Jesus Christ and him crucified.[20]

Paul summons "Corinthians," ancient and modern, to approach the cross and to trust the word of the cross to lead to life and community. Elizabeth Johnson has written that Jesus, "this crucified victim of state terror," raised from death to glory "through the vivifying power of the Spirit," defines the God in whom Christians believe as a God of endless surprise and boundless love, creator out of nothing, animator of "a koinonia of believers built up in joy and justice."[21]

Gospel

MATTHEW 5:1-12

"Jesus' First Public Word: 'Blessed'"

The Sermon on the Mount is the first public action of Jesus narrated in any detail by Matthew. After his baptism (Matthew 3), Jesus called four disciples to leave their fishing and their families (4:18-22), and then Matthew offers a brief sketch or outline of Jesus' activity: He taught and cured, attracting a great international crowd (4:23-25). When that crowd gathered, then Jesus went up onto the mysterious, unnamed mountain and sat down to teach them.

"Blessed" is the first word out of Jesus' mouth when he faces that vast throng, drawn to him by his proclamation of the kingdom and by his power to heal and make whole. And that word *Blessed* rings out nine times in a series of great "beatitudes." Instead of asking how a large crowd could possibly hear very much in the great outdoors, or what they made of that word spoken by a craftsman from Nazareth, it is better to ask what Christian readers are to make of it.

I don't think that *happy* is a very happy translation. And *blessed* has become a church word that carries a vague aura of religiosity or sacredness. One of the editions of the Good News Bible translates the underlying Greek word with the phrase, "Good for you!" at Matthew 16:17, where Jesus congratulates Peter on correctly confessing Jesus as the Christ.[22] But we need to unpack even that good English exclamation.

Ask yourself, "Who really is this who sits on the mountain and speaks this magisterial 'Blessed'?" All the way from beginning to end, and not just at the end, the Gospel of Matthew confronts us with the one who has "all authority in heaven and on earth" (28:18). In this word *Blessed* we are hearing the voice of none other than that resurrected and exalted one who is coming to judge the world.

The beatitudes stand in the first paragraph of the first of Jesus' five sermons in Matthew. The last paragraph of the last sermon brings us full circle. In it (25:31-46) Jesus plainly and unmistakably pictures himself as the judge of the universe, with "all the nations" gathered before him. Like a shepherd, he separates that throng, sheep at his right hand and goats on his left. Then, Jesus continues, the exalted judge will say "Come, you blessed" to those on his right, and "Depart, you cursed" to those on his left.

In the beatitudes we hear not just good proverbs spoken by some anonymous ancient sage. And even though the beatitudes are astonishing poetry, arranged in two stanzas with exactly thirty-six Greek words in each stanza (5:3-6, 7-10), we are listening to something greater than the rhymes and accents of a great poet. We hear the voice of the world's final judge, speaking a word of blessing ahead of time, saying to people on that hillside, "Good for you!"

But if he later approves of Peter as confessor, who exactly wins his approval here in the beatitudes? "The poor in spirit" (5:3) are folks who seem to themselves to lack charismatic endowments, and others also ignore them as deficient in spiritual gifts. But gifts of the spirit can inflate people's egos, deluding them into thinking they deserve special recognition on earth and in heaven (7:21-23). Jesus commends not those who boast of great gifts (see 1 Cor. 1:29) but rather those whose sole resource is God, who rely wholeheartedly not on their giftedness but on the Giver. Jesus commends them and declares that they possess the gift above all gifts: the immortal and gracious reign of God, the "kingdom of heaven" or "rule of God as opposed to all the rulings and dominations of human bosses and tyrants." That promise both opens and concludes the beatitudes, comprehending all the promises in an awesome embrace (5:3,10).

JESUS' WEAPONS ARE LOVE OF THE ENEMY, PRAYER FOR THE PERSECUTOR, AND A CROSS BORNE ON BEHALF OF ALL.

Those who "mourn" (5:4) weep at the world's atrocities and at the church's failings, including their own most grievous faults (cf. 1 Cor. 5:2). With cries and groanings they pray to God, "Deliver us [all of us] from evil!"

The "meek" (5:5) are not the tepid but the nonviolent, who, like Jesus himself renounce power and domination as the way of God's sovereignty. The same Greek word translated here as "meek" is used of Jesus himself in 11:29 (where it is translated "gentle") and in 11:29 (underlying "humble"). He was hardly soft, spiritless, or easily cowed. But he will not take up the sword to strike his enemies vicious blows. Jesus' weapons are love of the enemy, prayer for the persecutor, and a cross borne on behalf of all.

The first stanza of four beatitudes concludes on a note especially dear to the heart of Matthew's Jesus, "Blessed are those who hunger and thirst for righteousness" (5:6). We ache and yearn for so many things, even "spiritual" things like the power to prophesy, speak in tongues, perform miracles of healing, or have a deep personal experience of God. But Jesus commends those who sigh and pray and work for the coming new world in which righteousness dwells (3:15; 6:33; 2 Pet. 3:13). Here is echoed the programmatic utterance of Jesus in conversation with John the Baptist: "It is my job to bring righteousness to fullest expression" (3:15, my paraphrase). The first four beatitudes (5:3-6) and the second four (5:7-10) climax with sayings about "righteousness." It is the hallmark of God's gracious rule (6:33), and Matthew is the evangelist who has taken it as his job to remind us of that.

The second stanza speaks blessing upon the "merciful" (5:7). Their hearts are wide open in compassion toward the weak, the broken, the poor, toward all those cast aside by an unrighteous world. It is in this Gospel that Jesus cries, "Mercy not sacrifice!" (9:13; 12:7), and he speaks harshly of religious exercises like fussy and scrupulous tithing, if the worshiper neglects "justice, fidelity, and mercy" (23:23).

THE PRINCE OF PEACE WHO SPEAKS THESE BEATITUDES UNDERSTANDS THE POWERFUL DRIVE IN HUMAN HEARTS TO DOMINATE OTHERS, AND IN MATTHEW'S GOSPEL HE SHARPLY CRITICIZES THE QUEST BY THE STRONG IN THE COMMUNITY FOR TITLES AND STATUS AT THE EXPENSE OF "THE LITTLE ONES."

But aren't sacrifices or other recognizably "religious" exercises necessary? What would religion be without them? What about the perennial human fascination with ritual washings and lustrations? Jesus, however, blesses those who are washed and clean and "pure in heart" (5:8), whose minds and wills are wholeheartedly and undividedly fixed on God (6:24; James 1:6-8; 4:8).

The Prince of Peace who speaks these beatitudes understands the powerful drive in human hearts to dominate others, and in Matthew's Gospel he sharply criticizes the quest by the strong in the community for titles and status at the expense of "the little ones" (23:8-10 and 18:1-35). But he speaks blessing upon "peacemakers" (5:9), who work for a community of equals in church and society.

None of this is easy. These beatitudes are not the cheap and sentimental murmurings of a hopelessly naive rustic prophet. Jesus knows how powerful is the grip of evil on the world. So his final blessing is reserved for those who are "persecuted for righteousness' sake" (5:10). He blesses people who pray and watch and work for the coming of the new heavens and new earth in which righteousness is perfectly at home (3:15; 2 Pet. 3:13). But righteousness is not yet at home on our earth, and its friends will be scorned and misunderstood, probably as much in the church as in the world, until the new day dawns.

The "you" of the ninth beatitude pulls the reader into the sequence of blessings. When people suffer for the sake of Jesus, who speaks all these stunning beatitudes, they may still rejoice, confident that they are fellow citizens with the prophets, who greeted the new world from afar.

In the words of Brian Wren, Jesus who speaks the Sermon on the Mount is "Carpenter of the New Creation."[23] That description of Jesus strikes a poignant chord. Our Gospels call Jesus a craftsman, an artisan, a carpenter (Mark 6:3; Matt. 13:55 says that Jesus was the son of Joseph the craftsman). With what materials does Jesus construct the new creation? Key elements are the timbers of the cross. It is no surprise that artists have long pictured those timbers as supporting beams in the stable where he was born. In fact, the tremendously popular "Golden Legend" of the Middle Ages traces the wood of the cross back to the sacred tree in the Garden of Eden and then follows that wood through its use in Noah's Ark and the Temple of Solomon all the way down to Jesus' time, so pointing to the cross as the culmination of God's plan to renew creation.

FIFTH SUNDAY AFTER THE EPIPHANY

February 7, 1999

Fifth Sunday in Ordinary Time

Revised Common	Episcopal (BCP)	Roman Catholic
Isa. 58:1-9a, (9b-12)	Hab. 3:2-6, 17-19	Isa. 58:7-10
Ps. 112:1-9, (10)	Ps. 27 or 27:1-7	Ps. 112:4-9
1 Cor. 2:1-12, (13-16)	1 Cor. 2:1-11	1 Cor. 2:1-5
Matt. 5:13-20	Matt. 5:13-20	Matt. 5:13-16

"Liturgy and Light"

How do we honor our team? The "liturgy" hardly varies: players running out onto the floor and slapping the hands of teammates, all standing to sing the Star Spangled Banner, people cheering or booing in unison, every spectator wearing their team's colors.

How do we honor our nation's dead? Visiting the cemetery on Memorial Day or the Fourth of July, listening to patriotic speeches and to buglers playing taps, veterans in uniform saluting, all reciting the Pledge of Allegiance with hands resting on hearts, waving the Stars and Stripes.

And how do we honor God? What rituals or liturgies does God seek of us? How shall we come into the presence of God? And does God have a day like Presidents' Day or Mother's Day or Labor Day?

First Reading

ISAIAH 58:1-12 (RCL/RC)

"Rituals of Righteousness"

Once again (as in the Old Testament lesson and psalms of last week) we are confronted with strong words concerning true and false worship. In a series of vivid images Abraham Joshua Heschel conjures up pictures of fire burning on many altars, of animals offered up to the glory of the gods, sacred songs filling the air, pilgrims trudging along traditional paths as they make the ascent to their shrines and high places, priests burning incense and presiding over ancient rituals, worshipers caught up in moving pageantry.

Heschel interprets sacrifice as the experience of yielding oneself vicariously to God and of being received with favor by God. Sacrifice so conceived would appear to be a noble and excellent practice. And yet he notes how the preexilic prophets thundered against sacrifices in the most scathing terms (Amos 5:21-27; Hos. 6:6; Isa. 1:11-17; Mic. 6:6-8; Jer. 6:20; 7:21-23; Ps. 40:7; 50:12-13). At an early date Samuel had insisted on the primacy of obedience over sacrifice, but Amos and succeeding prophets went far beyond Samuel. They insisted that "the worth of worship, far from being absolute, is contingent upon moral living, and that when immorality prevails, worship is detestable."[24]

So in Isaiah 58 God cries out as in Micah 6:1 (last Sunday) and then commands the prophet to accuse the people of rebellion (v. 1). Immediately the prophet delivers God's complaint. These people come up to the temple piously enough: They "seek me" and "draw near" to me and they love to "fast." They perform their ritual, and then they demand that I rescue them ("they ask of me righteous judgments"). But they do not practice righteousness (vv. 2-3). They make a great show of their piety, fasting in sackcloth and ashes (see Matt. 6:16-18), but immediately they go out and continue their old wickedness and oppression (vv. 4-5). That is no fast!

THE PROPHET DESCRIBES THE FAST THAT GOD DESIRES IN WARM AND GLOWING COLORS: LOOSE THE BONDS OF INJUSTICE, SHARE YOUR BREAD, HOUSE THE HOMELESS, COVER THE NAKED.

The prophet describes the fast that God desires in warm and glowing colors: Loose the bonds of injustice, share your bread, house the homeless, cover the naked. These words echo down the corridors of scripture all the way to Jesus, seated on the Mount of Olives opposite the temple. His disciples had commented on the splendors of the temple. "Look," they said, at those great buildings, the monumental staircase, the Royal Portico, the Golden Gate, the Holy Place itself. See the clouds of incense rising into the air, listen to the sounds of trumpet and chorus swelling, and don't our nostrils thrill at the odor of the sacrifices offered by all those worshipers. Jesus squelched the enthusiasm of his disciples. He predicted coming disaster for the temple complex and shared with his disciples his vision of the day of judgment, when the sheep at his right hand would not be told, "Blessed are you because of proper ritual or dutiful fast." Rather they would hear the welcome words, "Come, you blessed ones, inherit the kingdom prepared for you from the world's first beginning, because I was hungry and you fed me." (Matt. 25:31-46).

When the people of God begin to celebrate liturgies of righteousness, then "light will break forth like the dawn" (v. 8), then "the glory of the Lord shall be your rear guard" (v. 9), then "your light shall rise in the darkness and your gloom will be like the noonday" (v. 10).

HABAKKUK 3:2-6, 17-19 (BCP)

"Might and Light"

Habakkuk was active in the dark days of Babylonian oppression, after Babylon defeated Egypt at Carchemish in 605 B.C.E., around the time of the first captivity of Jerusalem (597 B.C.E.). Nebuchadnezzar is triumphant. Babylon is crushing God's people. Habakkuk agonizes. Everywhere he looks, he sees "violence" (1:2, 3, 9; 2:8, 17). God is rousing those Chaldeans (Babylonians, 1:6), whose "own might is their god" (1:11), as the instrument to punish wickedness in the earth. Surely judgment executed by such a force cannot be God's final word.

The book concludes with a vision and a prayer (3:1-19). Habakkuk remembers God's ancient saving deeds and begs God to act now as in the past, praying in effect, "Break out, Lord, but show mercy!" (v. 2). The prophet is granted a vision of God's glory, which should be compared with the vision of glory celebrated in Psalm 29 (see the Baptism of Our Lord, First Sunday after the Epiphany), or even better with the imagery in the Song of Deborah (Judges 5) or the Song of Moses (Exodus 15; Deuteronomy 32) or the recitation of Israel's history in Psalm 68.

With his prophet's eye Habakkuk sees once again the ancient progress of God's glory leading the people from the southern mountains, Teman and Paran near Mount Sinai, proceeding north toward the Promised Land (v. 3). For the people of God that progress of glory meant "brightness like the sun" (v. 4), but for the enemies of the people the glory of the Lord meant "pestilence" and "plague" (v. 5). Pestilence and plague indeed went before and followed after God like the fierce escort of a general marching forth to do battle. At all the stopping places along the way, the earth shook and the nations trembled. The old eternal rocks and the everlasting hills sank low (v. 6). Nature convulsed, nations staggered.

The prophet also trembles, awestruck at his own vision, filled with horror, joy, and trust. He resolves anew to wait quietly on the Lord (v. 16). When enemies cover the land like locusts, when crops fail and herds have no offspring, when he can see no solid evidence of the presence of God or the favor of God, he will yet rejoice in the Lord (vv. 17-19). The prophet lives by faith, trusting in God (2:4). As his trust is shaped by his people's sacred memory of exodus, so Paul's trust is shaped by the word of the cross and resurrection (1 Cor. 1:18-31).

PSALM 112 (RCL/RC)

"No Fear of Evil Tidings"

Psalm 112, unlike Habakkuk 3, seems to celebrate in simpleminded fashion a direct and unambiguous connection between present righteous living and present riches. Those who fear the Lord are "blessed" (v. 1; cf. Psalm 1), and the psalm paints a rosy picture of the "blessed estate" of the ideal wise person. Good conduct leads straight to prosperity not only for the wise but even for their descendants, who will be "mighty in the land" (v. 2). The wise receive not only spiritual blessings, but "wealth and riches are in their houses" (v. 3).

How precisely does this psalm spell out the conduct that qualifies to be called "fearing the Lord"? Those who fear the Lord are "gracious, merciful, and righteous" (v. 4). They "deal generously and lend," they "conduct their affairs with justice" (v. 5), and they are people who "have distributed freely and given to the poor" (v. 9).

The psalm seems to promise that no evil can touch those who fear the Lord, and that they will gain a good reputation that will outlive them (vv. 6-7). And yet the psalm approaches the more hard-won trust of Habakkuk in other phrases. The time may come when even the righteous will receive "evil tidings" (v. 7), perhaps news as bad as that brought to righteous Job, news of disaster to the righteous person's flocks or business or family. And the psalmist reveals a realistic recognition that the righteous person will have foes (v. 8), because the wicked will be roused not to admiration but to envy and will plot ill against the righteous. Nevertheless the psalmist writes that those who fear God will in the end "look in triumph on their foes" (v. 8). And finally "the desire of the wicked comes to nothing" (v. 10).

PSALM 27 (BCP)

See the Third Sunday after the Epiphany, pp. 124-25.

ROBERT H.
SMITH

Second Reading

1 CORINTHIANS 2:1-12, (13-16)

"Nothing But Christ Crucified"

It was once widely thought that Paul's focus on the cross at Corinth could be chalked up to his lack of success in Athens. Paul had arrived in Athens after being driven out of Thessalonica and Beroea in northern Greece (Acts 17:1-15). There in Athens, in the ancient city of Socrates and Plato, Paul's religious sensibilities had been offended by the multiplicity of idols and altars in the agora, and he had entered into heated debate with Stoic and Epicurean philosophers. These latter thought that Paul was making propaganda on behalf of two new deities named "Jesus" and "Resurrection" or "Anastasis" (17:18). In addressing them at the Areopagus, Paul quotes no biblical passages but instead argues on the basis of "one of your own poets" (17:28). The upshot was that some scoffed, others showed mild interest in continuing another day, and only two people are named as persuaded by Paul, a man called Dionysus and a woman named Damaris (17:33-34).

Deeply discouraged, or so goes this scenario, Paul abandoned Athens and traveled south to Corinth (Acts 18:1). He arrived there "in weakness and in fear and in much trembling" (1 Cor. 2:3). There in Corinth, having learned his lesson in Athens, he no longer tried to argue like a philosopher. He changed his tactics and "decided to know nothing among [them] except Jesus Christ and him crucified" (2:2).

The truth seems to be that Paul always preached the crucified Christ, not only in Corinth but everywhere he went, not beginning in the '50s in southern Greece but from the first moment of his work as an apostle of the Lord Jesus starting fifteen years before he ever arrived in Corinth. And in Corinth Paul stresses the crucified as the heart of his proclamation not because he was burned in confrontation with philosophers outside the community of believers but because of sad experience with believers inside the Corinthian community.

The Corinthians defined "God" exactly the way most people still do today: "God" = "power." For the Corinthians the whole point of being believers is to gain access to God's exhilarating and liberating power mediated through the Spirit of the exalted Christ. They want to be in touch with higher powers. Why else seek communion with the Christian God? They want to be lifted up out of the mundane and the ordinary. In their celebrations, the Corinthians feel the transforming power of God and they rejoice in rich spiritual endowments. They especially love to speak in the tongues of angels (13:1). And they have begun to despise Paul for not endorsing their spiritual postures and for not guiding them into the deeper mysteries of God.

God is indeed "the world's mystery." All creatures experience the gift of life welling up, creating, giving, enlivening. And love sometimes oozes, sometimes erupts out of the depths, embracing and gracing our existence. And "hope springs eternal," as human beings in spite of crushing blows and terrible evil are ever and again coaxed out of bitterness and despair toward a fairer tomorrow.

But can we trust that mysterious and inescapable depth out of which life and love and hope flow into our lives? Will it one day run dry? Is it too weak or too fickle for us to trust? Is it anywhere near as strong as the flood of evil that continually sweeps through human history?

WHEN WE NAME THE WELLSPRING OF LIFE "GOD" AND BEGIN TO TRUST, WE DO SO NOT BECAUSE OF OUR PROBING INTELLIGENCE, OUR SENSITIVE WISDOM, BUT BECAUSE OF THE CROSS OF JESUS CHRIST.

When we name the wellspring of life "God" and begin to trust, we do so not because of our probing intelligence, our sensitive wisdom, but because of the cross of Jesus Christ. The cross is for us a sure, if paradoxical, sign that the mystery of God is an unfathomable well of grace. Paul stands before the cross like Moses before the burning bush. He takes off his shoes, for he knows that he is in the presence of holiness. The holy and life-giving mystery of the cross speaks to Paul's heart, embracing him in the divine agape. And the cross calls him, but not to the private cultivation and enjoyment of vivid personal religious experience; the cross calls him and us to participate in God's own suffering love on behalf of the life of the world.

Gospel

MATTHEW 5:13-20

"Who Is the Light of the World?"

In the whole history of the world no other piece of literature has been more studied than the Sermon on the Mount. Nevertheless, almost everything about the Sermon continues to puzzle and amaze. It is a bit like dragging the latest scientific equipment to the shores of Loch Ness in Scotland in order to examine one more time the depths of that mysterious body of water. Are the reputed sightings of the famed Loch Ness monster based on reality or are they evidence only of some form of hysteria? Is there more here than meets the eye, or less? What is it about those depths that stirs the waters and stirs also the imagination?

Even simple questions do not yield easy answers. For example, what is the theme of the Sermon on the Mount? Where is the topic sentence or paragraph?

Most students of the Sermon have been content to identify 5:17-20 as the topic paragraph. Jesus, they say, is expounding a "higher righteousness," something that exceeds the righteousness of scribes and Pharisees (5:20). And then they usually go on to define that exceedingly great righteousness as an unobtrusive inner quality, a truth lodged deep down in the inward parts, which may stir the surface but remains essentially hidden not only from casual but even from careful observers.

Interpreters then often continue by stating that this deep inner rightness desired by Jesus stands in sharpest contrast with the supposedly showy, ostentatious piety of the Pharisees. In the worst forms of this way of viewing the Sermon, all the Pharisees without exception are caricatured as hypocritical in their religiosity, as being full of bluster, always posturing and positioning themselves so that they can be seen and applauded by fellow human beings.

The result is a caricature of Pharisees and of the words of Jesus in this Sermon. The two simple comparisons of 5:13-16 should make us stop and consider. Here Jesus calls his disciples "salt" for the earth (v. 13) and "light" for the world (vv. 14-16).

Salt was not merely a delightful seasoning for food. It was an essential preservative, a necessity for sacrifice, and a sine qua non for binding the parties of a covenant (Mark 9:49-50; Exodus 30–35). Ancient sages praised Torah and Wisdom as the salt of the world. It would be provocative enough if Jesus had pointed, not to Torah and Wisdom, but to his own teaching as salt or to his life and death and resurrection as salt or to the essential teachings of scripture as salt. But he describes the people who hear his words and follow him as "the salt of the earth," and that means salt for the earth.

And then immediately after that high and shocking compliment, Jesus quite realistically admits that it is all too possible for his followers to fail to live up to their calling. If salt loses its saltiness, it is thrown out onto the street where it is trod underfoot. Those words "thrown out" have an ominous ring and remind us of the man without a wedding garment and the worthless servant, who were "thrown out" (22:13; 25:30). It is used of a fate reserved for unfaithful insiders (8:12).

Then Jesus uses the image of light. God is light (Ps. 27:1; 1 John 1:5), and the word of God is "a lamp to my feet and a light to my path" (Ps. 119:105). A teacher exemplifying righteousness can be called "a guide to the blind, a light to those in darkness" (Rom. 2:19). And of course no saying of Jesus is more familiar than his ringing "I am the light of the world" (John 8:12; 9:5), and Matthew has described Jesus as fulfilling the promise of "a great light" for all who sit in darkness and in the shadow of death (4:15-16). But it is astonishing that here in the opening of the Sermon on the Mount, Jesus points once again not to God or to Moses or to himself or to the word of God but to these anonymous followers on the mountain and calls them "the light of the world."

Whatever else we make of these declarations about disciples as salt and light, they certainly describe a robust role for disciples toward the world. Here are words that seem to be the opposite of going into your closet to pray or performing deeds of charity quietly and unobtrusively (6:1-18). Here nothing is said of cultivating an inner garden of the soul or of doing some kind of spiritual interior decorating. No one lights a lamp only to stick it under a basket. It is lighted so that it can shine and illuminate. So Jesus is not creating a new community only to sequester them from the rest of society.

What is their high and public calling? What flashes of light are they called to emit? The fire and thundering of a John the Baptist? The lightning bolts of rebels and Zealots? The white-hot brilliance of Qumraners and desert monks? The dazzling pyrotechnics of exorcists and miracle workers? Jesus turns from metaphor to plain prose and says that the salt and light which the world badly needs are the disciples' "good works." We may be tempted with Charlie Brown to cry, "Good grief!" Good works seem so dull, so unexciting, so moralistic. Some Reformation Christians are allergic to "good works" and react to the very words as they would to an attack by killer bees. They take flight and run. But Jesus calls them back.

SOME REFORMATION CHRISTIANS ARE ALLERGIC TO "GOOD WORKS" AND REACT TO THE VERY WORDS AS THEY WOULD TO AN ATTACK BY KILLER BEES. THEY TAKE FLIGHT AND RUN. BUT JESUS CALLS THEM BACK.

It will take the whole Sermon, in fact the entire Gospel, to define what Jesus means by "good works." But right here is the theme of the Sermon. The foils are usually thought to be "the scribes and Pharisees" (v. 20), but it is much nearer the mark to read these opening paragraphs (5:13-20) in closest relation with the closing paragraphs of the Sermon (7:15-27). There Jesus warns about false prophets, described as coming in sheep's clothing while they are actually ravenous and ravaging wolves (7:15). "Sheep's clothing" means that they are Christian false prophets, members of God's flock, not outsiders. That makes them all the more dangerous. They call Jesus by his correct title, "Lord, Lord" (7:21), and they expect to enter the kingdom on the last day. They will point to their spiritual gifts of prophecy, exorcism, and wonder-working, all of which they performed "in Jesus' name" (7:22). They revel in those gifts as the most brilliant proofs of the power of God in Christ. But Jesus (like Paul in 1 Corinthians 13) says that all those great and ecstatic bursts of power are nothing, because these inspired Christians are careless about God's will. All through the Sermon and all through the Gospel of Matthew, Jesus interprets that will in his dealings with others, in his healings and eatings, in his teaching, and in his dying. In all of that, Jesus says and shows that the will of God is agape or love. And love, love of God and love of neighbor, expresses itself in good works on behalf of the world, as naturally as a lamp gives light, as naturally as salt is salty.

Jesus says that it is a fatal mistake to think that he has come to cancel the law of God (5:17). We are accustomed to hearing about prophecy being fulfilled. But Jesus speaks here of fulfilling not only the prophets but also the law. His mission is not to annul the law or to do an end run around the law of God but to bring law and prophets to their highest and deepest expression. At his baptism (see the First Sunday after the Epiphany, pp. 109–11) Jesus described his work as "fulfilling all righteousness" (3:15). And that word *righteousness* surfaces here once more. Through Jesus, God is laying healing hands on the world to make it "all right" and to summon us to live lives of "all rightness." Jesus does not throw out and trample under foot (v. 13) the sincere concern of scribe and Pharisee for doing the will of God. He will lift their care to a higher plane or carry it to astonishing depths (5:20). But all that waits further description in the Antitheses (5:21-48) in weeks ahead.

In the Sermon on the Mount, Jesus promotes what we call "ethical living," and in doing so he criticizes certain leaders who prefer ecstasy and practice ecstasy to such an extent that they have neither time nor energy for ethics. It may be hard for us to relate to the ancient situation. In our own day eleven o'clock on Sunday morning is not widely regarded as a time for joyous entering into the sphere of the ecstatic, but it is known as a time when ethical pronouncements of all kinds come pouring out of the pulpit in a never-ending stream so strong that the faint glow of the ecstatic is completely extinguished.

But it may be too facile merely to contrast ethics and ecstasy. After all, Jesus promotes a certain kind of ethic and does not reject all ecstasy. Jesus speaks the Sermon on the Mount only after he himself has been born of the Spirit, baptized and drenched in the Spirit, and, in the power of the Holy Spirit of God, has waged war on the evil spirit, who tempts Jesus with a series of ecstatic visions. So it is a spiritually powerful and ecstatic Jesus with inspired vision who addresses us in the Sermon. He is not a philosopher who comes to us from the library to teach us the lessons of his dusty scholarship. He comes to us from the womb of God and the heart of God after hard testing in the wilderness. Jesus comes to share with us not rules or commands, not ordinances or injunctions, not teachings or lessons, not advice or counsel. He comes to share his vision of a new world of new relationships, and he comes to share the power of his love.

SIXTH SUNDAY AFTER THE EPIPHANY

February 14, 1999

Sixth Sunday in Ordinary Time/Proper 1

Revised Common	Episcopal (BCP)	Roman Catholic
Deut. 30:15-20 or Sir. 15:15-20	Sir. 15:11-20	Sir. 15:15-20
Ps. 119:1-8	Ps. 119:1-16 or 119:9-19	Ps. 119:1-2, 4-5, 17-18, 33-34
1 Cor. 3:1-9	1 Cor. 3:1-9	1 Cor. 2:6-10
Matt. 5:21-37	Matt. 5:21-24, 27-30, 33-37	Matt. 5:17-37 or 5:20-22, 27-28, 33-34, 37

"Field of Dreams"

Believers are God's "field," says Paul. And that makes me think of the movie "Field of Dreams."Then I find myself wondering what dreams disturb or delight God's slumbers, what images rising up put a frown on God's brow or a smile on God's face. Does God dream of having a powerful people? Or a numerous people, like grains of sand on the seashore? Or perhaps a deeply pious people? God's dreams may or may not be our dreams. How does God's garden grow? What is God's dream?

[Editor's note: These lessons may be used by those churches that do not celebrate this Sunday as the Transfiguration of Our Lord.]

First Reading
DEUTERONOMY 30:15-20 (RCL)

"I Have a Dream"

Deuteronomy is Moses' farewell speech to the people of Israel. Although he has led the people out of their Egyptian slavery to Mount Sinai, and through the wilderness up to the very threshold of land promised long ago to Abraham, Isaac, and Jacob, he himself will not enter. He will die without ever setting foot in the land toward which he has journeyed so many years. There at the border, on the edge of Israel's new world, he stares hard into the future. And he has a dream. In fact he has a dream and a nightmare.

Moses sees two possibilities, two ways, two paths the people might travel (see Psalm 1; Matt. 7:13-14; *Didache* 1:1), and he spells them out chapter after chapter. Now he says, "I have set before you this day life and death, prosperity and adversity, blessings and curses" (vv. 15,19). They surely are the people of God, delivered by the arm of the Lord from Pharaoh, granted glorious freedom, and guided along an arduous path to the cherished goal of their striving and dreaming and wandering. They have been blessed mightily, but future blessing is anything but automatic.

The people must renew the covenant. Moses names heaven and earth as witnesses on the solemn occasion and then calls to the people. "Choose life," says Moses (v. 19). And the people can do that by loving God and not being led astray to other gods. The people will love God when they quite concretely keep the commandments, decrees, and ordinances of God.

All these words of Moses were written down long centuries after Moses lived and died. These words were set down in the book of Deuteronomy at a time when Israel had suffered the bitter and stinging loss of the Promised Land. How is it that the Holy Land could be taken from the Holy People? Such an eventuality was nearly incomprehensible. But Deuteronomy, through the dream and warning of Moses, offers an explanation. It happened because they did not choose life. They went aside to other gods, chasing other dreams, losing their way by wandering down the other path.

THE PEOPLE WILL LOVE GOD WHEN THEY QUITE CONCRETELY KEEP THE COMMANDMENTS, DECREES, AND ORDINANCES OF GOD.

What happened to Israel could happen to any nation, including our own. Years ago one of my professors at seminary could not sing the stanza of the patriotic hymn "America," which asks God to "crown thy good with brotherhood from sea to shining sea." The line not only smacks of a commercial relationship with God. That would be bad enough. It also paints a naïvely bright picture of American community that completely ignores the darker realities of American life.

What song can the churches sing about our nation? Some years ago I remember driving along "church row" on Skinker Boulevard in St. Louis. Houses of worship, Adventist and Scientist, Episcopal and Presbyterian, Jewish and Vedanta, are all lined up where Wydown connects with Skinker. What they say of themselves is always intriguing. One house of God had a sign on its lawn, "A Safe Summer is a Happy Summer." Practically next door was another church with another sign bearing a word of the prophet Isaiah: "Righteousness exalts a nation, but wickedness is a rebuke to any people." The first sign is just plain sappy, while the latter encapsulates a deadly serious vision. It was impossible to drive past that sign without asking, What is our dream? What is our dream for our family, for our church, for our city and for our nation?

SIRACH 15:11-20

"Permission Denied"

Sirach echoes themes of Deuteronomy 30 (above). Sirach says, the Lord has placed before you "fire and water" (v. 16). Immediately Sirach glosses the image and speaks more directly of "life and death" (v. 17). So here again, as in Deuteronomy, are two doors, two paths. In Sirach's day some were attempting to squeeze out of the responsibility of making a choice. They were saying, "Why blame me if my acts are evil? God made me do it!"

Sirach takes that protest seriously. He answers that the Creator has given each person "the power of their own free choice" (v. 14). People have it within their ability to make right choices, to observe God's commandments, and to act in a faithful fashion (v. 15). If they fail to walk the path of life and righteousness, then they have misused their power. Therefore they are to be blamed, not God.

We might argue with Sirach's apparent optimism about the moral powers of human beings. But Sirach is not writing a systematic theology. What Sirach clearly wants to do is to combat the notion that our failings are somehow God's fault, and what he just as clearly urges is the love of the Lord and the fear of the Lord (v. 13), expressed in a life of dutiful action.

It is awkward and can be dangerous to teach positive lessons with negative statements, but Sirach concludes with the arresting comment, "God has not commanded anyone to be wicked, and has not given anyone permission to sin" (v. 20).

Responsive Reading

PSALM 119:1-19, 33-34

"Fullest Obedience"

Each of the twenty-two sections of the psalm begins with a successive letter of the twenty-two-letter Hebrew alphabet, and each section contains precisely eight verses. That's the easiest thing to say about Psalm 119. But that orderly progression of the alphabet, from beginning to end, from *aleph* to *tau*, *alpha* to *omega*, A to Z, is not just interesting poetic architecture. The psalm as a whole is an orderly celebration of the law of God that orders all things well and calls us to surrender not just some but all the elements of our lives to God. In that it is reminiscent of Jesus' definition of the "first and greatest commandment" as loving God "with our whole heart, our whole soul, our whole mind, and our whole strength" (Mark 12:30).

The opening stanza (vv. 1-8) echoes the themes of Psalm 1, although using less powerful images than Psalm 1, as it declares "happy" (see Matt. 5:3-12, Fourth Sunday after the Epiphany) those whose feet walk in the law of the Lord. At stanza's end (v. 8) the psalmist in very realistic fashion entertains the possibility that the pious might not be able to keep the law and might experience forsakenness rather than blessedness. The following stanza (vv. 9-16) turns to God seeking help. "With my whole heart I seek you" (v. 10), "teach me" (v. 12), "open my eyes, so that I may behold wondrous things out of your law" (v. 18).

Verses 33-34 conclude the portion of the psalm selected for this Sunday with the prayer, "Give me understanding." That same cry for understanding punctuates this long psalm at regular intervals all the way to the end (vv. 73, 125, 144, 169). What should we "understand"? The psalmist prays for a heart that is open to the beauty and the wisdom of the law of the Lord and that he might then perform that law with his "whole heart" (v. 34; cf. Matt. 22:34-40). In very realistic terms the psalmist acknowledges that God has serious competitors for his allegiance, and as chief among those competitors he names selfish gain and vanities (vv. 36-37). Nothing could be more relevant to the modern American scene than the competition Jesus saw between "God" and "Mammon" (Matt. 6:24). The psalmist knows in his heart of hearts that real life (vv. 37, 40) is walking in the way of God's commandments. But he also knows that such a walk is a difficult path, beset by constant temptation, and so he prays for God's help. It really does seem to require a charism to be able to "delight in the way of [God's] decrees as much as in all riches" (v. 14) in our consumer society.

The Psalm Prayer aptly sums up central features of the psalm, although it neatly avoids the issue of wealth, precisely mirroring the way many denominations avoid the issue:

> Lord, you are just and your commandments are eternal. Teach us to love you with all our hearts and to love our neighbor as ourselves, for the sake of Jesus our Lord.[25]

1 CORINTHIANS 3:1-9 (RCL/BCP)

"God's Field"

The Corinthians complain that Paul is a great disappointment. He never gave them the lofty teaching about spiritual things, which they crave. Other teachers have brought it to them, so now finally they feel enlightened, illumined, enriched, strong (4:8-10). Now, they think, they are mature, but no thanks to Paul.

Paul replies that everything about the Corinthians reveals not their maturity but the opposite. They are still babies, "infants in Christ" (3:1), and like any intelligent and caring nurse (see 1 Thess. 2:7-8), Paul gave them milk to drink. Solid food will come in due time (1 Cor. 3:2). Paul uses "mature" (v. 6) and "spiritual" (v. 1) as synonyms, and these two terms are the opposites of "infants" and "people of the flesh" (v. 1).

Their disunity and factionalism, arising out of jealousies and quarrelings, prove that they are fleshly and not spiritual, infantile and not mature. They are "behaving according to human [not spiritual] inclinations" (v. 3). That sounds like Jesus' rebuke to Peter, when Peter rebuked Jesus (!) for saying that it was God's determined will and plan that he go to Jerusalem and die on the cross. When Peter showed more interest in Jesus having power than in his having a cross, Jesus said that Peter was thinking the thoughts of human beings and not thinking the things of God (Mark 8:33; Matt. 16:23).

When the Corinthians say, "I belong to Paul" or "I belong to Apollos" (v. 4), they are bragging about human connections. That kind of talk proves that they are "merely human." Isn't it odd that they do not boast of spiritual connections! Their own slogans convict them.

It is wrong to think that Paul and Apollos are rivals, like the successors of Alexander the Great. When Alexander died prematurely in 323 B.C.E. at the age of 33, about the age of Jesus when he died, his generals began carving up the vast territories that the Macedonians had conquered. Ptolemy, Seleucus, Antigonus and the others each bit off as much as he could grab, even warring with former comrades, and each set himself up as king and established a dynasty.

Something of that sort had crept into the minds of James and John with their celebrated request that they might be members of Jesus' cabinet when he established his kingdom (Mark 10:35-45). But Jesus did not have domination on his mind, the way Alexander did, much to the consternation of Peter, James, and John.

Paul writes that he and Apollos and all the other missionaries (9:5) are "servants" (3:5,9) with differing tasks assigned to them by the one Lord. The Corinthians themselves are "God's field" (v. 9), God's garden. Saying that, Paul is using an old biblical image. It emerges in Isaiah's "Song of the Vineyard" (Isaiah 5). In Psalm 80, Israel is a vine brought by God out of Egypt, one for which God cleared the ground by driving out the nations who previously held the land! But the vineyard had been devastated by invaders, and the psalmist prays that God would again have regard for the vine (cf. Ezekiel 19). Jesus spoke of Israel as the vineyard and of Israel's leaders as rebellious workers (Mark 12:1-12 and parallels).

Paul uses the old image in altered fashion, declaring that he had done the planting, and then Apollos came later and watered. And God? "God gave the growth" (v. 6). One of the basic points Paul wants to make is that, far from being rivals, he and Apollos share a common goal: the health and maturation of the Corinthians. But what they contribute is nothing compared with what God the Creator alone can give: the life, the increase, the growth.

Paul goes on to talk about receiving wages from God (v. 8). He certainly does not mean that he and Apollos are working only for what they can get out of it. Elsewhere he will speak of the laborer being worthy of his hire (1 Corinthians 9). But here his point is that God is the owner of the field. It belongs to God. And God has sent both Paul and Apollos out to work. God, not the Corinthians, "hired" Paul and Apollos. God, not the Corinthians, will "pay" Paul and Apollos. That is to say, Paul and Apollos are responsible to God and must strive to please God their "boss" or lord, not the Corinthians.

The life of the community at Corinth does not rest on the creative genius of Paul or Apollos. God and God alone is the mysterious creative power flowing out through Jesus Christ to give life in all its "maturity" or fullness to the Corinthians. The image of the field with vines growing to maturity is compatible with Paul's other image of a human being growing from infancy to maturity. The word *maturity* also connects the reading this week both with the epistle designated for last Sunday and with one of the Gospel selections (Matt. 5:38-48).

The Greek word translated "mature" in 1 Cor. 2:6 and 14:20 is the same word translated as "perfect" in the Sermon on the Mount at Matt. 5:48 and in Jesus' reply to the rich man, "If you wish to be perfect" (Matt. 19:21). In 1 Cor. 13:10 the same word is used in Greek, but there it is translated as "complete" in contrast to the partial, the childish, and the infantile. For the Corinthians, being complete or mature spiritual beings meant being a religious elite, knowing great mysteries, and reveling in powerful charismatic endowments. For Jesus and for Paul, being mature spiritual beings, being a complete man or a complete woman, means being merciful as God is merciful, loving as God is loving.

While the Corinthians say, "We belong to Paul, or to Apollos, or to Cephas," Paul replies, "You belong to God in Christ." "You are God's garden, God's field."

And in following paragraphs he will continue by declaring, "You are God's house," as he switches from agricultural to architectural images. With both sets of images Paul has in mind the work performed by God and the labors of Paul and his fellow apostles in the wake of the work of God. God is the "ground of our being" and the creative wellspring of all life. Paul and Apollos are farmers in God's field, planting or watering, weeding or hoeing. And God is the architect and master builder who has laid a good foundation. Paul and Apollos and all the others need to exercise care as they build on that foundation.

Paul and Apollos need to know their place in the economy of God, and the Corinthians need to know the source of their life and the kind of life to which they are called. Implicit in Paul's images, and sometimes surfacing, is the idea that a garden should bear fruit. And it is no accident that Paul describes God as building not a palace or a hut. Paul seems to worry that he and his coworkers and the Corinthians themselves might build straw on God's solid foundation. Then it would be no stronger than those flimsy structures erected by the first two of the three little pigs.

In God's mind, in God's dream, the Corinthian community is no hut made of straw. And it is nothing like the proverbial "house of cards." It is rather God's own temple, a sanctuary indwelt by the Spirit of the living God. As such it is holy to God and precious. Any assault on that temple is an attack on God! That thought should sustain the Corinthians. As field or as temple, they belong to God. Not to Paul, not to Cephas, not to Apollos, not even to themselves. If they could just realize who it is to whom they belong, then they could stop their bragging about human sponsors, human baptizers, human initiators, and human leaders. What need would they have to boast about connections with human beings? And why fear any human power or for that matter any earthly or heavenly power in the entire cosmos? The whole universe belongs to them, because they belong to Christ, and Christ belongs to God (1 Cor. 3:21-23).

FOR JESUS AND FOR PAUL, BEING MATURE SPIRITUAL BEINGS, BEING A COMPLETE MAN OR A COMPLETE WOMAN, MEANS BEING MERCIFUL AS GOD IS MERCIFUL, LOVING AS GOD IS LOVING.

We hear plenty these days about self-esteem, and it does not all come from the Rev. Jesse Jackson, who teaches disadvantaged children (and adults) to say emphatically, "I am somebody!" When people operate out of a shrunken sense of self, they easily fall prey to demagogues. Agitators are never in short supply. They love to take advantage of weakness in their followers by offering them a twisted sense of self, stirring them up to identity with others of the same color or same language or same class against other groups of people. Ethnic groups, linguistic groups, racial groups, and interest groups are all practicing "identity politics" these days, fragmenting the body politic, pitting one group against another in the name of "rights" owed to them. Paul's vision embraces all people—Jew and Gentile, male and female, slave and free—precisely because he finds his own identity in belonging to Christ, who belongs to God, who is the Creator and Redeemer of all people without exception.

1 CORINTHIANS 2:6-10 (RC)

See the Fifth Sunday after the Epiphany/Fifth Sunday in Ordinary Time, pp. 146–47.

Gospel

MATTHEW 5:17-48

"But I Say to You!"

After pronouncing his infinite blessing and calling the blessed to be a blessing (light and salt, 5:1-16) and to yield the fruit of an exceeding righteousness (5:17-20), Jesus begins to expound on that salty, shining righteousness in six paragraphs, which have long been called "Antitheses." They got that name because they all begin with statements of contrast: "People long ago were told . . . but I now say to you."

Who offered that old teaching long ago? Is Jesus contradicting some catechetical tradition, popular understandings, scribal interpretations? Could Jesus possibly be contradicting Moses? Surely Jesus would not contradict scripture, the word of God? But is he really contradicting? Is the nomenclature "Antitheses" accurate? Aren't some of these statements of Jesus better designated "radicalizations"?

Jesus is here pictured as spelling out in sometimes shocking detail how his followers should act in such basic areas of human and social life as worship, marriage, courts, politics, and business. If the shackles of sin have been broken, if God's sovereignty is bursting in, if God is really laying healing hands on the world to make it all right in and through the life and death and resurrection of Jesus, how should and how can the disciples live their lives? It is important to note that it is not a matter only of "should." Something new has arrived: a new time, a new creation, with new wine and new energies and new potencies. The old is passing away with its old advice and old rules and old arrangements.

These "antitheses" are not pieces of sage advice to the confused, nor are they laws aimed at curbing the unruly. These are not the kinds of ordinances that the police might be called on to enforce. Maybe angels could enforce them! They would have to look into the depths of the human heart. Jesus speaks about sudden thoughts and feelings of anger, lust, resentment, and hate. These move deep down in the inward parts. They are not always easily detected, and how could they possibly be regulated by any board of supervisors or police force? We are dealing here with the language of the visionary. If we don't recognize that, then we easily get caught up into moralizing interpretations and turn Jesus into a fussy lawgiver or pitiless legislator.

But the Jesus who speaks in this sermon shares with us his vision of new human community. He envisions a world free not only of murder, but free even of insults and angry words. They do not disappear because of additional police, harsher sentencing, or more prisons. They cease because people touched by the healing hand of God seek peace and reconciliation (5:21-26).

Jesus sees a new world coming where men and women experience the oneness for which they were created in the first place. He is not offering marital advice, and he is certainly not laying down a law, even though his words on divorce influenced legislation for centuries. He is lifting eyes to God, to the power of God, to the new world of God, challenging his followers to share his vision of a great and glorious peace beyond the battle of the sexes (5:27-32).

Jesus lifts our eyes to a wondrous world where personal and corporate transactions no longer require batteries of lawyers and reams of documentation, where such safeguards are no longer necessary, where deceit and half-truths and downright lies are unknown, where our speech is simple, direct, and completely honest (5:33-37).

The lectionary appoints only four of the six Antitheses (5:21-37) for reading and reflection in this particular year, holding back the last two Antitheses (5:38-48) for use in years when Epiphany has one more Sunday. But it would be a mistake to ignore the end of the series which is in fact its climax.

> SOMETHING NEW HAS ARRIVED: A NEW TIME, A NEW CREATION WITH NEW WINE AND NEW ENERGIES AND NEW POTENCIES. THE OLD IS PASSING AWAY WITH ITS OLD ADVICE AND OLD RULES AND OLD ARRANGEMENTS.

In the fifth Antithesis (5:38-42) Jesus offers his vision of a society that moves beyond equity ("an eye for an eye" is a form of balanced justice) to stunning generosity. And that is not yet the end. In the sixth and culminating Antithesis (5:43-48) Jesus shares his vision of a society that loves as God loves. "I say to you, Love your enemies!"

The Jesus Seminar confers its decree of authenticity very sparingly. The members of the Jesus Seminar studied some 1500 sayings of Jesus culled from ancient Christian sources of the first three centuries. Out of all those sayings, they count only six sayings of Jesus recorded by Matthew as having actually been spoken by Jesus. Those six are the long parable in 20:1-15 and then some very few other words of Jesus: 5:39-42a; 5:44a; 6:9a; 13:33; 22:21. So two of the six "authentic" words of the historical Jesus (as counted by the Jesus Seminar) occur in this portion of the Sermon on the Mount.

The members of the Jesus Seminar are convinced that the words and deeds of the historical Jesus (as distinct from the canonical Jesus or the credal or liturgical or devotional Jesus) "cut against the social grain." So by printing in red the saying about turning the other cheek, giving away cloak with coat, and carrying a soldier's pack a second mile, they are labeling the sayings as outrageous and unnatural. And so also they regard those three simple words, "Love your enemies," as eminently and even shockingly countercultural. They remain so in our own societies today. This climactic word among the Antitheses, "Love your enemies," is not just one more command or law. It encapsulates the whole divine drama by which the loving God has reached out to embrace a wayward humankind in order to lead it toward universal shalom.

Mitri Raheb, pastor of an Arab Christian congregation in Bethlehem (the Evangelical Lutheran Christmas Church), tells the story of two ten-year-old Israeli children who missed their bus stop and were dropped off at the end of the line, far from home as night fell. They began to walk but headed off in the wrong direction and were soon lost. Finally they came to a gas station and asked for help. The Arab station attendant phoned the children's frightened mother, who was terrified to learn that her children were not simply lost but were among Arabs across the street from Dehesha refugee camp, known as a center of resistance to Israeli occupation. Isa, the station worker, turned on an electric heater for the children, got food and drink for them from his own home, and took care of them until a car full of Israeli men, prepared for the worst, came to fetch the children. The Palestinian Muslim gas station attendant saw the Israeli children not as enemies but as neighbors. Of course, says Raheb, "The story did not make the headlines. It was not shown on television, for no blood had been shed. Only two newspapers, one Israeli and one Palestinian, reported it."[26]

The beatitudes introducing the Sermon on the Mount (5:3-12) pronounce the approval of the world's judge upon all who hunger for righteousness, and that righteousness is defined as something "exceeding" the highest known forms of righteousness in that ancient culture, that practiced by the scribes and Pharisees with their passion for the will of God (5:17-20). When Jesus then sets out to define the higher, exceeding righteousness, he assaults our imaginations with image after shocking image (5:21-48). It is not until the final paragraph in the series of six that Jesus uses a word that can serve as an adequate synonym for "righteousness," and that is the word *love.*

This wonderful word has suffered loss of purchasing power, so that one of my pastoral colleagues has dropped the word from his homiletical vocabulary, preferring to use the English transliteration of the Greek *agape.* This agape is something out of the ordinary, as its use by Jesus indicates. He knows we love those who are near us or like us, members of our own family or clan, nation, or denomination. All of those represent our own egos written large. Jesus shocks by speaking of love for the enemy, of prayer for our own persecutors.

Jesus speaks of agape and then underscores his statement by saying that those who practice the difficult art of loving show thereby that they are children of God, for it is the nature of God to love widely and wildly. God causes warming sun to rise and nurturing rain to fall not on good people only, not on the friends of God alone, but on all, the good and the evil, the righteous and the unrighteous. God's generosity is boundless, and so ought our own love to be.

Concluding this portion of the Sermon on the Mount, Jesus paraphrases the old saying from Leviticus 19:2, "You shall be holy as I the LORD your God am holy." Jesus says, "You shall be perfect, as your heavenly Father is perfect" (5:48). "Perfect" is not an easy word. The Greek word underlying *perfect* has in it the root *telos,* which means a goal or target. So the word *perfect* suggests a plant growing up and maturing so that it bears its fruit. Or a human being growing and maturing not only in physique but also in heart and spirit. It's as if Jesus were to say, "Grow up and grow out of your childish egotism and pettiness; grow up into the life and spirit of God."

By his living and his speaking, Jesus calls us to imagine a transfigured world, where agape is the rule rather than the exception, where righteousness is no alien but is perfectly at home, a new time and a new space where we are all completely caught up into God's own suffering love freely entered into on behalf of the life of the whole world.

Throughout the Sermon on the Mount, and especially in these strange Antitheses, Jesus is giving us not good laws and good rules and good advice in place of bad. He is shaking his head at the fallen state of our lives that requires prisons and courts and laws and oaths. He shows that he understands the reality of deep human divisions and knows about brothers and sisters injured by insults (5:21-24), women as objects of male exploitation (5:27-30), warfare between husbands and wives (5:31-33), neighbors suing neighbors (5:33-37), occupation forces oppressing the vanquished (5:38-42), insiders indifferent or hostile to outsiders (5:43-48).

He knows all that, and so do we. But how shocking, how sad, if that is all we can see and all that we know. The Epiphany season asks whether we can see the great new star over the place of Jesus' birth (2:1-12). Can we hear the voice of God, "This is my Son" (3:17)? Do we see Jesus' victory over Satan in all the wildernesses of the world (4:1-11)? Do we see Jesus as a great burst of light for all who live in darkness and the shadow of death (4:12-17)? Do we see new power in his proclamation of God's sovereignty and in his cures and healings (4:23-25)?

Do we see and experience blessing, as he shares his vision of God's new world in the Sermon on the Mount (Matt. 5-7)?

The Sermon on the Mount as a whole is not a piece of new legislation, promulgated by Jesus like some New Moses. It is a mighty word of the resurrected one, designed to shatter our old assumptions and our tired old ways of thinking. Jesus would stimulate our moral imaginations to think new thoughts and dare new deeds.

THE TRANSFIGURATION OF OUR LORD

FEBRUARY 14, 1999

LAST SUNDAY AFTER THE EPIPHANY

REVISED COMMON	EPISCOPAL (BCP)
Exod. 24:12-18	Exod. 24:12, (13-14), 15-18
Ps. 2 or 99	Ps. 99
2 Peter 1:16-21	Phil. 3:7-14
Matt. 17:1-9	Matt. 17:1-9

"DOMINATION, ILLUMINATION, MATURATION"

THE READINGS TAKE US TO THE HEIGHTS, to Mount Sinai, to the Mount of Transfiguration, and oddly even to Mount Calvary. In the rarefied air of those high places we enter the presence of holiness, burning and brilliant and awesome. On those mysterious heights, holiness breaks out of darkness, out of silence, and illumines our lives and our dreams with startling speech. Holiness addresses us, not overpowering us but wooing us, nudging us, calling us by name. The speech of God and the one whom we call "the Word of God" invite us to step into the flow and stream of God's own life. The life of God is an awesome flow of wind and water and word that would carry us together with our whole world toward peace and perfection, toward maturity and reconciliation. But do we swim against the stream? Are we afraid of the water? It is deep and it is sometimes cold.

FIRST READING

EXODUS 24:12-18

"The Finger of God"

Exodus surrounds ethical living with an aura of holiness. It does not picture Moses as getting the Ten Commandments by convening a conference of all senior Israelites, and setting them the task of regulating their personal and common lives. Nor does he invite Aaron and Miriam to one side and with them draft a questionnaire, which he then circulates among all male tribesmen over the age of fourteen, seeking consensus on the ten most-needed rules for life in the wilderness. Nor did he send emissaries to foreign courts on a quest for codes and rules found to be useful by other nations. Those are all possible and even sensible ways of doing business, but that is not the way it happened according to the sacred text. Exodus says that God, Creator of earth and sky, Liberator from Egyptian serfdom, initiated talks with Israel, speaking through Moses. God summoned a small delegation to come away from the rest of the people. So Moses with Aaron, Nadab, and Abihu (sons of Aaron, Exod. 6:23), and seventy elders of the people went off a little way from the people, but Moses is the one with whom God spoke (24:1-2).

Exodus offers in rapid succession two stories of the way that the people received the words of the Lord and bound themselves to do them. In one account (24:3-8) Moses built an altar at the foot of the holy mountain, offered burnt offerings, dashed blood on the altar and on the people, and heard the people's pledge to obey all that God commanded.

In the other, (24:9-11) Moses and Aaron, Nadab and Abihu, and the seventy elders go up onto the mountain, where they are granted a vision of God. They are pictured as looking up to the sky, to the vault of the firmament (that thin but opaque dome separating the sky-waters above from the earth-waters below) fixed in its place by the Creator near the world's first dawn. But suddenly the firmament was rendered transparent, and they found themselves looking straight through it into heaven's throneroom. The firmament appeared to be a translucent sapphire pavement, seen by other visionaries as a thin dome of crystal (Ezek. 1:22) or a crystalline sea (Rev. 4:6). They were able to see the glory of the Lord, like a massive storm of cloud and lightning, covering the mountain for six days, and then on the seventh day God called Moses to enter the cloud. Looking from below, they found they were gazing through the firmament at the soles of God's feet and the base of God's throne. It is not possible to come so close to pure holiness without dying, and yet their lives were spared. They ate as God's table-guests, protected by the law of hospitality. In exactly the same way those who offered sacrifice in the preceding story also ate of their sacrificial offerings, sharing a meal with one another and with God at that altar surrounded by twelve pillars.

> THE GOD OF SINAI SUMMONED MOSES UP ONTO THE MOUNTAIN, NOT TO INITIATE A NEW CULT BUT TO INAUGURATE A NEW HUMAN COMMUNITY, MARKED BY SINGLE-MINDED DEVOTION TO GOD AND PASSIONATE CARE FOR THE NEIGHBOR.

Then God summoned Moses alone to "come up to me on the mountain" (24:12). Joshua went with Moses part way, and then Moses ascended alone. The glory of the Lord, like a massive storm of clouds and lightning, settled on the mountain and shrouded it for six days. Then on the seventh day God called

Moses to step into the cloud. There on the mountain heights God spoke with Moses for forty days and forty nights. At last the Lord ceased speaking. Before retreating once more into total silence, the Lord gave Moses two stone tablets, written with the finger of God (31:18).

As Jesus says in Mark 12:30-31 (Matt. 22:37-39) the central and core command is that we love God with our entire being. But that command comes with a second—or a second is its other side, bone of its bone and flesh of its flesh, indivisible from it—that we love our neighbor as ourselves. The God who appeared to Moses on Mount Sinai seeks no adoration, no worship, no hallowing of the divine name in isolation from doing God's loving will on earth toward real earthly neighbors. And yet the "religious" impulse is strong, and human beings repeatedly reenact part of Moses' ancient smashing of the commandments. We continually find ways to divide the two tables of the Law and smash one or the other.

Gandhi is reported to have offered a list not of ten commandments but of seven social sins. In some interesting ways they reflect the two tables of the Law, or Jesus' response to the question about which is "the first and great commandment." Gandhi put his finger on seven fatal divisions that mirror Jesus' own concern for holding in a sacred union love for God together with love for neighbor. Gandhi's seven deadly sins are these: politics without principle, wealth without work, commerce without morality, pleasure without conscience, education without character, worship without sacrifice. The God of Sinai summoned Moses up onto the mountain, not to initiate a new cult but to inaugurate a new human community, marked by single-minded devotion to God and passionate care for the neighbor.

Responsive Reading
PSALM 2 (RCL)

"You Are My Son"

Psalm 2 is a royal psalm, chosen to accompany the account of the Transfiguration in Matthew 17. The psalm celebrates the coronation of a new king. Talk of conspiring nations and rulers taking counsel against the Lord and his anointed (vv. 1-2) indicates that rebellion has broken out somewhere at news of the old king's death.

God who sits in the heavens terrifies the nations, saying to them, "I have set my king on Zion, my holy hill" (vv. 5-6). And the Lord has addressed the king, "You are my son; today I have begotten you" (v. 7). That address is accompanied by the promise that God will give the nations into the hand of the king (vv. 8-

9). Subject kings or rulers contemplating rebellion against the Lord's anointed are warned to submit themselves or prepare to be smashed into pieces.

The Psalm Prayer focuses not on the response of nations far away but on the response of insiders:

> Lord God, you gave the peoples of the world to be the inheritance of your Son; you crowned him as king of Zion, your holy city, and gave him your Church as his bride. As he proclaims the way of your eternal kingdom, may we serve him faithfully, and so know the royal power of your Son, Jesus Christ our Lord. Amen.[27]

PSALM 99

"Lover of Justice, Agent of Equity"

The psalmist praises God as king, enthroned upon the cherubim (cf. Ps. 80:1). Israel had no molten image of God in its sanctuary. The ark of the covenant—surmounted by cherubim, those half-human, half-beast bodyguards of God, in the holy of holies—served as the footstool (Ps. 99:5) of the invisible God (1 Sam. 4:4). The sanctuary stood on God's "holy mountain" (99:9), namely Mount Zion at Jerusalem (v. 2). The psalmist uses the traditional language of God as king and lord, but more important is the way this "Mighty King" is named "lover of justice," who has "established equity" (v. 4). God spoke "in the pillar of cloud" (v. 7) and takes seriously the decrees given to Israel through Moses. The thrice-holy God (vv. 3, 5, 9) is "a forgiving God" but also "an avenger of wrongdoings" (v. 8), so having mercy or punishing people, as necessary.

The Psalm Prayer is succinct and to the point:

> Lord our God, King of the universe, you love what is right. Lead us in your righteousness, that we may live to praise you; through your Son, Jesus Christ our Lord. Amen.[28]

SECOND READING
2 PETER 1:16-21 (RCL)

"On the Holy Mountain"

Second Peter is cast in the form of a biblical farewell speech or last will and testament. Jesus' farewell in John 13-17 may be the best known of the biblical farewell speeches, but others also come to mind. Jacob (Genesis 47-49), Moses (Deuteronomy 1-3, 28-31), and Paul (Acts 20:17-35 and 2 Timothy) uttered famous farewells. Farewell speeches have a number of features in common: a head of a family or religious leader on the threshold of death gathers his children or followers, announces his imminent departure, describes internal and external dangers threatening the unity of the fellowship, rehearses his own past teaching and his life as compass and anchor in the storms to come, prays with and for the fellowship, and then shares a final meal with his family or friends.

Second Peter exhibits many of these features; it is certainly the speech of an elder worried about the coming generation. The author announces that his death is near and speaks of dying in terms that echo the Transfiguration: "I will soon put off my tent, my earthly dwelling" (v. 14). He writes to people to whom he has written in the past (3:1) and whom he calls "beloved" several times, even though we are ignorant of his precise relationship with them.

He is clearly troubled at the rise of false prophets in the community. He compares them to Balaam, who took money to utter his mad ravings and was rebuked by a donkey (2:15-16). In the name of Christian "freedom" (2:19, perhaps a twisted version of Paul's accent on Christian liberty, 3:15-16), the false prophets undermine godly living (goodness, self-control, agape, righteousness) and they scoff at the notion of a future judgment as some kind of "cleverly designed myth" (1:16).

The author holds up Noah ("herald of righteousness," 2:5) and Lot ("a righteous man," 2:7-8) as extraordinary exemplars of two fundamental virtues that 2 Peter espouses: (1) living godly lives and (2) exhibiting joyful confidence in God's future. Noah and Lot lived lives of godliness and hope, even though Noah was surrounded by "a world of the ungodly," while Lot dwelled in Sodom and Gomorrah.

GRACE AND HOPE ARE SOURCES OF A SPECIFIC LIFESTYLE, FOR THEY EVOKE NEW BEHAVIOR FITTING BOTH WHAT GOD HAS DONE AND WILL YET DO.

At the time of the transfiguration Peter and his companions were not great exemplars of Christian virtues. Peter had just been rebuked in words stronger than those used here of the false teachers. He had been called "You Satan!" by Jesus (Matt. 16:23). But Peter came to know "the power and coming of the Lord Jesus" (2 Peter 1:16) at the Transfiguration. At that moment, he saw the glory of God dwelling in this Jesus, whose words about traveling to the cross (Matt. 16:21) had so offended him. He came to see glory in Jesus' lowly and loving path to the cross (the basis of all Christian "ethics") and in Jesus' powerful resurrection from the grave (the basis of Christian patience and hope).

Peter calls that mountain "holy" (v. 18), but the thrust of his words is to insist that living in the present toward the future following the transfigured Jesus renders anyone's life "holy" and guards against all "ungodliness." So he calls the community to hold firmly to his luminous word about Jesus as Lord, as they continue their journey through what he calls "a dark place" (v. 19). Peter wants his readers to share his confidence that we are not traveling toward greater darkness and nothingness but toward the dawn of a brilliant new day, when "the morning star" will rise in our hearts (v. 19). Then and only then, when the Light of the world directly illumines hearts, will we be able to dispense with the shining testimony of his word. Until then it is a lamp unto our feet.

PHILIPPIANS 3:7-14 (BCP)

"Called Up"

Paul speaks the language of the accountant, poring over books, scanning his assets and liabilities. Thinking in purely human terms, Paul can make an impressive list of his spiritual assets: a member of God's ancient people Israel; born into the tribe of Benjamin and even bearing the name of Saul the first king of Israel who was of that same tribe; circumcised on the eighth day; knowing Hebrew, the language of the sacred scriptures; an observer of the law in the manner of the Pharisees; so zealous for the traditions of his people and party that he was a persecutor of the upstart church, and in fact he could not think of any way in which he was not blameless, completely innocent of any transgression against the law, righteous in terms of law. He "boasts" in similar language at the beginning of the "fool's speech" in 2 Corinthians 11:21-33 (cf. Rom. 11:1).

Again in the language of accounting, Paul continues by saying that all those credits of his he now counts as debits. In fact he has gladly disposed of all his old assets and credits because of the supreme value of knowing Christ Jesus as his Lord. This begins to sound like a sort of commentary out of Paul's own life on Jesus' parable of the one pearl of great price (Matt. 13:45-46). What Paul once valued most highly, he values no more. In fact, in comparison with knowing Christ, he now thinks of all he once prized as just so much refuse or garbage. The word can even be translated as "dung" or "excrement."

Paul has gladly suffered great loss. He has been willing to be wiped out, because he has experienced a miraculous gain. Paul's gain, his new asset, is Christ, being in Christ, having a relationship with God based not on the law, not on his own achievements, not on what he has inherited from his parents and ancestors, but only on what God in Christ has done for him. That is pure gift, and it is his not by laboring and striving but by faith, by simply opening his hands like a child delighted to receive a present.

Paul's deepest desire is to "know Christ" (v. 10). Christ is "known" not by electrical currents in the brain cells, but by the experience of the power of Christ's resurrection. And the path to participation in Christ's resurrection life leads, strangely enough, through sharing in his sufferings and his death. To know Christ, to take Christ seriously, is, as Dietrich Bonhoeffer said, to "participate in God's own suffering on behalf of the life of the world." That is a suffering that leads to living. Indeed it is both living and life-giving.

With these words Paul turns from contemplating his past renunciation of old assets and even from meditating on his present knowledge of Christ. He begins to face toward the future. He wants to "attain the resurrection from the dead" in the deepest, most full-bodied sense (v. 11). Whatever he has or is in Christ today, he has not yet reached the goal.

Here he switches from commercial to athletic metaphors. Paul pictures himself as running a race. The goal lies out there ahead of him. Like a good runner, he forgets everything that lies behind him and strains forward to the finish line. Not everyone who enters a race wins a prize. In Corinthians Paul says that he does not run "aimlessly" or erratically (1 Cor. 9:24-27). The lanes are marked, and anyone who runs a crooked course, crossing into another lane, will be disqualified. And of course a runner who just wanders off the track and out of the stadium is hopeless. Paul exercises athletic self-discipline and presses toward the goal.

At the end of a race in a Greek stadium, a herald announced the name of the victor together with his father's name and the name of his city. Called up, the winner stepped forward to receive his prize. Paul disciplines himself, because in the end he hopes to be called up by Christ, acting as herald of the "games" presided over by God. Greek athletes competed in hopes of winning a perishable wreath; Paul seeks one that is imperishable (1 Cor. 9:25). In Philippians 4:1 Paul speaks of fellow Christians at Philippi as his "crown." Paul seems to be saying that the crown he most hopes for is the unending fellowship of the whole company of people whom he has led to Christ.

Gospel

MATTHEW 17:1-9

"Sovereign But Servant"

Whatever mountain it was (Tabor? Hermon?) the author of 2 Peter is correct: It was a "holy mountain" (2 Pet. 1:18), because there they encountered the Holy. And whatever the "six days later" refers to, the event occurred in the nick of time for Peter, James, John, and all the others.

Near "Philip's Caesarea" at the foot of Mount Hermon (not the other Caesarea, called "Maritima" because of its location on the Mediterranean coast),

Simon declared Jesus to be "the Christ, the Son of the Living God" (Matt. 16:16), and Jesus returned the compliment by giving Simon his new name, "Peter" (16:17-18).

Simon had spoken the truth and nothing but the truth, but it fell short of being the entire truth. So Jesus sealed his disciples' lips and ordered them not to speak of him as Christ, at least not yet. They still needed to be initiated into deeper mysteries than those revealed in Jesus' commanding words, his shocking parables, and his potent deeds.

Reading awesome power in his varied self-expressions, they were caught up in messianic fervor and fairly exploded with pride to announce their personal commitment to him and to his coming messianic reign. Unlike their duller contemporaries (16:13-15), they understood Jesus. Or so they thought.

Jesus rudely burst the bubble of Peter's enthusiasm with his call to hard discipleship: He began to unveil the necessity of a tragic journey to Jerusalem where he was destined to suffer at the hands of civic and religious authorities and even be killed (16:21a,b). They hardly heard the final few syllables promising resurrection (16:21c).

Peter acted swiftly to silence the unwelcome announcement. He dared to "rebuke" Jesus (16:22), whereupon Jesus hurled the harshest epithet at him, calling him no longer a solid "rock" on which he might build but "Satan" and a "scandal" or stone of stumbling, an obstacle in Jesus' destined path. Peter had his heart set not on divine but only on human, all too mundane and human, things (16:23).

Capping it all off, Jesus then called Peter and the others to hoist their own crosses on their shoulders and follow him in a parade of crosses, Jesus with his going ahead and they with theirs following joyfully behind (16:24). The literal reality in Jesus' case is no harder than the use of crucifixion as a metaphor for discipleship. In poetry as in prose, *cross* is a perplexing word.

In the disciples' lexicon the word *cross* was defined as defeat, as ignominious death, as dread destruction of all their high hopes. The disciples were mystified by Jesus' insistence on finding an inner connection between cross and kingship, servanthood and sovereignty. To them these pairs of words were antonyms, not synonyms. They were blind to the blessed synergy that Jesus saw and articulated. Peter, their spokesman, expressed their shared confusion and earned rebuke for all of them.

How can Jesus so strongly insist that in the cross is hidden the deep mystery of life and glory and the kingdom (16:25-28)? Perhaps we need to look again at those "six days" (17:1). Did the disciples mope for six days? Did their distress or their density begin to weigh heavily on Jesus? Or just wear him down? Or are the "six days" a way of naming a bleak period of brokenness, a time of incompleteness, something less than a full and complete "biblical seven"?

At any rate Jesus walked from the plain up onto the mountain, a place of holy experience so often in the biblical story. There light and glory broke through the disciples' doubt and confusion. Suddenly Jesus was transformed, metamorphosed, transfigured. The face of Jesus, this weak and vulnerable pilgrim journeying toward the cross, this master of theirs whose head would be tortured with a crown of thorns (27:29), began to shine with all the brilliance of the sun at high noon. (Compare the way John of Patmos describes the glorified Christ in his inaugural vision in Revelation 1:9-20.) And Jesus' poor clothing, later stripped from his body and divided by his gambling executioners (27:35), began to glow with unearthly light.

Then the disciples saw that Jesus was not alone in solitary splendor but was flanked by two men, not by two criminals as at the cross (27:38), but by Moses and Elijah, those two great ancient worthies out of Israel's past. Moses and Elijah had each met God on the mountain. Moses went up to receive a vision of God and the tablets of the Law (Exodus 24), and Elijah in his flight from earthly sovereigns Ahab and Jezebel had ascended Sinai/Horeb to be strengthened by God in the "still small voice" (1 Kings 19).

Moses and Elijah had served God diligently and suffered persecution (5:12; 23:29-37). At the end, like Enoch (Gen. 5:24), Moses and Elijah were caught up by God from an undeserving earth, and in popular piety of Jesus' day both were thought to have continuing service as God's living and lively agents. Their presence on the Mount of Transfiguration indicates that Jesus also will be rescued from his unjust death by the finger of God in resurrection.

> OUR VAST, INTRICATE SYSTEMS OF DOMINATION, SO POWERFUL AMONG US TO THIS DAY, HAVE COME DOWN TO US NOT FROM GOD BUT FROM SOCIAL REVOLUTIONS OF THE THIRD MILLENNIUM BEFORE CHRIST.

All the signs and all the words on the Mount of Transfiguration affirm that the way of the cross trod by Jesus is the righteous path of deathless life. That glorious moment was pure gift to the befuddled disciples, illuminating for them Jesus' high rank and holy task and encouraging them to follow him in his unrelenting journey to the cross.

Peter, so recently called "Satan" (16:21-23), now volunteers to make three booths for the three agents of God. It is hard to say whether Matthew approves or disapproves of Peter's enthusiasm. Does Peter now understand? Does he now see that Jesus with his cross is the true path to life? (Jesus' word in John 14:6 could be translated either "I am the Way, the Truth and the Life" or "I am the true path to life.") Or does Peter want to freeze the moment, stay on that mountain, avoid heading back down to resume the journey to Jerusalem?

Whatever Peter's intention, he is interrupted when a bright cloud (Exod. 24:16–17) hovers over them, and the three disciples hear a voice speaking from the cloud, exactly as at Jesus' baptism, "This is my beloved Son" (cf. 3:17), and this time the voice adds, "Listen to him!" As the Gospel proceeds, readers must wonder whether anyone ever will listen to Jesus. Who will really hear and heed the word which he speaks and the word which he is? Finally a centurion listens carefully to Jesus' own final cry and sees great signs surrounding Jesus' death, and he confesses, "Truly this man was God's son" (27:54).

Golgotha (at the end) and the Mount of Transfiguration (here at the midpoint) teach identical lessons: Suffering love is the path of glory, servanthood is the way that God's sovereignty insinuates itself into our world, and the cross (Jesus' and our own) is victory and not defeat.

So Transfiguration says that the cross (16:21-28) is altogether splendid, endorsed by God's own voice trumpeting from heaven, signed and sealed as the way God means to conquer kingdoms, topple fiefdoms, and establish the divine in the midst of human communities. Transfiguration does not say that an eternity of glory will follow a brief and fleeting time of suffering service. It does not say, "Jesus will be glorious sometime later on." It says, "Jesus on the way to the cross is already glorious, if only you have the eyes to see it." And for a moment on the mountain God let those three disciples and all of us see it.

The message of Matthew 16 and 17 is a hard lesson. James and John were on the mountain, but they still don't get it. This section of Matthew's Gospel will close with the mother of James and John begging Jesus to install her two sons in places of honor in this "kingdom" Jesus is always talking about (20:20–27). I suppose she wants James to be minister of finance, and John should be in charge of foreign affairs. The other disciples are outraged, not at the brothers' misunderstanding, but because they wanted those posts themselves (Matt. 20:24).

They all wanted to be in charge, to sit on seats of privilege and power. It is not only pharaohs who build pyramids. All the nations do it. Corporations do it. Churches and schools organize hierarchies, and families and clans do it. It all seems so natural. It happens so regularly, so easily, so universally, that we find ourselves thinking, "Of course the few were born to give orders, and the many were made to obey!"

But is it natural? Where does it all come from? From God? Did God order the universe in such a way that humankind should exercise a ruthless dominion over the trees and rivers, over birds and beasts? Did God's voice really call out that men should rule over women? That people of the Northern Hemisphere should dominate the poorer nations to the south? Did the finger of God write that we should have social systems that are rigidly hierarchical, authoritarian, and patriarchal? Walter Wink believes that "it is difficult to date the rise of systemic domination and its legitimations," but he points to the rise of massive city-states in Sumer and Babylon around 3000 B.C.E. There for the first time, he says, we see the advent of autocracy legitimized by myth and ritual and supported by standing armies equipped with new bronze weaponry.[31]

Our vast, intricate systems of domination, so powerful among us to this day, have come down to us not from God but from social revolutions of the third millennium before Christ. Clever people learned a long time ago to shore up their privileged place within these systems by offering "authoritative" readings of the Bible in support of hierarchy.

The practice of Jesus in his ministry and the death of Jesus on Golgotha have always struck a minority of Christians in every age as the most powerful evidence that God intends Christian communities to be fellowships of agape and not little pyramids of the domineering and the dominated.

All this strange news on the mountain caused the disciples to flop down on their faces, overcome by the weight and terror of it all (17:6). Jesus did not stalk off in disgust. He approached and touched them. He told them to lay aside their fears, stand upright on their two legs, and take up the journey once more as his companions (17:7). And they did journey with him, offering their very imperfect best.

Afterword

"Declaring the Glory"

A rabbi neighbor of mine some years back told of a congregant crossing back over the border from Canada to the United States after a vacation trip. He was asked, "Do you have anything to declare?" He put a prophetic spin on the question and responded, "I declare the glory of God!" That reply was costly. The border agent could see neither humor nor prophecy in that answer, and so he pulled him out of the line and delayed him with extensive bureaucratic questioning.

I can understand that security guards at airports take a dim view of efforts to make jokes about bombs. But the glory of God? If the traveler had spoken jauntily of the glory of Canada or the glory of America, no doubt that would have earned him a pat on the back.

But wait a minute! Maybe it should make the nations uneasy when citizens go around declaring the glory of God. It should make all our big and little thrones and dominions and petty tyrants nervous, in governments and businesses, in schools and even in our families. The glory of God is the honor of God and the power of God and the victory of God and the sovereignty of God, before which all other sovereignties and powers pale and by which they must be judged.

That Epiphany star is a criterion and crisis confronting every earthly "lord" or "boss," critiquing and asking hard questions. And that star is also deepest consolation, summoning us to a bright place of great light, a place of joy and justice.

Notes

1. *Webster's Third New International Dictionary*, ed. Philip Babcock Gore (Springfield, Mass.: Merriam-Webster, 1961), s.v. *Star.*

2. John Henry Hopkins Jr.,"We Three Kings," hymn 646 in *With One Voice* (Minneapolis: Augsburg Fortress, 1995).

3. Dorothy Sayers, *Creed or Chaos?* (New York: Harcourt, Brace , 1949) 5.

4. Brian Wren, *What Language Shall I Borrow?* (New York: Crossroad, 1989), 134.

5. Hopkins, "We Three Kings," op. cit.

6. Karl Rahner, *The Great Church Year* (New York: Crossroad, 1993), 105

7. Barbara Kingsolver, *High Tide in Tucson* (New York: HarperCollins, 1995), 7.

8. Wren, *What Language Shall I Borrow?* 128-29.

9. Kingsolver, *High Tide in Tucson,* 105.

10. Robert Bellah et al., *Habits of the Heart* (Berkeley: University of California Press, 1985).

11. Abraham Joshua Heschel, *The Prophets* (New York: Harper and Row, 1962.) 171.

12. Psalm Prayer no. 305, p. 356 in *Lutheran Book of Worship: Ministers Desk Edition* (Minneapolis and Philadelphia: Augsburg Publishing House and Board of Publication, Lutheran Church in America, 1978). Hereafter cited as LBW: MDE.

13. Psalm Prayer no. 417 in LBW: MDE, 434.

14. Heschel, *The Prophets,* 102.

15. Juan Alfaro, *Justice and Loyalty* (Grand Rapids: Eerdmans, 1989).

16. Hans Walter Wolff, *Micah,* trans. Gary Stansell (Minneapolis: Fortress Press, 1990), 183-84.

17. Heschel, *The Prophets,* 207.

18. Jerome Murphy O'Connor, *1 Corinthians* (Wilmington: Michael Glazier, 1979), 15.

19. Martin Buber, *The Eclipse of God* (New York: Harper and Brothers, 1952), 4-6.

20. Quoted by J. S .Whale, *The Protestant Tradition.* (Cambridge, U. K.: Cambridge University Press, 1955), 18-20.

21. Elizabeth A. Johnson, *She Who Is* (New York: Crossroad, 1994), 139–140.

22. *Good News for Modern Man: The New Testament in Today's English Version.* Third Edition. (New York: American Bible Society, 1971), 44.

23. Brian Wren, "God of Many Names" (Carol Stream, Ill.: Hope Publishing Company).

24. Heschel, *The Prophets,* 195.

25. Psalm Prayer no. 397 in LBW: MDE, 426.

26. Mitri Raheb, *I Am A Palestinian Christian.* Tr. by Ruth C. L. Gritsch. (Minneapolis: Fortress, 1995), 102.

27. Psalm Prayer no. 280 in LBW: MDE, 341.

28. Psalm Prayer no. 377 in LBW: MDE, 406.

29. Walter Wink, *Engaging the Powers* (Minneapolis: Fortress, 1992), 39.

THE SEASON OF LENT

WILLIAM H. WILLIMON

It is a story that tells of the confluence of "many rivers of tears," as one character puts it. *Dead Man Walking* is a movie about people in the middle of life's worst pain, life's deepest tragedy. Sister Helen Prejean teaches in a Catholic mission house in New Orleans. When asked by a prison ministry leader to write to a death row inmate, she agrees. The prison's seasoned, tough chaplain warns Sister Helen that the inmates are a low, despicable lot of humanity.

We learn how right he is in his assessment when we meet the prisoner whom Sister Helen writes, Matthew Poncelet—guilty as sin of the rape and murder of two young lovers. In order that we in no way romanticize Poncelet, the film has brief, horrible intercuts of the crime and its costs. Poncelet is no Robin Hood. He is a cheap, heartless loser, who is, as the chaplain says, despicable.

The murderer has only a couple of weeks to live. Sister Helen listens to him, finds him a new lawyer, protests his death penalty, and becomes his spiritual counselor as death approaches. The film spares us a simple-minded, do-gooder treatment of its theme. Sister Helen, the death penalty opponent, meets the heartbroken parents of Poncelet's victims. Even as she stands for the criminal at his pardon board hearings and death penalty vigils, she is made to look into the eyes of these horribly hurting people who accuse her of caring more for a bestial thug like Poncelet than for the innocent victims of his crime.

In confronting Poncelet, there is none of Hollywood's usual "whore-with-a-heart-of-gold" sentimentality. Poncelet is bad, bad as can be, bad to the core. Almost to the end, he scavenges, grabbing what he can from a world for which he has contempt. He swaggers in his badness, boasts, mouths off to the judge during his trial, even taunts his victims' parents. Even at the last, he shows no remorse, insisting that he is the real victim.

Yet we find that Poncelet the murderer is not nearly as tough as Sister Helen the nun. She wants, in the face of his approaching death, to save his soul as much as his life. She swallows none of his self-justifying, macho evasiveness. Even when he invokes Jesus as his door to heaven, Sister Helen ridicules his sentimentality, telling him that salvation involves honesty and repentance, which he is probably too cowardly to muster.

When Poncelet dares compare his execution to the cross of Jesus, Sister Helen rejects his comparison, noting how his act merely ruined so many lives while Jesus' cross "changed the world with love."

Finally, with the gallows approaching, Poncelet comes to remorse, even to a kind of repentance, saying he sees he must now "die to find love." Sister Helen pronounces even him a "son of God," saying that he can dare to look upon the face of God because "Christ is here."

Dead Man Walking is a story, a journey, not unlike that which we enact during the forty days of Lent. The journey begins in ashes, in the dark recognition that "we are dust and to dust we shall return." We are all, according to this stark story, "dead people walking." How odd, how utterly countercultural for us to begin in such dismal regions of the soul. Forty days is a long time, when you experience it in church. Honesty, in a world of lies, takes time. During these forty days, the church, through its sacred texts and liturgy, forces us to encounter what we spend most of our days avoiding.

DURING THESE FORTY DAYS, THE CHURCH, THROUGH ITS SACRED TEXTS AND LITURGY, FORCES US TO ENCOUNTER WHAT WE SPEND MOST OF OUR DAYS AVOIDING.

The journey ends on a cross at Golgotha, in death, violence, and utter abandonment. Or does it end there? The disciples of Jesus assumed that it did, as well they should, knowing what we all know of despicable human nature and the hard realities of this life. After Good Friday, the story becomes a drama about who shall write the last act of the play—God or the Devil, life or death.

Dr. Johnson accused Shakespeare of never knowing how to end a play. "Having got so much right throughout the play, he makes a muddle of it at the end," said Johnson. We wait forever for Hamlet to do something, for Lear to finally go and die. *Dead Man Walking* struggles with how to end its story. The end of the movie is not as good as the problems it initially poses. Most modern stories have problems with endings. Having succeeded, through art, in addressing large human questions and deep human problems, contemporary films, novels, and plays often seem unable to deal effectively with reality.

Yet even Hollywood, in attempting to be faithful to a true story, can be subsumed into the story that ends in Easter. The film does not end with the murderer being wheeled away to his death, strapped to a gurney. After Poncelet's death by lethal injection, there is the funeral where Sister Helen encounters, once again, a victim's father. He is a man whose life has been ruined by his loss. He is moving toward a divorce. The murderer has begged the man for forgiveness, but forgiveness is not something the father can, as yet, give. Something tells us, here at the end of the film, that Sister Helen and this poor man are preparing to begin another journey together. Perhaps it will be a journey beyond grief and anger, a journey toward reconciliation and new life. Perhaps.

The Lenten Journey

Lent tells the church that any journey toward life, toward rebirth, toward God makes its way through forlorn regions of darkness, honesty, and hopelessness. Let us be honest. We are all "dead people walking." God gives us life, yet we seem bound and determined by death. Goodness is set before us, yet why do we so often revel in the wrong? The somber colors of the congregation's sanctuary during Lent, the restrained, sober hymns that sing of the cross, pain, and suffering—all work together to turn us toward the painful parts of our lives that we expend so much energy avoiding. This is Lent.

Yet Lent does not end there, because, in the words of Sister Helen—words derived from the cumulative effect upon her of the Sunday gospels "Christ is here." Even here. Even in the darkness, the desert, especially here. In the wilderness, on the First Sunday of Lent, we meet Satan, the accuser, who offers us what our hearts desire. The story is one of threat and accusation. Yet where is Jesus, the Messiah, the Christ? There with us in the desert, in the wilderness, beating Satan at his own game of biblical interpretation. We can dare to admit to the reality of our wilderness because he is there with us, even there.

Perhaps we preachers ought to move into the season of Lent honestly admitting that the moves of the Lenten journey do not come naturally for us feel-good, positive-thinking, sin-denying modern Americans. The message we have to proclaim to the congregation through the Sunday lessons is countercultural. Yet the word of the cross can be proclaimed in the face of a death-dealing, death-denying culture because it is true and because it is here, at the depth of our need, that Christ meets us.

Fortunately, we have great resources for our countercultural Lenten preaching. We are blessed during these Sundays with some of the church's richest narrative treasure. There are Sundays in the church year when we preachers must heroically labor to engage a skeptical congregation with the Bible, but not during Lent, not in Year A. They will listen willingly to the stories we have to tell because these are truthful stories about them, about their temptation, their confusion, their questions, their redemption. When, at the end of this season, Jesus proclaims to grieving Martha with a strong, confident voice, "I am the resurrection and the life," they shall surely hear him speaking to them.

The first two Sundays of Lent, beginning with texts from Genesis, depict our primordial condition. From our first opportunity to choose, we chose wrong. What shall be done about our propensity toward the wrong?

After the traditional First Sunday of Lent story of the temptation of Jesus, we follow Jesus through some of the most vivid and enigmatic moments in the Gospel of John. Our sin is deep, so should we be surprised that the One who came to meet our sin is also an enigmatic, ambiguous savior?

Our task and our joy is to open up these biblical riches for the faithful, to tell the story of a journey from ashes toward Easter, through death to life, a story we are able to tell without flinching, because "Christ is here."

ASH WEDNESDAY

FEBRUARY 17, 1999

REVISED COMMON	EPISCOPAL (BCP)	ROMAN CATHOLIC
Joel 2:1-2, 12-17 or Isa. 58:1-12	Joel 2:1-2, 12-17 or Isa. 58:1-12	Joel 2:12-18
Ps. 51:1-17	Ps. 103 or 103:8-14	Ps. 51:3-6, 12-14, 17
2 Cor. 5:20b—6:10	2 Cor. 5:20b—6:10	2 Cor. 5:20—6:2
Matt. 6:1-6, 16-21	Matt. 6:1-6, 16-21	Matt. 6:1-6, 16-18

LOTS OF PEOPLE SAY THEY COME TO CHURCH to "get close to God." Sunday is "the Lord's Day," the day when we, who have avoided God most of the week, attempt to get close to God. Be forewarned that the God we get close to on Ash Wednesday may not be the God we desire to meet.

FIRST READING

JOEL 2:1-2, 12-17

Interpreting the Text

Israel had long hoped for a "Day of the Lord," that day of days when Yahweh would at last make war upon the enemies of the Lord. Joel says that the Day of the Lord is at last upon Israel. God is coming close to us. Yet it will not be the day we had expected. It will be a day when the Lord comes in power to put to rout God's enemies. To our dismay, we have met the enemies of the Lord and they are us (2:11).

The trumpet sounds (2:1), signaling the approach of a powerful enemy, "a great and powerful army" (v. 2). The sound of the trumpet is an ambiguous sign. It is both a summons to worship and a threatening alarm.

The prophet calls upon Israel to turn, to "return" (vv. 12, 13) in fasting, weeping, and mourning. Elsewhere, such actions are appropriate grief responses to death (1 Sam. 31:13). Grief is grief work, public processing of pain, actions and gestures expressive of sorrow too deep for words.

An intransigent member in one of my congregations would emerge from our Ash Wednesday service muttering, "Hmph! Rend your hearts and not your garments!"—his low-church protest against our ritual display of ashes upon foreheads. Repentance ought to be a personal, private, internal matter, he thought. Joel permits no such either/or reading of repentance. Joel calls for corporate, public, ritualized sorrow before God with signs of turning and returning to God. Yet Joel also names such action as having personal, ethical, social consequences—"Rend your hearts and not [just?] your clothing" (v. 13). (See Responding to the Text.)

ISAIAH 58:1-12 (RCL/BCP)

Interpreting the Text

The Isaiah text is nicely paired with Joel 2, for Isaiah also opens with a "voice like a trumpet" (58:1). The prophet is to announce the sin of the people (vv. 1-2). Furthermore, the main aspect of their sin is the falsity of their worship. Bad worship is being scathingly rebuked here (vv. 3-5). On what basis? Does the Lord want purple vestments on Ash Wednesday rather than black? Are we to be high church or low? No. That's not the concern. The problem is ethical more than liturgical. Our works invalidate our worship.

What God wants, according to the prophet, is not elaborate, showy services, but rather justice, compassion, righteousness (vv. 6-7). The demands are excruciatingly specific, having to do with matters of bondage (debt, property ownership), hunger, and homelessness. Here is a text that dares to name the specific shape of our infidelities.

Then the prophet piles one conditional clause upon another: If you do this, then this (vv. 9-10). The demands of this righteous God are quite specific, having to do with money, politics, and law. A "day acceptable to the Lord" (v. 5) is not just the day of a full house at Ash Wednesday worship, but a people ready to put their money where their mouth is in regard to their worship.

Responding to the Text

Joel does not enumerate the sins for which Israel ought to repent, and neither need we. What is summoned forth is a turning, a right orientation toward God. The Lord has turned toward us—which is not necessarily good news, for the Day of the Lord is a dark day when the Lord names God's own people as God's enemy, when God makes war upon our unrighteousness and rebelliousness. Yet the good news is that we can turn, return to the God who has turned toward us. God's judgment against us is the other side of God's love and mercy toward us.

Why, we might ask on Ash Wednesday, does this God not simply let us be and allow us to stew in our own juices, proceeding along our own merry way, without turning toward us in judgment? Our text ends with Joel's answer. This God "is gracious and merciful, slow to anger, and abounding in steadfast love. . . ." (v. 13).

We say we want to get close to God. Yet both of today's readings from Joel and Isaiah say to us that when God gets close to us, it is not always the closeness we desired. The God who comes to us is not some pale, limp projection of our highest human aspiration, not some idealized image of ourselves. This God stands against us, makes war upon us, reduces our vaunted images of ourselves to ashes, so that he might love us, make us, have us as his own.

When that happens to people like us, on Ash Wednesday in church, or on any day anywhere, then that is truly a "Day of the Lord."

Responsive Reading

PSALM 51 (RCL/RC)

Interpreting the Text

Ash Wednesday's psalm is one of the most eloquent expressions of repentance in the entire psalter. Tradition has ascribed it to David, relating it to David's repentance after his seduction and rape of Bathsheba. Its appeal is universal.

The psalmist cries for a "clean heart," a "right spirit" (v. 10). In great devastation, one has no hope except hope in a God who acts. Therefore the psalmist wastes few verses on what he may or may not do for God, pleading instead that God might act for him, begging God to "have mercy," to "blot out," to "wash me thoroughly," and to "cleanse me." (vv. 1-2).

In verses 3-5, the psalmist declares his sin in honest, open confession. Sin is named as offense against God, therefore it is up to God to heal the relationship. In verses 6-12, the results of God's healing presence are cited. Cleansed, renewed, the psalmist is able to resume relationship with a forgiving and steadfast loving God. Finally, in verses 13-17, the lament claims that the forgiven person is a virtually new being. By God's grace, the old self is laid aside that a new self may begin again.

Responding to the Text

Carl Sandburg begins one of his poems by asking, "Can we be honest for five minutes even though this is Chicago?"

Honesty, in the Windy City or anywhere else, is in short supply. Today one does not hear poetry as heartfelt and honest as Psalm 51. Not because there are no longer poets, but rather because modern people are not overly burdened by their sin. Sin is seen as a minor mix-up, a mistake, not as a fundamental severing of our relationship to God. Therefore the psalm, chanted together on Ash Wednesday, is an invitation to journey into territory that may be strange for us.

Second Reading
2 CORINTHIANS 5:20b—6:10

Interpreting the Text

"Be reconciled to God!" Is that a direct enough imperative for Ash Wednesday? The Corinthians, having begun their journey with Christ, show in their life together that it is possible to deviate badly after baptism. Paul is concerned that, on the basis of their present behavior, the Corinthians appear to have accepted "the grace of God in vain" (6:1).

Paul's call to repentance and change among the Corinthians picks up tempo as he urges, "See, now is the acceptable time; see, now is the day of salvation!" (6:2). Then Paul proceeds to list the troubles endured by those who, like Paul, have ministered among the troublesome Corinthians. His list is a wonderful catalogue of the trials and tribulations, along with the great glories, of ministry in Christ.

THE ASHES UPON OUR FOREHEADS ARE A VIVID, STARK REMINDER THAT FOR EACH OF US THERE WILL NOT ALWAYS BE A TOMORROW. WE ARE ALL TERMINAL.

This urgent call to repentance repeats itself throughout Paul's Corinthian letters. When Paul is urging his congregations to do something, he reaches for a wide array of rhetorical devices to move his hearers to action. Elsewhere, Paul's call for personal and congregational change is based upon other appeals. Here Paul seems to be setting himself up, as well as his fellow ministers at Corinth, as motivation for Corinthian change. From time to time, Paul was not above offering himself as an example to his people. "Imitate me," he would say, "you have a worthy example in us" (see Phil. 3:17).

Responding to the Text

Could we contemporary ministers of the gospel offer ourselves to our people as encouragement for their repentance? One might wish that a person's repentance be based on some more noble, higher theological rationale. Yet motivation arises where it arises. Affection and high regard for the pastor may prod us toward greater righteousness. As Augustine said, speaking of Christ rather than Christ's ministers, "We imitate whom we adore."

Here on Ash Wednesday we might also juxtapose Paul's urgent plea for repentance with our rather relaxed, endlessly deferred attitude toward repentance. "There will always be a tomorrow," we say to ourselves. Why the rush? Change can be costly. So we keep our distance, ponder, reflect, coolly consider. In so doing, Paul might say we risk "accepting the grace of God in vain" (6:1), insulting, in our slothfulness, the sacrifice of Christ, as well as the sacrifices of those who minister to us in Christ's name.

The ashes upon our foreheads are a vivid, stark reminder that for each of us there will *not* always be a tomorrow. We are all *terminal*. The most important business of our lives may not be endlessly deferred. The day for reconciliation to God is this Wednesday.

Is this day's sermon an occasion to forsake subtlety and simply to say, "Be reconciled to God!"?

Gospel

MATTHEW 6:1-6, 16-21

Today's Gospel has an ironic twist, placed in context with Ash Wednesday's service. Most Ash Wednesday worship includes the imposition of ashes. The ashes on the forehead are a sign to the world that we have been in church, that we have repented and confessed at the beginning of Lent.

Interpreting the Text

The Gospel warns against piety that is performed for an admiring audience of peers rather than quiet, secret piety seen only by God (6:1). Religion practiced for the crowd's approval, rather than for God, is hypocrisy. Almost all of us do it. When we are hypocritical in our faith, we can be unaware of our hypocrisy. Have you ever known anyone who set out deliberately to be a religious hypocrite?

The repetitive quality of this passage, as well as its use of hyperbole, are literary devices used to grab our attention. A stark contrast is evident between worship whose audience is other people, and worship offered solely for the pleasure of God. Because the language uses hyperbole, we preachers must not indulge in detailed instructions, new rules for prayer in closets, or worship without instrumental accompaniment. A general warning is being sounded here.

What impresses is how often the term *reward* is used throughout this passage. The text opens with the warning that those who practice hypocritical piety have no reward from the Father (6:1). Three times we are told, "Your Father who sees in secret will reward you" (vv. 4, 6, 18). Matthew is not above advocating faithfulness related to reward (see Matthew 25). If there be those who have scruples against serving God in order to receive a reward, Matthew is not among them. The specific nature of this "reward" is not mentioned. Rather, the emphasis seems to be that the Father does see and the Father will reward.

> THOSE WHO, IN A CONSUMPTIVE, CAPITALIST SOCIETY, DECIDE NOT TO LIVE ON THE BASIS OF THEIR POSSESSIONS CERTAINLY OUGHT TO BE REWARDED BY GOD BECAUSE THIS WORLD WILL GIVE THEM FEW ACCOLADES.

Those who dare to follow Jesus' demands will need some "reward." The concluding verses of today's Gospel (6:19-21) moving from acts mostly within worship like prayer and almsgiving, to specific economic matters, raise the demands of discipleship considerably. Following Jesus is a matter not only of how you pray in church but also what model car you drive. Material possessions are presented in sharp, either/or contrast. Thus the passage, before it ends, moves from liturgy to ethics. Or does the passage imply that our ethics are liturgical—our use of possessions (or their use of us!) is a matter of which God we worship?

Responding to the Text

"I don't mind what a person believes," people sometimes say, "as long as that person is sincere." Yet what does it mean in one's innermost heart to be "sincere"? Have you ever known anyone who admits in the middle of worship, "I am contributing to the offering in an insincere manner"? Perhaps we need not become entangled in an attempt to sort out "sincere" from "insincere" religion. Rather, we ought forthrightly to ponder the place of "reward" in the practice of our piety.

We who have frequently fulminated against crass, cause-effect, instrumental religious practices in the expectation of divine reward, we who have previously urged our people to serve God for intrinsic reasons, without thought of future reward, may be challenged by this text. In a passage so full of warnings and prohibitions against improper piety, we ought gladly to proclaim the good news contained in this talk of piety rewarded. Those who, in a consumptive, capitalist society, decide not to live on the basis of their possessions certainly ought to be rewarded by God because this world will give them few accolades.

Two great, comforting affirmations are repeated amid the warnings: God sees our attempts to be faithful, and God rewards our fidelity.

I know someone who challenged her company's policy on promotions. She noted that, when there was a promotion into management, no persons of color had ever been promoted. She carefully thought out her position and thoughtfully presented her objections to the boss. He listened. He said he would think about what she said. A week later, she was fired.

"Just not a team player," someone said.

I wish the story might have ended differently. I wish that I could tell you that her fidelity was seen and affirmed by the world, that it always pays to do what is right. Let's be honest. Such goodness and fidelity is rarely rewarded by the world.

For struggling believers who are fighting to be faithful against great odds—the ridicule or outright persecution by those less faithful—Ash Wednesday's Gospel is a comforting word. Good news. Though the world may neither note nor praise our piety, God sees, God rewards. If there were a time when acts of faithfulness—almsgiving, prayer, fasting, care in our use of material things—were seen and rewarded by the world, that time is over. The world's response to such piety today is more often ridicule than admiring acclaim. Therefore, it is good for the faithful to hear the good news that God sees, God rewards.

FIRST SUNDAY IN LENT

FEBRUARY 21, 1999

REVISED COMMON	EPISCOPAL (BCP)	ROMAN CATHOLIC
Gen. 2:15-17; 3:1-7	Gen. 2:4b-9, 15-17, 25—3:7	Gen. 2:7-9; 3:1-7
Ps. 32	Ps. 51 or 51:1-13	Ps. 51:3-6, 12-14, 17
Rom. 5:12-19	Rom. 5:12-19, (20-21)	Rom. 5:12-19 or 5:12, 17-19
Matt. 4:1-11	Matt. 4:1-11	Matt. 4:1-11

ALL TOO FREQUENTLY FEW PEOPLE ATTEND Ash Wednesday services. Let's face it, sin, finitude, dust, and ashes are not popular themes in contemporary American religion. Many follow the faith of the "Be-Happy-Attitudes," "Possibility Thinking," onward and upward, better and better every day in every way.

If they missed the ashes on Wednesday, this First Sunday in Lent gives them another opportunity, through the various lenses of the texts, to stare at their sinfulness and finitude. That's one great thing about the Bible; it refuses to leave us alone in our denial.

No wonder so few read the Bible.

FIRST READING
GENESIS 2:15-17; 3:1-7

Interpreting the Text

After the starkness and dust of Ash Wednesday, the Old Testament lesson on the First Sunday of Lent finds us in a garden—*the* Garden. As Walter Brueggemann has noted, in the Garden we are given a task (2:15). God has graciously granted us the opportunity to participate in sustaining the life of the Garden. Furthermore, we are given permission to enjoy, to "freely eat" of the good bounty of the garden.

Yet God also gives a prohibition. In 3:9 an ominous tree offers "knowledge of good and evil." Why is this particular tree prohibited? We are not told directly, except that it has something to do with the disruptive human presumption to be like gods unto ourselves. Who has complete knowledge of what is good and what is not, except God?

The serpent appears as the embodiment of human presumption. The serpent is not represented as especially evil, just savvy, crafty, and smart. Humans are naïve, childlike, and inexperienced. The serpent does little more than raise questions, "Did God say . . . ?" (3:1). Yet quickly the serpent moves from these cool questions to outright defiance of God's word: "You shall not die" (3:4).

The man and the woman are equal in their rebellion. They both participate in defiance of God's order and plan. And when questioned, the pitiful blaming begins. The man blames the woman who in turn blames the serpent.

Responding to the Text

Ash Wednesday continues in this story. Life in the lush, freely given Garden is disrupted by our failure to accept that we are creatures rather than Creator. We want to know, to control, to strive, to be like God. Paradoxically, our innate human desire to grow, to explore, to be curious, is also our undoing. There is a caughtness about us. We know, from the moment we are told that we must not eat of the Tree of Knowledge of Good and Evil, that we shall do what we have been told not to do. This is therefore not so much a story of a "fall," as it is a story of how, once given a chance to rebel, we rebelled. The man and the woman are not presented as sinless, just as naïve, innocent, inexperienced.

Thus the story depicts human sin as the human predicament. We want to know, yet that same knowing and striving is our undoing. The whole world is thus disrupted by our rebelliousness, the garden is choked with thorns, and we get death rather than life.

The story ends in irony. At first we were naked and unashamed, as innocent as a toddler romping about after a bath. But we wanted to know, to see, to understand, on our terms rather than on God's terms. By the end of the story our "eyes are opened;" we see, we gain the insight we so desperately desired. We know, but how little we see! The eyes of the man and woman are opened and all they see is their genitals! They now "know" their nakedness, their vulnerability, and they are ashamed. Their primordial innocence is turned to shame and fear. They cower before the presence of the God who gave them the garden. God the friend and co-creator is now the enemy.

Today's first lesson, Genesis 2 and 3, is a portrait of our caught condition, the situation for which we need salvation. We have acted, decided, ventured forth on our own, and look at where it has gotten us. Our eyes have been opened, and how little we see. Who shall save us from the mess we have made of our story?

Responsive Reading

PSALM 32 (RCL)

Interpreting the Text

Today's psalm is, appropriately, one of the great penitential psalms. Yet the psalm begins, not in confession, but with beatitudes. Happiness is the gift to those who know that they are forgiven, that their sin is not the last word in their lives (verses 1-2).

Verses 3-5 offer a nice meditation on the virtues of open confession of our sin, rather than keeping it within. As such, the psalm is a good selection for this First Sunday in Lent. We are invited to come forward to corporately confess our sin before God and one another. Our God is a one who surrounds us "with glad cries of deliverance" (v. 7).

Responding to the Text

We often think of confession of sin as a dour affair, a matter of sad, doleful honesty about the wretchedness of our condition. It is therefore worth nothing that this psalm of penitence begins in happiness, in beatitude, in blessing for the gift of repentance. Because our God is steadfastly gracious, we need not lie about ourselves, need not be filled with pretense. The psalm also ends in gladness and rejoicing (v. 11), in a great shout. Is it possible for us to proclaim the good news of repentance and confession?

PSALM 51 (BCP/RC)

See above under the comments for Ash Wednesday, pp. 183–84.

SECOND READING

ROMANS 5:12-19

Interpreting the Text

"All have sinned and fall short of the glory of God," proclaims Paul (3:23). This is the primal insight arising out of today's Old Testament lesson and is the condition that is the concern of today's epistle.

Paul's typological argument, comparing and contrasting Christ and Adam, sounds rather foreign to our ears. How is it that the sin of one leads to the sinfulness of all? We do well to treat his argument metaphorically. Today's first lesson tells us that Adam and Eve sinned, and thereafter every human being, like our forebears, once given the chance to rebel against God, did so. We need not become entangled in an Augustinian argument about how and why this is so; rather, reference to Adam confirms what each of us knows (when we are honest) within each of our lives—all have sinned (5:12). In a sense, each of us recapitulates, in our own lives, the same dynamic which we read of in Genesis 2-3. Our innocence does not last long. We all, in some fashion or another, come to resemble our forebear Adam.

We pervert all that we touch to our sinful ends. Even something so sacred as Torah, "the law," becomes an occasion for our sin (5:20).

Then Paul compares the Adam to Christ. Just as Adam brought sin and death, so Christ brings justification to God and life (5:16). Our bondage to sin, in Adam, is broken through the power of the new man, Christ (5:18-19). Paul's argument becomes rather involved and difficult to follow at this point. We preachers ought not get too involved in its explication. The metaphorical weight of the argument is enough. We are caught in sin, caught since our beginning (as demonstrated by this Sunday's first lesson). Sin, in Paul's rendering here, is not some slipup, not some temporary, momentary mistake. Sin is our fundamental, innate disposition.

Responding to the Text

Elsewhere Paul asks the rhetorical question, "Who will rescue me from this body of death?" (Rom. 7:24). Here he gives a strong answer. Our innate, primordial tendency toward sin is strong, yet the grace of Christ is even stronger. Thus, Paul affirms two ideas: sin is pervasive, unavoidable, deep, and relentless. Thanks be to God, the power of God in Christ is more pervasive, triumphant, liberating, and certain. Any homiletical word on today's epistle ought to contain this twofold affirmation, an affirmation derived from Paul's juxtaposition of Adam and Christ.

Carlyle Marney loved to tell of being asked by some student in a dormitory discussion, "Where is the Garden of Eden?"

Marney responded, "220 Elm Street, Knoxville, Tennessee."

"What?" the students asked. "It's some place in Asia Minor, isn't it?"

"No," replied Marney, "for it was in Knoxville, Tennessee, as a child, that my mother sent me to the store with a quarter to buy some milk and I took the quarter and bought candy and ate the whole lot before I got home. And when I got home I was so ashamed that I hid in the closet. It was there that she found me and asked, 'Where are you?' Then, 'What have you done?'"

Our propensity to sin is deep, innate, primordial, with us from the first. If something is to be done about our sin, it must be deep, not of our own devising, a radical newness outside ourselves—some new Adam, some new humanity built from the ground up.

Gospel

MATTHEW 4:1-11

Interpreting the Text

Much is revealed by Matthew in the eleven verses of this Sunday's Gospel. Linked with the preceding account of Jesus' baptism, here is a rich adumbration of a growing portrait of Jesus.

The voice at his baptism declared Jesus to be God's Son (Matt. 3:17). But what sort of Son of God is Jesus? Through a series of three tests, we learn what it means for him to be called Son of God. To have the very power of God at one's disposal, to be able personally to harness awesome divine forces, who could want for anything more? Jesus will be known, in his temptations in the wilderness, by what he rejects.

Rather surprisingly, behind all of Satan's proposals is the satanic proposition that Jesus take matters into his hands and do good—all that Satan offers Jesus is beneficial for humanity—bread, political power, and spectacular religious signs. The tests are therefore not simple. What Satan offers is not self-evidently bad. Generally, the Bible knows that temptation is rarely a simple matter of rejecting something that is bad in order to receive something that is good. Temptation is far more subtle than that; Satan often masquerades as an angel of light. Is bread not necessary for life? Shouldn't we utilize political power for the order and benefit of humanity? What is the harm in a sign, a self-evident sign of the reality and power of God? And besides, Satan backs it all up with citation from scripture!

To our surprise, Jesus rejects all of Satan's suggestions. He quotes scripture back to Satan. He refuses public, self-evident demonstration of his relationship to

God. Even more dear to him than public, irrefutable validation of his vocation, more important even than "doing good" as we define goodness, is obedience to the Word of God. Citing Deuteronomy, he will be obedient to the Word of God, whether that obedience is publicly validated or not. He refuses power as this world defines it. Utterly rejecting "the kingdoms of the world and their splendor" he sets his face toward a different realm.

With striking consistency, Matthew depicts Jesus as a faithful child of Israel. Jesus, according to Matthew, is the fulfillment of the promises of God to Israel. When Jesus, in encounter with Satan, cites scripture, falls back upon the demands of Torah, he is being very "Jewish." Through countless times of testing, all Israel had was the Word, the Word of God.

Hungry, in the wilderness, Israel had asked, "Is God there for us or not?" Hunger was a cause of temptation for Israel then, and eventual apostasy. Jesus has not eaten for forty days and is famished (4:2). Yet he does not yield to temptation, even in great hunger. Something even more than food is loved by Jesus, namely to do the will of his heavenly Father. In response to Satan's offers of concrete, useful, even potentially beneficial powers—food, political influence, religious spectacle—Jesus counters with nothing but the Word. He really is the best of the hopes of Israel, Matthew seems to say in that he knows, lives by, and if necessary is willing to die by the Word.

Responding to the Text

Matthew's story of Jesus' temptation first tells us something about the nature of Jesus by showing us what Jesus rejects. By implication, the story says something about us, the followers of Jesus, in our various temptations. Any of us would have readily accepted Satan's tempting offers—after all, bread, political power, and miraculous signs are all good things.

But first we preachers ought to focus on what is learned about Jesus through this story. Jesus rejects what we would expect him to embrace, certainly what we would embrace. Thus, at the beginning of Lent, Matthew has placed some distance between us and Jesus, a distance we shall have ample opportunity to ponder as we make our way through these forty days.

> ONE REASON FOR PREACHING IS TO TAKE US AS WE ARE, ALONG WITH OUR WRONG REASONS, AND TRANSFORM, TEACH, AND TRAIN TOWARD THE CHRIST, THE CHRIST AS HE IS IN HIS SOVEREIGN FREEDOM RATHER THAN AS WE WOULD HAVE HIM TO BE.

Later in Matthew's Gospel and in Lent, Jesus shall take bread and feed his disciples, he shall be hailed as "King," and people will urge him to prove that he is really Messiah by throwing himself down from the cross (Matthew 26-27). There is no "Satan" present in that story, no need for one. The voices that cry for him at last to stand up and act like a real King will be our voices. We will have taken the role of Satan in the story. We will be screaming, at the foot of the cross, for Jesus to act like the god we want, to seize power, as we define power, to give us what we want, and give it now. Again, Jesus will reject the tempting offers. He will remain obedient to God's Word, even obedient unto death.

Yet today's gospel ends in triumph, not defeat. Jesus takes charge. "Away with you, Satan!" and with that, Satan's suggestions for a successful messianic campaign cease. Right at the beginning of our Lenten journey, Satan and Jesus have squared off. There will be other perils to be encountered along the way of Lent, but we journey in confidence, knowing that Jesus reigns and that the journey shall come to a good end. Although Satan, and we, his willing assistants, will continue to bedevil Jesus to the end, here, at the beginning, we see that Satan's power, along with that of "the kingdoms of the world and their splendor" are in great peril.

The way I see it, most people come to church for the wrong reasons. They are there because they lust for a quick fix to what ails them. They want to be healed, now. They desire some sure, absolutely fail-proof set of rules that will help them to negotiate the pitfalls of life, they want to be liberated, free, and unbound from any care greater than themselves.

We preachers must take them as they are. One reason for preaching is to take us as we are, along with our wrong reasons, and transform, teach, and train toward the Christ, the Christ as he is in his sovereign freedom rather than as we would have him to be. In his love, he takes our reasons, right or wrong, and turns them toward himself.

SECOND SUNDAY IN LENT

FEBRUARY 28, 1999

REVISED COMMON	EPISCOPAL (BCP)	ROMAN CATHOLIC
Gen. 12:1-4a	Gen. 12:1-8	Gen. 12:1-4a
Ps. 121	Ps. 33:12-22	Ps. 33:4-5, 18-20, 22
Rom. 4:1-5, 13-17	Rom. 4:1-5, (6-12), 13-17	2 Tim. 1:8b-10
John 3:1-17	John 3:1-17 or Matt. 17:1-9	Matt. 17:1-9

"I'm losing my faith," he said.

"What is the faith you are losing?" I asked.

In further discussion with him, it appeared that he had been knocked around a bit in a college philosophy class and this had caused him to question much that he had assumed about the Christian faith.

"Perhaps 'losing my faith' is not exactly accurate to describe what's happening to you," I suggested. "Perhaps God is simply leading you into a new dimension of your faith journey."

Today's lessons, in different ways, all struggle with the nature of faith in the God of Israel and Jesus.

FIRST READING
GENESIS 12:1-8

Interpreting the Text

"In the beginning was the Word . . ." (John 1:1). Without the Word, God's word, intruding into our silences, there would be no world. Word creates world. This is the Genesis story that John echoes in the prologue of the Fourth Gospel.

Today's first lesson claims that word also creates family. Abraham and Sarah are "barren" (Gen. 11:30)—without children, without future. God speaks, and their future is radically altered. Newness, not of their own devising, is created amid their barrenness. A promise of God transforms their fixed lives into pilgrimage, a journey of faith toward the Promised Land.

The beginning is the word. It is a word "from above" (compare with John 3:4), that is, a word not initiated by Abraham or Sarah. It is a word from outside their caught, conditioned existence (Luther spoke of the *verbum externum*, the "external word" of God). Hebrews cites Abraham as an exemplar of faith (Heb. 11). The word creates a new world. The word is the beginning of the journey from barrenness to fruitfulness and hope. Here is a creative, intrusive God who (in the words of this Sunday's epistle) "gives life to the dead and calls into existence the things that do not exist" (Rom. 4:17).

Responding to the Text

We, who have set forth on this Lenten journey are here not, we believe, from our own initiative, but in response to the summons of God. We have been convened, called together for a journey. It is a journey full of peril and dangers to our vaunted, modern self-esteem and its shaky construction. Who would dare risk such a journey except by the summons of God?

The story of Abraham and Sarah begins with a promise. God promises to guide us, to go with us, but that promise must be received in faith—there are no guarantees. Abraham trusts. He ventures forth, late in life, toward a future not of his own creation. Nothing is said explicitly about "faith" in this primordial narrative. Nothing need be said. We here learn significant things about faith simply by being encountered by the narrative. Coupled with the other readings for this Sunday, this first lesson, Genesis 12, provides a rich feast of reflection on the meaning of faith in a God who calls, promises, leads, evokes, creates, and makes a way when there seems to be no way.

Might you think of examples of people, right in your congregation, who have ventured forth of faith in God, like Abraham and Sarah, toward an uncertain future, certain of the sustaining, trustworthy love of God?

Responsive Reading
PSALM 121 (RCL)

Today's psalm was possibly a pilgrim hymn, sung by pilgrims making their way to Jerusalem to worship. As such, it fits nicely with today's first lesson in which Abraham and Sarah are made into journeying pilgrims.

In the context of this Sunday's various lessons, we would do well to focus upon the central question of this psalm in v. 2: "From where will my help come?" Our help, it would appear from the words of this hymn, lies not in ourselves, but in God who comes and helps us. The Creator who created heavens and earth continues to create, continues to make new and to evoke new worlds, even in us. No other gods can save (vv. 3-4).

The psalm affirms a God who does not slumber, rest, or cease keeping his own (v. 5). Yahweh is a fulltime God, relentless, jealous in care of God's people. In v. 7, three times it is reiterated that this God "keeps." In an age of selfmade religion, where our relationship to God is so often presented as our responsibility, this psalm affirms that our keeping next to God is first a matter of God keeping us.

You will find similar affirmations of God's providential care and guidance in the Episcopal and Roman Catholic appointed psalm (33) and the Lutheran psalm (105).

Second Reading

ROMANS 4:1-5, 13-17 (RCL/BCP)

Interpreting the Text

Reaching back into Israel's story, Paul retrieves Abraham as an example of faith in God and its effects. Abraham, the Father of Israel, is enlisted by Paul in his argument and made significant not only for Jews but also for Gentiles, a major concern of Romans.

Paul expands the significance of Abraham in his extended discussion of how we are made "righteous," that is, how we are made right with God (Rom. 4:2-5). Quoting from Genesis 15:6, Paul argues that Abraham's relationship to God was based, not on what Abraham did, but in his trusting obedience to God in faith. Never mind that this may not be Genesis' meaning of the Abraham saga, or that Genesis might not understand Paul's belabored distinction between "faith" and "work." Paul unfolds it for his own purpose of explicating the relationship between faith and righteousness.

In the second part of today's epistle, Paul praises the superiority of faith over the law (4:13-17). He makes Abraham significant, not just for Jews, but even for Gentiles, declaring Abraham to be a prototype of the person who lives by faith.

Care ought to be taken here not to make simplistic distinctions between Christian faith and Jewish "legalism." Recent thought on Pauline theology indicates that Paul's objection to Torah was not that it was "legalistic," but rather that it was not Christ. In the present context we might say that just as God came to Abraham, giving him a new life through divine promise, so Paul says that God comes to us in Christ giving us new life, a new way toward righteousness.

It is therefore not that the law is "legalistic" (though some appropriations of Torah may be just that) but rather that Torah can (in Paul's mind) deter us from the new promise, the fresh path, the Christ. Paul is using his story, the story of Israel, the story of Abraham and Sarah, to unfold the significance of Christ. He is arguing, not that the story of Christ supersedes the story of Abraham or negates it, rather that the story of Christ is surprising fulfillment, enlargement of that story.

Responding to the Text

In pondering the significance of Christ for us, Paul goes so far as to say that God "justifies the ungodly" (4:5). Paul thus underscores the radical, utterly gracious nature of faith as gift of God to the undeserving. We are righteous because we are made righteous by a gracious act of God, not by our own doing. Ending his reflection upon the call of God to Abraham as example of faith and its effects, Paul declares that the story shows God to be the one "who gives life to the dead and calls into existence the things that do not exist" (4:17).

FROM OUT OF NOTHING, NOTHING BUT JEWS AND GENTILES, JEWS STRUGGLING TO BE OBEDIENT TO THE LAW, AND GENTILES KNOWING NOTHING OF THE LAW, GOD IS CREATING A FAMILY CALLED CHURCH.

The call of Abraham is true creation ex nihilo. From out of nothing, God created a family. From out of nothing, nothing but Jews and Gentiles, Jews struggling to be obedient to the law, and Gentiles knowing nothing of the law, God is creating a family called church.

It would be appropriate, therefore, for you to link a sermon on the epistle with the Abraham and Sarah story from Genesis. This God is determined to have a family, even if that family must be created by sovereign, divine intervention and promise. Gathered in our congregation today, we are a sign that God's interventions continue.

Thus the epistle underscores the sovereign, free, unconstrained grace of God, that is, grace to the undeserving and the unrighteous. We have faith in Christ, not as our own achievement, but rather as the creative gift of a sovereign and gracious God. In a self-help, self-made man and woman world, proclamation of the sovereign grace of God is countercultural, prophetic, and, we believe, *true.*

GOSPEL

JOHN 3:1-17 (RCL/BCP)

Interpreting the Text

One of the joys of Lent, Year A, is a series of Sundays that feature some of John's greatest stories. Before we read Jesus' encounter with Nicodemus, let us venture a few hermeneutical principles to guide us in our Lenten encounter with John:

1. John's narratives are "thick." There are layers upon layers of meaning. Details are significant. Our desire for simple explanation is frustrated by the richness of John's manner of presentation.

2. Rarely does John mean for this material to be read "straight." Irony, paradox, and metaphor are favorite Johannine devices. Again and again, people "see" but don't see, they "hear" but don't hear. More is going on in these stories than meets the eye or the ear. Remember the "Energizer® Bunny" from the battery advertisement a few years ago? You thought you were watching a TV ad for a car or chewing gum, then, across the bottom of the screen, there came this pink bunny banging a drum, and the words, "It keeps going, and going, and . . ."

That's the Johannine way of approaching the truth of the gospel. Gail R. O'Day has noted the skillful way in which John uses ambiguity to engage the reader/hearer in the message of the gospel. In so doing, John recreates in the contemporary reader the same dynamic of awakening faith which occurred in those who first met Jesus.

3. Reading these stories is like being privy to an insider's joke. From the first of this Gospel, we know who Jesus is. He is the eternal Word, Word straight from God, in the flesh, dwelling among us. Nobody else knows that—not Nicodemus, not the Woman at the Well, or even the disciples—but we know it. It is fun for us to see those who thought they saw, seeing nothing. It also confirms our faith. We have graciously been given eyes to see what they looked for, but did not see. This is what Alan Culpepper has called the "wink, smile, or scowl" through which the evangelist "creates a bond of secret communication."[2]

Now let us attend to John 3:1-17. First read the story aloud. Use different voices for the two characters in the story. The dialogue here is one of John's best. Jot down your first impressions.

Nicodemus is there as a representative, a "leader of the Jews," a "teacher of Israel." In context, he seems to be one of those folk of whom Jesus complained earlier (John 2:23), those who hanker after "signs." Nicodemus comes to Jesus because he has been somewhat impressed with Jesus' "signs." In his wonderment over Jesus' miraculous deeds, he is superficially impressed with Jesus. He is curious, trying to figure all this out for himself. Intellectual curiosity is surely an important attribute for one who is a "teacher of Israel."

Yet Nicodemus seems to have gotten the thing all wrong. He comprehends little that Jesus says, tangling himself up in Jesus' maddening doubletalk about anew (RSV)/above, Spirit/wind, lift up/crucify. How is he intellectually to figure all of this out?

Intellectually figuring it out is beside the point, apparently. Jesus tells him that "No one can see the kingdom of God without being born from above" (3:3). Only an action "from above," a miracle, can enable Nicodemus to see.

Responding to the Text

The Greek word *anothen* figures prominently in this discourse. Delightfully, it means either above, again, or anew (3:4). Everything about Jesus and the "kingdom of God" seems to be either delightfully or exasperatingly ambiguous, multifaceted. I think Nicodemus is exasperated. Like us, he wants his world flat, in five basic fundamentals, onward to the kingdom through three easy steps. Living in a one-dimensional world of "the flesh" (not a bad interpretation of "the flesh"—one dimensional), Nicodemus is ill-suited, intellectually speaking, to perceive a plenteous world where things are not closed, fixed, finite. Yet, the "Spirit" is untamed, not limited to our flat concepts. The good news is, the Spirit blows where it will.

So Nicodemus begins with a fixed, authoritative declaration, stating what he knows about Jesus (3:2). The dialogue ends with a "How?" question (3:9), to which Jesus responds, not with some new three-step program for Nicodemus to follow, but rather by a declaration of God's effusive, uncontainable, indefinable grace (3:10).

The answer to Nicodemus's "How?" is not one of "the flesh." The answer lies not in us and in our programs and methods but rather in the exaltation/humiliation (there, that ambiguous, Johannine Jesus doubletalk again) of the Son of Man (see John 12:32-33). When the world humiliated Jesus by crucifying him, God was busy unleashing a new, life-giving power into the world by exalting him. Thus the Gospel joins hands with the epistle in its declaration that God is the one who "from above," "gives life to the dead and calls into existence the things that do not exist" (Rom. 4:17). It also ties nicely into this Sunday's psalm and its thematic question, "From where will my help come?" We keep thinking that our help lies in ourselves. We have difficulty in being born "from above."

In turning from exegesis of the text to exegete myself, I find that I like definition, control, self-initiated progress, method, and certitude. I would as soon be born out of my own effort rather than as gift "from above." Auto-salvation is my earnest hope. Is it yours? All of which suggests that my problem, in interpreting today's Gospel, lies in me rather than in the text. In turning from exegesis of myself to exegesis of the congregation, I find that many contemporary strategies for church growth are just that—strategies. The gospel is a reminder that the church grows not through our savvy corporate planning and strategizing, but rather "from above"—as a gracious act of a sovereign and free Lord.

MATTHEW 17:1-9 (RCL/RC)

See the Gospel for The Transfiguration of Our Lord/Last Sunday after the Epiphany, pp. 169–73.

THIRD SUNDAY IN LENT

March 7, 1999

Revised Common	Episcopal (BCP)	Roman Catholic
Exod. 17:1-7	Exod. 17:1-7	Exod. 17:3-7
Ps. 95	Ps. 95 or 95:6-11	Ps. 95:1-2, 6-9
Rom. 5:1-11	Rom. 5:1-11	Rom. 5:1-2, 5-8
John 4:5-42	John 4:5-26, (27-38), 39-42	John 4:5-42 or 4:5-15, 19-26, 39-42

Water appears in nearly all of this Sunday's lessons. Yet it would probably be a mistake for the preacher to make too much of that. A more prominent theme is our dependency upon God. Just as we are utterly dependent upon water for survival, so we are dependent upon the love and care of a beneficent Creator. In today's Gospel, Jesus is revealed to be a mysterious, enigmatic One who both attracts us, and still confuses us. Water is deep, primordial, powerful, mysterious. Just like Jesus.

First Reading

EXODUS 17:1-7

Interpreting the Text

Lent begins in the wilderness with Jesus' temptation. Wilderness is not a place, in scripture, for back-to-nature ecological romanticism. Wilderness is a place of deprivation, temptation, and crisis. Death. Free of the Egyptians, liberated from slavery, one might think that Israel is free of all difficulties. Liberation, curiously, is the beginning of Israel's real problems rather than their solution. Israel has been freed from slavery, not so the people might be free to do whatever they want, but so they might better serve Israel's true God.

In the wilderness without water, the blaming and unrest begin, taking the form of complaint against Moses (17:2). Slavery, as tough as it was, at least provided three meals a day. Freedom, in the wilderness, is perilous.

Moses, attacked by the people, turns and attacks God (17:3-4). What sort of God would have brought us out here to die in the wilderness?

Yahweh responds to Moses' complaint with a decisive command. Strike the rock. It is a weird order, incongruent with human experience. Water from a rock? Of course, human experience, human ingenuity are beside the point. Yahweh has, with a mighty hand, brought forth Israel from slavery. Now it is demonstrated that Yahweh has no intention of leaving Israel to its own devices. Yahweh promises (or threatens?), "I will be standing there in front of you." Yahweh precedes, rather than follows, Israel.

The narration is decisive, direct. On what commodity are we humans more dependent than water? In the story, dependency is acknowledged, a solution is proposed (back to slavery!), and Yahweh enters, commands, and provides.

Behind the narrative is a threatening, risky question: "Is the Lord among us or not?" (17:7). Is God on our side, subject to our summons? No. Yahweh is free, sovereign. We are at the disposal of Yahweh, not vice versa. Yahweh will provide, will sustain, even in the wilderness, but not through our methods and not at our summons. Yahweh commands, provides, but is not servile to us.

Responding to the Text

We live in a capitalist, utilitarian, pragmatic culture. When faced by any new person or experience, what is our first question? What good will this do me? We judge and value all persons, experiences, and events on the basis of their utility. Little wonder that, in our hands, religion becomes a means to an end, a method for getting what we want.

The Israelites need water. They come to God expecting their needs to be met. Their needs are met, but in a strange, unexpected way. The defining and the meeting of need are in God's hands, not our hands.

Wilderness may be interpreted as metaphor, as place of deprivation. We, who live in an age that thinks of freedom, or liberation, as the supreme human goal, the solution to all of our problems, might well ponder the story's implicit claim that liberation is the beginning, rather than the end of our difficulties. There is something quite comfortable about slavery.

The central question of Israel in today's first lesson ("Is the Lord among us or not?") is thus subtly rephrased. The question, the question behind the text is now, "Will we be with God, trusting God, or not?" Can God be trusted to provide a way when there seems to be no way? Will we trust God's means of meeting our need more than we trust our own definitions of our need? In other words, this lesson seems to continue an exploration begun last Sunday on the nature of faith.

Responsive Reading

PSALM 95

Interpreting the Text

The lectionary has obviously chosen Psalm 95 due to its reference (vv. 7-11) to today's Old Testament lesson from Exodus. If we think of Lent exclusively as a time of penitence and confession, we may be somewhat surprised by this psalm's shout of praise. Praise is the natural response of those who have been graciously delivered. If Lent is a time for deliverance from slavery to sin and death, then praise is appropriate.

Yahweh is praised as Creator. The Lord who formed the world did not leave the world, in Deist fashion, to fend for itself. Israel's God is no absentee clockmaker who fashioned the well working clock, then left it alone. Yahweh continues to care for creation (vv. 4-5).

Yahweh is acclaimed as King (v. 3). In an age in which our views of God are somewhat detached and distant, where there has been a critique of monarchial language, we ought to note that God as King proclaims a powerful, active God who cares for the world because the world is God's creation.

Moreover, Israel is also the beloved creation of this creative God (vv. 6-7). We praise because God is our Creator, our maker and keeper (v. 7).

Before ending, the mood of the psalm shifts to a somber note of warning (vv. 7-11). The warning, based upon memory of Israel's troubles in the wilderness, fits well with today's first lesson.

Responding to the Text

Acclamation of God's creativity has ethical implication. Recognition of our creatureliness implies our utter dependency upon God. The meaning of our existence is not of our creation; rather we are created for loving, responsive obedience to the One who is source of our being.

Obedience is not much in fashion these days. This is not necessarily, the psalm might imply, because we are big on "freedom," but rather because we have little sense that our lives are created, owned, claimed by anything, anyone greater than ourselves and our needs.

SECOND READING
ROMANS 5:1-11

Interpreting the Text

Today's epistle is full of joy and rejoicing, particularly during the somber season of Lent. It begins (5:1) with a conclusion. Because we are justified, made right with God through Christ, therefore we rejoice at the following implications.

Joy is a reflexive emotion, dependent, and in response to something else. Here, joy is in no way self-induced. The lesson therefore fits well with the lesson from Exodus and Psalm 95, both of which affirm the benefits of being loved by a God who cares and who acts.

Believers may boast and rejoice in three ways in this passage. First, we rejoice in hope (5:2). This hope is no mere "wishful thinking." It is hope based upon sure confidence in the ultimate triumph of God. Here in Lent, where there is much focus upon the real difficulties of life in this world, we do well to ponder the source of and the nature of Christian hope.

Paul goes so far as to say that we should also rejoice in our suffering. Suffering is in no way defined as a positive good, as something to be sought as an act of piety. Rather, inevitable suffering produces endurance, endurance produces character, and character leads to hope (5:3-4). Perhaps Paul is saying that, in the loving hands of God, set in context with our ultimate confidence in the triumph of God, even so sad and tragic an experience as suffering is redeemed and given significance through our ultimate hope in Christ. Suffering, which is often terribly destructive, becomes redemptive when set in the context of ultimate Christian hope.

> PERHAPS THE MOST VIVID VISIBLE EVIDENCE THE WORLD HAS FOR OUR CLAIM OF REDEMPTION IN CHRIST IS OUR MANNER OF LIFE, THE CHARACTER DISPLAYED BY REDEEMED PEOPLE.

The rationale for Christian hope and joy is given specificity in vv. 6-10. Paul's argument is a bit difficult to follow, yet the thrust is clear. We, who are helpless, sinful, and ungodly (typical Lenten themes), are loved, justified, saved, and reconciled by the death of God's own Son (an appropriate Lenten theme). That reconciliation is asserted rather than explained. Clearly, in describing us as helpless, sinful, and ungodly, Paul makes clear that our rejoicing does not arise out of our nature, but rather in response to the work of God in Jesus Christ. This puts Paul's talk of boasting in proper context.

Responding to the Text

Perhaps the joy of today's epistle seems more notable set in the context of Lent. We live in an age in which joy, real joy, is a rarity, often chemically or commercially induced. To have done for us that which we could not do for ourselves, namely, to be brought close to God, is a joyful experience. G. K. Chesterton called joy "the gigantic secret of the Christian." Paul says that we ought to let the secret out, to boast to all the world what God has done for us in Christ.

Implied in today's epistle is that one way we Christians "boast" is through the manner of our lives. Elsewhere, it was said of Christians, "see how they love one another." Might the world also say of us, "see how they rejoice in their suffering"? Perhaps the most vivid visible evidence the world has for our claim of redemption in Christ is our manner of life, the character displayed by redeemed people.

"You must look much more redeemed," said Friedrich Nietzsche to the church, "if I am to believe in your redeemer."

GOSPEL
JOHN 4:5-42

Interpreting the Text

Today we are blessed with another wonderful, rich story from John, one of the longest dialogues in the Fourth Gospel. We naturally recall Jesus' encounter with Nicodemus in reading today's story of Jesus and the Samaritan woman. Like Nicodemus, the woman has difficulty comprehending Jesus, understanding him, seeing him for who he is. As is typical of so many narratives in John, Jesus' words seem to sail past her. We quite easily identify with the woman in her frustration to figure out who Jesus really is. After all, it is rather early in John's Gospel. Jesus has revealed himself to be a strange, unpredictable, difficult-to-categorize figure. Through John's supreme artistry, we are kept (with this woman) off balance. The mystery and the ambiguity draw us into the tale, set in motion our own attempts to join with her in attempting to figure out who is this Jesus.

At the well, Jesus is the first to speak. Throughout the dialogue, Jesus both requests and commands, seeking something from the woman, drawing her out, treating her as someone with resources and ability.

We are in Samaria, that shadowy, marginalized region. Ironically, Jesus seems (in John) to have more success in Samaria than even among his own people. The Samaritan woman is therefore a woman, an outsider, a Samaritan, which will make all the more striking her comprehension of Jesus, as well as Jesus' initiative with her.

The woman is full of questions. Jesus seems to do that to people. How is it that you, a Jew, are speaking to me, a Samaritan woman? Where can I get this "water" of which you speak? Who is this? The woman is undeterred by the difficulty of Jesus' speech. She hangs in there, interacting with Jesus, determined to wrestle meaning out of an ambiguous encounter.

As in the exchange between Jesus and Nicodemus, there is much double-talk on the part of Jesus. He speaks of "living water" and the woman thinks of water and a bucket. The reader therefore realizes that this conversation is functioning on a number of different levels. The question of verse 9, "How is it?" permeates the entire dialogue.

As we move through the conversation, we sense that the woman's recognition of Jesus is unfolding. Perhaps Jesus is some sort of miracle worker who will produce an unending supply of water so that she need never have to return to this well again. In a sense, she is right. In a sense, she still does not see who Jesus is.

Responding to the Text

What John does so skillfully, and what we preachers might also seek to do, is to involve the hearer every step of the way with the woman in the conversation. Gradually, Jesus is disclosed to us. We are allowed to make the discovery for ourselves, with the woman, in a way that is more engaging than if John had simply made the direct statement, "This is who Jesus is. . . ."

JESUS HAS BEEN MET, YET HE IS NOT YET FULLY GRASPED, INDEED, HE CANNOT BE FULLY GRASPED. THE CHRIST IS LARGER THAN OUR CONCEPTS AND EXPERIENCES.

At the end, the ambiguity and mystery are not completely resolved. The woman stands there, having been engaged by Jesus, recognizing much about him, yet still unsure. "This can't be the Messiah. . . . Is he?" Things are left open-ended, still in process. Jesus has been met, yet he is not yet fully grasped, indeed, he cannot be fully grasped. The Christ is larger than our concepts and experiences. Many in your congregation will be able to empathize with the woman's encounter with the ambiguous Christ.

Gail O'Day, in her wonderful exposition of this passage, comments that the ending question ends the story tentatively. "This tentativeness has an important function. because it is not a definite assertion, it leaves room for individual response. In reflecting on the woman's question, the reader is drawn back to Jesus' own self-revelation."[3]

In our homiletical treatment of this rich story, we might also want to leave our hearers with some sense of the incomprehensible largeness of Jesus, the mystery, the ambiguity that inheres in one who is from God and with God (John 1) rather than a mere projection of our own egos.

Who is this? He's not the long-expected Messiah. Is he?

FOURTH SUNDAY IN LENT

March 14, 1999

Revised Common	Episcopal (BCP)	Roman Catholic
1 Sam. 16:1-13	1 Sam. 16:1-13	1 Sam. 16:1b, 6-7, 10-13
Ps. 23	Ps. 23	Ps. 23:1-6
Eph. 5:8-14	Eph. 5:(1-7), 8-14	Eph. 5:8-14
John 9:1-41	John 9:1-13, (14-27), 28-38	John 9:1-41 or 9:1, 6-9, 13-17, 34-38

First Reading
1 SAMUEL 16:1-13

Interpreting the Text

Today's first lesson begins in rejection. Saul has failed miserably to be the king Yahweh had intended for Israel. Out of rejection and the ending of the old order comes a fresh beginning. Both the ending of the old and the beginning of the new are clearly in the hands of Yahweh.

Yahweh initiates a palace coup. Samuel is hesitant—the prophet knows how kings like Saul behave when their power is threatened. Reluctantly, he goes to Bethlehem, a small, insignificant village, an unlikely place to find a king.

While the sons of Jesse pass by for consideration, Yahweh and Samuel discuss the virtues of each candidate. Yahweh is not moved by external appearance. What matters is in "the heart," the inner inclination of the person.

No suitable candidate is found. Then Jesse remembers his youngest son, little David. When the eighth son appears (vv. 12-13), Yahweh speaks. "This is the one."

Responding to the Text

The story is at first childlike, naïve, engaging. It is the sort of story in which we delight. Power moves from the proud and the powerful down toward the lowest and the least. Reminiscent of the story of David and Goliath, it is a story of reversal, with the little, vulnerable son arising from the little, insignificant town to claim the crown.

As such, it may be interpreted as one of the Bible's many topsy-turvy accounts of the ways in which God lifts up the lowly and brings down the proud. In any congregation, there are those who are young, insignificant, and powerless who ought to be encouraged by such a story.

Yet upon closer examination, the story of the anointing of David also has a somber cast. Saul is being displaced, cast down. There is a rebellion being worked here, a coup, led by none other than Yahweh. The maker of kings is also the ruination of kings. Yahweh is sovereign. Those, like Saul, who disappoint and deceive, shall be displaced. This is a politically charged account of shifts in power, initiated and guided by God.

We who in Lent walk behind One who was called "King" ought to take note. King Jesus came from the same town as King David. Jesus appeared lowly, insignificant, no match for the kings and kingdoms of this world. Yet in him, God is working a rebellion, a coup. The kings of this world are being replaced by the one called Son of David. Lent, like First Samuel, is full of politics, based upon stories with political implication.

The one who hangs from a cross at the end of Lent was hung there, in great part, because he was perceived as a political threat. The kings of this world are not kind to those who would displace their earthly power.

Responsive Reading

PSALM 23

Today is one of a number of times in which Psalm 23 is appointed for the day. Following on the heels of the Old Testament lesson, Psalm 23 underscores the nature of God's peaceful kingdom. To the shepherd is described all of the action of the psalm. The psalm is a consistent affirmation of the sure and certain goodness of a strong and caring God. The good shepherd is the one who makes, leads, restores, gives, and protects. Here in Lent, as we walk at times through the "valley of the shadow," it is good to be reminded of an active, resourceful shepherd who guides and cares for the sheep.

Also during Lent, when we ponder human sin and the countless ways in which we stray from the right path, the twenty-third Psalm's depiction of the shepherd as guide is most relevant. Yahweh gives guidance and certain direction through the meanderings of life. The shepherd is the one who will eventually bring the sheep safely home.

Set in context of the Lenten season, Psalm 23, which may in our minds have been worked and overworked, might take on fresh significance. Lent begins with Jesus tempted in the wilderness. There, the wilderness is presented as a dark and foreboding place. Here, the wilderness is also presented as the place where the shepherd cares, guides, and keeps us. Even in the darkest valley, the shepherd leads, especially there.

Second Reading
EPHESIANS 5:8-14

Interpreting the Text

The "darkness" and "light" of today's epistle fits well with today's Gospel. The passage is replete with strong contrast. Any notion of the Christian life as a slow, gradual, developmental journey is shattered by the sharp contrasts of the images of the epistle. Here are words addressed to persons who have been uprooted from former patterns of existence. They have been jolted, plucked up, shattered by light. When they think of their lives, everything is divided into before/after.

Having been moved to a new level of existence, the realm of light, these new Christians are to live differently, taking no part in the works of darkness (5:11). Conversion has ethical implications.

Verse 14 appears to be taken from an early Christian hymn, possibly an Easter hymn, possibly a hymn sung at baptism. Ephesians has been described as an early baptismal treatise, possibly used in the instruction of baptismal candidates. Here baptism is described as nothing less than transference to a new world of light, a move from death to life.

Responding to the Text

Any sermon derived from today's epistle must be a dichotomy, a division between life before Christ and life after Christ, drawn in the sharpest contrast.

When the Christian community has spoken of conversion to Christ, it has often used the language of darkness and light. Less dramatic speech fails to do justice to the disjunction between life before Christ and life after Christ. It is life lived in darkness then in light, nothing less than a movement from death to life (5:14). Coupled with today's Gospel, the healing of the man born blind, today's epistle provides vivid images to describe the new life in Christ.

Contemporary congregations may be somewhat discomforted by the sharp distinctions between the life of believers and the life of the world. We ought to consider if our discomfort in Ephesians' severe boundaries between church and world lies in our church's compromised and accommodated relationship to the world. Besides, even with our most compromised congregations, there may be individuals whose dramatic faith journey can be adequately described only as a movement from darkness to light, from life to death. The epistle thus reminds us that contemporary characterizations of the Christian life tend to be too tame, too smoothly drawn to do justice to the life-changing, world-dismantling nature of conversion into Christ.

A morning prayer from the fifth-century Leonine Sacramentary captures the spirit of the epistle:

> O God, who divides the day from the night, separate our deeds from the darkness of sin, and let us continually live in your light, reflecting in all that we do your eternal beauty. Amen.

Gospel

JOHN 9:1-41

Interpreting the Text

Another great story from John engages us this Sunday, the healing of the man born blind. Or is that the story? Even to give the story a title (which John does not) is to prejudice our reading. As usual, we begin the story thinking that we know what "blind" means. By the end of the story we, who thought we were quite able to "see" what is going on in the story, see that we, like the religious authorities of any age, have trouble with vision.

John 9:1-41 is a smooth, carefully crafted, dramatic creation. It ought to be read aloud. In the service, try making it into a vignette with readers assigned to various parts of the play. Of course, part of the power of any drama is the way in which the actors and their various parts make us, the audience, into the actors. We quite naturally find our parts in the play, identifying with various roles.

Once again, John gives us preachers so rich a feast that our problem, in preaching on this text, lies in limiting what we will say about so rich a text.

Surely a major theme of the story, particularly in our Lenten context, is sin. That is the disciples' question that provokes the episode, "Who sinned, this man or his parents?" (9:2). It is the disciples' question, therefore let us say that it is our question, since they are there for us.

The religious authorities have an answer (is not this the function of religious leaders, to give answers?). Jesus is the sinner (9:24). Jesus is sinful in that he does not appear to adhere to official religious answers. Yet by the end of this drama, they are called "sinners" (9:41).

Sin is here described as the inability to see. Quickly the dramatic action shifts from the man who has been born blind to the religious leaders who, by their attacks upon Jesus, and the recipients of his healing, show that they are blind. The whole episode seems to have something to do with Jesus' contention that the reason he came into the world was "for judgment so that those who do not see may see, and those who do see may become blind" (9:39). The light which came into the world enables some who sit in darkness to see light (like the man born blind) yet, ironically, blinds others (like the religious authorities).

Knowledge is also described here as the ability to see. Seeing is knowing. The blind man says at the beginning that he doesn't know the meaning of what is going on here (9:12). He only knows one thing (9:25), that he was once blind but now sees. Jesus enriches the blind man's interpretation of his experience by suggesting to him that something more than blindness/sight is going on here, something having to do with faith (9:35), something related to worship of the true and living God (9:38).

Thus, throughout the argument, the once-blind man progresses in his knowledge. All he knows in the beginning is that he was once physically blind. Now he sees. All he knows about Jesus in the beginning is that he must be some sort of prophet (9:17), then perhaps a man from God (9:33). Finally, when Jesus discloses himself to the man, he sees (9:37).

THE LIGHT WHICH CAME INTO THE WORLD ENABLES SOME WHO SIT IN DARKNESS TO SEE LIGHT (LIKE THE MAN BORN BLIND) YET, IRONICALLY, BLINDS OTHERS (LIKE THE RELIGIOUS AUTHORITIES).

The parents of the blind man see and know, but are frightened into saying that they do not know. The Pharisees have sure and certain knowledge (9:24) and yet do not see what is so clearly breaking in upon them. In a wonderful touch of irony, these blind Pharisees (John really does seem to be saying that there are two kinds of blindness—physical and spiritual—one as bad as the other) become the instruments whereby God pushes the blind man toward sight, toward true knowing, toward faith. First he acclaims Jesus as prophet. Then, when pushed by the Pharisees, the blind man taunts them suggesting that if they are so interested in Jesus, perhaps they ought to sign up as his disciples (9:27)! Their attacks upon him have forced the blind man better to define his own relationship to Jesus. Even the critics of Jesus are being used for his sovereign purposes.

Responding to the Text

Curiously, unlike last Sunday's episode with Nicodemus, Jesus is rather absent from this Sunday's action. His act of compassion is the catalyst that sets the argument in motion. So we are seeing Jesus reflected through the reaction of his critics and those who attempted to make sense of him. Jesus is thus depicted as the one who intrudes among us with signs of power, signs from above, and who provokes controversy and contention in the world.

Religious authorities, parents, those who devise and defend the world's conventional explanations do not come off well in today's Gospel. Those of us who are preachers—we authorities, devisers, and defenders of official explanations—ought not to expect to come off well either. Faced with concrete human pain, like the disciples, we pose detached, cool, religious questions. Faced with the unexpected, uncontainable, intrusive grace of God, we, like the Pharisees, tend to get nervous. Encountered by the censure of the establishment we, like the parents, are not sure whether or not we want to affirm the inappropriate religious experience of our children.

So G. K. Chesterton commented that "the mark of Faith is not tradition; it is conversion. It is the miracle by which men find truth in spite of tradition and often with the rending of all the roots of humanity." New life in Christ is characterized, in today's epistle and in the Gospel, as a life full of discordancy, disjunction, and rending of the old.

Yet we should note this: The story ends not with mere condemnation of those who are really blind. The story ends not with the simple tragedy of the once-blind man now sighted, yet now cast out of the religious community, pushed away from family and friends. The story ends with Jesus, reappearing, coming back, as if to Easter, to comfort the blind man, to offer him the gift of relationship, faith, to defend him against the attacks of the misunderstanding religious leaders. Pushed by the healing grace of Jesus to the boundaries, the margins, the man finds out there, not simply rejection, misunderstanding, and ostracism. He finds Jesus, waiting to be worshiped.

FIFTH SUNDAY IN LENT

March 21, 1999

Revised Common	Episcopal (BCP)	Roman Catholic
Ezek. 37:1-14	Ezek. 37:1-3, (4-10), 11-14	Ezek. 37:12-14
Ps. 130	Ps. 130	Ps. 130:1-8
Rom. 8:6-11	Rom. 6:16-23	Rom. 8:8-11
John 11:1-45	John 11:(1-16), 17-44	John 11:1-45 or 11:3-7, 17, 20-27, 33-45

A recent presidential candidate characterized himself as "a doer, not a talker." That's me. I like to do, to achieve, to accomplish. Isn't that the question on the minds of many who come to church? "Tell me, preacher, what should I do now?"

Yet throughout Lent we have found the scriptures speaking primarily about God and only secondarily (and even then) derivatively, speaking about us. This manner of characterizing our situation is especially true on this Fifth Sunday of Lent. All our lessons speak of the power of God to do for us that which we cannot do for ourselves. We are, according to our first lesson, little more than dead, dry bones. We await a life-giving breath of God. In today's Gospel, that breath comes as the strong voice of Christ, a voice loud enough, and with enough power, even to awake the dead.

First Reading
EZEKIEL 37:1-4

Interpreting the Text

In a strange valley, the prophet sees dry bones. These bones are not only dead, they are "dry," that is, completely, utterly without life. In conversation with God, an urgent question is posed by the prophet (37:1-3). Can these dry bones live? Does the power of the God of Israel extend even over the dominion of death?

Ezekiel is enough of a prophet to know that only God knows the answer. The power of life over death is God's, not ours.

In response, God makes a promise (vv. 4-6). I will breathe . . . I will make . . . I will cover . . . I will put. The repetition underscores that that initiative and power are with God.

The promise is quickly kept (vv. 7-8). The bones reassemble, awaiting breath. That life-giving breath now comes (vv. 9-10). The holy breath broods over the valley, summoned by the prophet, reminding us of the breath in Genesis 1 that brought creation into being, reminding us of all that talk with Nicodemus back in Lent 2 about wind and Spirit. Here is a God who calls forth creation out of nothing, life out of death, possibility when there is nothing. It is a vision, a metaphor meant to be enjoyed and remembered, not to be explained or laboriously explicated.

Responding to the Text

The preacher who speaks on today's first lesson is faced with the need to speak of "resurrection" when we are still deep in Lent. Coupled with today's Gospel, we are forced to speak of a God who does not wait on our calendar to work newness. Whenever this God blows in, life breaks forth.

Application will involve the naming of those circumstances within the life of the congregation, or of individuals in the congregation where there is death, dead end, and no potential or possibility of our own devising. My last time on this text was in a small southern town where, the day before, workers at the local textile mill, the town's largest employer, had just been told that their mill would be closed. Management called it "downsizing," but everyone at church that night knew it meant "death." To preach on a God who makes a way when there is no way, who brings the breath of life even in the valley of death, takes an act of faith on the part of preacher and congregation. Have we enough faith to preach such life in the teeth of omnivorous death?

Letting the mode of the message determine its presentation, any sermon on this text ought to be evocative and metaphorical, not explicated, explained, or argued. Once one has walked through the Valley of the Shadow of Death, and seen the dry bones, and felt the dust in the throat; then to feel the breeze, the wind, the miraculous reconfiguration of the body, the movement, the life, one can never forget it. In such visions lies the truth of resurrection, a truth toward which we are moving. Yet it is a truth to be encountered only by first walking through the Valley of the Bones.

RESPONSIVE READING

PSALM 130

Today's psalm begins in heartfelt, passionate cry to God. Nothing here is cool or reasoned. The cause for this passionate outburst is not specified. Therefore this psalm has served, down through the ages, as the epitome of the soul, in any age, needy, empty before God.

The psalm is a cry for forgiveness (vv. 3-4). Yet it is first a cry for God, for the ears of God, for a God so intimately involved with our lives as to be attentive to our need (vv. 1-2). Forgiveness is assumed of a God who takes the trouble to listen.

The psalmist then compares his situation to that of the night watchman, the sentry who guards the city (vv. 5-6), looking toward the horizon, waiting for dawn. Dawn is a gift, something for which we must wait rather than something for which we must strive.

Although the psalmist claims to be seeking God "out of the depths" (v. 1), the psalm ends in strong assurance, in an address to all of Israel to hope in the Lord. Thus the psalm [130] becomes, not so much a penitential cry for forgiveness, but rather a call to hope. Wherein is the source of our hope? Not in ourselves, in our penitence, or in our expectant watching for God. Our hope is in the *hesed*, the "steadfast love of God."

John Calvin called Israel's psalter "an anatomy of the whole soul." In psalms like this one, we see the soul laid bare. However, today's psalm might also be called the whole gospel in miniature. The psalm begins with earnest plea to God, a God who hears. It affirms the forgiveness of God. Then it speaks of the soul's wait for God, waiting as if waiting for morning. Finally, the psalm affirms the ultimate hope to be had through faith in the redemption of God.

Here, in the moves of Psalm 130, we see not only the whole gospel, but also an overview of the journey we have been making during the days of Lent.

SECOND READING

ROMANS 8:6-11 (RCL/RC)

Interpreting the Text

In this section of Romans a comparison is being made, a comparison between life in the "flesh," that is, life according to the old order of domination by sin and death, and life "according to the Spirit."

The chief metaphor that begins this section (Rom. 8:1) is "condemnation." We, who stand under the condemnation, the doom of sin and death, ought to be condemned to the hopeless domination by our sin. Yet sin and death are condemned to death by the work of Christ, therefore there is no condemnation among us.

Some care ought to be taken in interpreting the words *flesh* and *spirit* here. Paul is not talking about two aspects of human personality. Rather, Paul is speaking about two ways of life, two different dominions. The world of the flesh is all the ways of the world that are organized against God.

While Paul does not specify the exact contours of life according to the flesh, having our minds consumed by fleshly matters, it is clear that this is a realm which is "hostile to God" (8:7).

Contrary to life in the flesh is life in the Spirit. Paul makes the rather bold declaration that the Christians at Rome already have the Spirit of Christ presently dwelling within them (8:9). The believer and Christ are so intimately related that deep within us is a power greater than ourselves by which we are already free from the dominion of sin and death. Resurrected life is not something we must wait for until some future day. Resurrection, life in the Spirit, life not determined by the powers of the world, is possible now. The life-giving Spirit of God that brought worlds into being, that breathed over the dry bones in the Valley of Death, now breathes within us, making all things new, creating life in a world of death.

Responding to the Text

The people to whom we preach this Sunday know well life "according to the flesh." They may not have the words yet to put the matter in this way, but they know what it means to have lives that are determined by shadowy powers and inclinations over which they have little control. Have not the contemporary social sciences shown all the subtle but powerful ways in which our lives are determined by sociological, psychological, economic, and political forces outside ourselves?

True freedom comes only when we are driven by some more powerful, deeper domination. Paul claims, in his proclamation to the Romans, that the Spirit of Christ lives in us, so intimately connected to our thinking and willing that we are thereby freed from those powers that enslave us.

When Christian activist William Stringfellow spoke at Harvard Business School, he talked of the reality of the biblical principalities and powers, of "life in the flesh." Stringfellow said he was surprised that the future businesspeople knew exactly what he was talking about. They had no doubt that the world was under the determinative influence of godless powers. Yet when he went over to Harvard Divinity School, students there thought that terms like "world of the flesh" were "archaic imagery having no reference to contemporary realities."[4]

The preacher, faithful to today's epistle, will want to name those ways in which we know what it means to be caught in the strictures of "life according to the flesh." Yet, to be true to Paul's joyous proclamation, the preacher will also want to name, as a presently experienced reality, what it means for us to have the Spirit of Christ dwelling in us. Romans 8:7 ought to serve as the key to our interpretation.

Gospel

JOHN 11:1-45

Interpreting the Text

This is another great story from John. So often Johannine stories are full of irony, and today's Gospel, the raising of Lazarus, is not an exception. Yet this Sunday's text, set among us just before Holy Week, is peculiarly ironic. A man is being raised from the dead here. Shouldn't this be a text for Easter rather than Lent?

Yet there is also much death in this story. The episode opens with the announcement of illness (11:1). Jesus' reaction to the announcement is rather peculiar. He remains where he is for three more days. The disciples certainly have death on their minds—their deaths if they continue to follow Jesus into hostile territory (11:7-16). Lazarus is dying; so are the disciples. By the time they finally get to Bethany, it is all over. Lazarus has been entombed four days (11:17). There is much weeping and grieving, much because there is much death.

Wading into all of this death is Jesus. His disciples seek to deter him, Martha misunderstands and rebukes him, time keeps him from rescuing Lazarus before death. Jesus confronts, moves beyond all the misunderstanding, rejection, and mourning. He brings life to those in the land of death.

John's Gospel begins with the statement, "In the beginning was the Word"

(John 1:1). Echoing Genesis 1, John says that everything, all life, begins with the Word. Today's Gospel is also a creative echo to Genesis 1. Jesus speaks and there is life. New worlds, previously unavailable, spring into being. With a voice loud enough to wake the dead, Jesus cries, "Lazarus, come out!" (11:43). Then, "Unbind him, and let him go."

And we expect that here is the interpretive clue to the whole rich, wonderful story. The disciples are bound on their way to death. Martha and Mary are bound, in grief, to death. The crowds out at the cemetery are bound in cynical, disbelieving enslavement to death. Lazarus is bound in the bands of death.

Then comes Jesus, speaking, calling forth, creating possibility and life where there was none.

Responding to the Text

Ironically, all of this happens deep into Lent. The timing is wrong. Shouldn't this story be deferred until Easter? Yet the time is never right to overcome death. Just as timing is a problem in the story, with Jesus appearing to come out to Bethany too late, so here life in Christ comes to us too soon in Lent. Placing this story here in Lent enables John to say, "I know this story should have been saved until later in my Gospel, until after resurrection, until Easter, but no, whenever Jesus shows up, corpses rise, life breaks out, death is defeated, and people get unbound."

Despite all the power of death in this story, Jesus intrudes, moves out to the cemetery, and has the last word. His is a word of life. Thus our Gospel joins hands with this Sunday's epistle in proclaiming, "If the Spirit of him who raised Jesus from the dead dwells in you, he who raised Christ from the dead will give life to your mortal bodies also through his Spirit that dwells in you" (Rom. 8:11).

Our problem with this story is not the modern, "How could a dead man be raised back to life?" Our problem is that we are (according to last week's Gospel) blind to the glory of God (11:40). We have come to believe that, if there is going to be any life in this world of death, if there is going to be any shred of glory, it must be of our own devising—self-created, auto-initiated.

The people to whom I preach have a problem with death, as any congregation to whom the gospel has ever been proclaimed. Yet their problem may be peculiarly modern and North American. Many of my people feel that there is no problem that they cannot solve. Even death. After all, they have their master's degree!

Today's Gospel suggests that death, the deadliness of this world, life "according to the flesh" (Rom. 8) is a problem not to be solved by our sincere, capable, earnest efforts, but rather by the intrusive grace of a living Lord. Our Lord breaks through all our barriers and misgivings and blindness and calls to us, speaks, creates, makes new, gives life. The question that ought to give rise to this Sunday's sermon is not the conventional North American "What can I do?" but rather the more appropriate evangelical "What does God in Christ do for me which I cannot do?"

SUNDAY OF THE PASSION PALM SUNDAY

MARCH 28, 1999

Revised Common	Episcopal (BCP)	Roman Catholic
Isa. 50:4-9a	Isa. 45:21-25 or Isa. 52:13—53:12	Isa. 50:4-7
Ps. 118:1-2, 19-29	Ps. 118:19-29	Ps. 22:8-9, 17-20, 23-24
Phil. 2:5-11	Phil. 2:5-11	Phil. 2:6-11
Matt. 21:1-11	Matt. 21:1-11	Matt. 21:1-11

After the sobriety and restraint of Lent, Palm Sunday's jubilation comes as a relief to the congregation. Joyfully we celebrate Jesus' triumphal entry into Jerusalem. Yet today's lessons reinterpret our notions of what a "triumphal entry" would look like when the triumph is that of Jesus. "Look, your king is coming to you, humble . . ." (Matt. 21:5). The juxtaposition of "king" with "humble" prepares us for other discordances within today's texts and the worship of the congregation. The King who moves toward us in triumph is also moving toward a cross. Thus we name this day both Palm and Passion Sunday.

First Reading
ISAIAH 50:4-9A (RCL/RC)

Today's first lesson is a word to "sustain the weary." The "weary" is Israel in exile, the predominant audience in Isaiah. Sustenance for the weary is offered in the form of a word about a reality that is greater than the weariness of exiles. Israel in exile is portrayed as suffering servant. Faithfulness to the true God can be costly in a land of false gods.

Those who are burdened, oppressed, persecuted need to hear of a God who helps (50:7, 9). That is the God who is proclaimed in this passage. Every morning this God comes, teaches, sustains (50:4). Without such sustenance, God's faithful people would not have the resources they need to resist the Empire and its seductive ways.

Verses 8-9 move us into a courtroom in which a disputation is in progress. The faithful feel as if they are on trial, falsely accused, assaulted. The servant has confidence in ultimate vindication because the servant has confidence in the ultimate rule of Yahweh. God's purposes shall not be defeated therefore God's faithful ones shall not be defeated.

Isaiah 50:4-9a has obviously been chosen for this day because it was remembered by the church in the church's coming to terms with the passion of Christ. The image of Israel as faithful Servant was applied to Christ, the one who was persecuted and derided yet who was fully faithful. We are justified in applying the passage to believers in general, those who are faithful despite the harassment of the world. The passage is honest in its naming of the real powers that are arrayed against the faithful, yet also confident in its faith in the ultimate triumph of God.

Responding to the Text

Isaiah speaks of the vindication and triumph of God's people on exile. Exile is an appropriate term for how many Christians feel in late twentieth-century North America. Exile is not too strong a term for our feeling of being strangers in a strange land.

Yet Isaiah also speaks of the triumph of God's suffering servant. Those who suffer and who serve God despite the will and the ways of the world will triumph. Their triumph will not be without pain, without risk. Yet they will triumph.

Every pastor knows people who exemplify the path of suffering servanthood in exile.

"Dr. Willimon, are you up yet?" a hoarse, tense, young voice asked.

"Yes."

"I need to see you right away. I've had a terrible night and need to talk."

"I'll meet you at the chapel in thirty minutes," I said.

Upon arriving at the back door of the chapel, the student greeted me and fell into my arms in tears.

"What's happened?" I asked.

"It's terrible. I've had the worst night of my life. Last night, after the fraternity meeting, as usual, we had a time when we just sit around and talk about what we did over the weekend. This weekend, during a party we had on Saturday, I went upstairs to get something from a brother's room and walked in on a couple who were, well, 'in the act.'

"I immediately closed the door and went back downstairs, saying nothing. Well, when we came to the time for sharing at the end of the meeting, after a couple of the brothers shared what they did over the weekend, one of the group said, 'I understand that Mr. Christian got a real eyeful last night.'"

"With that, they all began to laugh. Not a good, friendly laugh; it was cold, cruel, mean laughter. They were all laughing, all saying things like, 'You won't see nothin' like that in church!' and 'Better go confess it to the priest,' and stuff like that.

"I tried to recover, tried to say something light, but I couldn't. They hate me! They were serious. I walked out of the meeting and stood outside and wept. I've never been treated like that in my life."

I said something like, "That's amazing. And you're not the greatest Christian in the whole world, are you? And yet, just one person running around loose who can say No is a threat to everyone else, has to be put down, ridiculed, savaged into silence. This campus may make a Christian out of you, despite yourself!"[5]

Faithful suffering servants are yet among us who need to hear Isaiah 50:4-9a.

ISAIAH 45:21-25; 52:13—53:12 (BCP)

See Gail O'Day's comments below on Palm Sunday/Passion Sunday (Isa. 45:21-25) and Good Friday (Isa. 52:13—53:12).

Responsive Reading
PSALM 118:1-2, 19-29

Today's psalm beautifully portrays the tension inherent in Palm/Passion Sunday. It begins with great joy, much as this Sunday's service may begin, with praise to the God whose steadfast love is forever (Ps. 118:1-2).

Yet quickly the psalm moves toward talk of persecution and even death (vv. 10-12). Although these verses are not included in today's psalm, they do help to make sense of the joyous note which is sounded again in verses 19-29. These verses proclaim this to be a day which the Lord has made (118:24), the result of the Lord's doing.

Set in context of Palm Sunday, the psalm proclaims joyous entry into the Temple. The King and his entourage are moving joyously in procession toward God, the King. Moreover, it proclaims God's creation of joyous new possibility, possibility which is not the result of our efforts but rather the result of God's steadfast, active love.

After our long Lenten journey, the end of our pilgrimage is in sight. The vindication of the purposes of God is about to be worked for all to see. Therefore, despite whatever trials there may be in the present movement, we are able to sing:

> O give thanks to the Lord, for he is good,
> for his steadfast love endures forever. (Ps. 118:29)

PSALM 22

See Gail O'Day's comments below on Palm Sunday/Passion Sunday.

Second Reading
PHILIPPIANS 2:5-11

Interpreting the Text

Some things are best said in poetry rather than in prose. Today's epistle illustrates that truth. In pondering the nature and work of the Christ, only a hymn will do. Paul cites what must have been a beloved early Christian hymn in order to portray the dynamic which is at the heart of the gospel. Even as we are witnessing a move in which the great, highly exalted Christ "empties himself," "taking the form of a servant," during the events of Holy Week (Phil. 2:7-8), we also have confidence that he shall be lifted up, exalted, seated at the right hand of God (Phil. 2:9-11).

Yet mere depiction of the person and work of Christ is not this passage's full intent. The passage begins in imperative. Paul urges the Philippians to "have this mind among yourselves" (Phil. 2:5). They are so to internalize this mind, to make it so much a part of their actions and decisions, that their lives conform to the life of Christ. This is the theme which Paul has begun in the opening verses of this chapter.

The hymn is probably meant to be sung, to be enjoyed, to be joyously proclaimed, rather than argued or explained. The Palm Sunday church, come together to celebrate the great triumph of God in Christ, is chastened by this hymn to remember that the one who is to be exalted is also the one who us humbled, persecuted, crucified. Or, in our Lenten sobriety, are we reminded, in this passage, that the one who partook of our flesh, our earthly existence, the one who ultimately triumphs, defeating all those powers who would defeat God?

Responding to the Text

There is a movement within these beloved verses of Philippians 2. The passage begins high, in the grandest reaches of eternity with the Word, the eternal, preexistent Word who was and is God (John 1). Then there is descent, "downward mobility" as this exalted Word humbles himself and becomes obedient. This is the downward movement we have witnessed during these days of Lent.

Finally, the one who was obediently humbled is faithfully exalted. Paul does not claim that if we will be obedient, we shall also be exalted. Nevertheless, in proclaiming the movement of Christ—downward, then upward again—Paul hopes to draw our lives into a similar move. In our times of humbling, we have confidence, having witnessed the final triumph of Christ. This knowledge enables us to go on, despite the often dark and difficult realities of this fallen world.

As Karl Barth put this matter, "The only advantage of the Church over against the world is that the Church knows the real situation of the world. Christians know that non-Christians do not. . . . It belongs to the Church to witness to the Dominion of Christ clearly, explicitly, and consciously."[7]

Gospel

MATTHEW 21:1-11

Interpreting the Text

Jesus has been working in the hinterland, in places like Galilee (Matt. 4:23). Throughout Matthew's Gospel, tension has been steadily building as he moves step by step toward Jerusalem, the capital city. Jesus' final entry into Jerusalem is literally an "earth-shaking event." Matthew says that "the whole city was in turmoil" (21:10). The Greek verb here is used more typically to describe violent changes in the weather, like storms and earthquakes. Jesus enters, and the whole city shakes. Thus the scene is full of apocalyptic undertones. A day of reckoning is upon us, judgment day, the end of the journey. In Jerusalem he will encounter his fate. Judgment will be rendered in the case of Jesus of Nazareth. Behind the story, a judgment is also being rendered upon us. Will we follow him down his narrow path or not?

In one way or another, the question on the lips of the Palm Sunday crowds in Jerusalem is our question: "Who is this?" In these Sundays of Lent, John's Gospel has had its own peculiar answer to this question. Now, back to Matthew, and we seem to stand on firmer ground. The narrative is straightforward, well known, spare. Perhaps, in this story, relatively little is revealed about Jesus in order that the story may turn back upon its hearers in order to reveal something about us.

The story opens, in typical Matthean fashion, by citation from the Hebrew scriptures. The citations are royal, enthronement acclamations. The king is coming. Israel, so often oppressed by the kings of other nations, dreamed of a time when a king would come and establish Israel. Palms, cloaks in the road, palm branches waved, and shouts of "Hosanna!" all signify that at last the secret about Jesus is out. Here comes the king. Zechariah 9:9 is quoted, with allusion to Isaiah 62:11. Interestingly, this citation (quoted also by John) is omitted by Mark and Luke. Quoted by Matthew, it is surely meant to set this scene in appropriate context. We are meant to see Jesus as the fulfillment of the promises of God to Israel. Two prophets are quoted. Furthermore, two animals are summoned! It is as if Matthew wants to drive home that, in Jesus, not only a "king" is riding into the capital city, but our king, the one on whom we have waited.

BOUNCING ON THE BACK OF A DONKEY, HUMBLE, JESUS IS NOT THE TRIUMPHANT WARRIOR KING WE EXPECTED.

One other detail should be noted. Matthew omits Zechariah's words about the king, "triumphant and glorious is he." By omitting this royal acclamation, does Matthew mean to highlight that this king is "humble" (21:5), that he bounces in on the back of a donkey rather than upon a warhorse? Earlier in Matthew, in summoning disciples, Jesus said that he was "gentle and humble of heart" (11:29).

Responding to the Text

Thus Matthew means for us to ponder a striking juxtaposition. At last Jesus has entered the capital city, the place of pomp and power. The heading atop this page in my NRSV speaks of this as "Jesus' triumphal entry into Jerusalem." The acclamation of the crowds and their waving palm branches, are signs of triumph, to be sure. Yet Matthew is busy rearranging our ideas of the triumph of God. Bouncing on the back of a donkey, humble, Jesus is not the triumphant warrior king we expected.

Matthew began his Gospel by calling it "An account of . . . Jesus the Messiah, the son of David, the son of Abraham" (1:1) and we thought we knew what that meant. He is Messiah, Anointed One of God, son of David, King of Israel. Yet we know how the story of this, his finest week in Jerusalem, will end. He will not be enthroned in a palace, but hanged from a cross on Golgotha.

So the joyous crowds, shouting, "Hosanna to the Son of David!" (21:9), have it partly right and mostly wrong. Jesus is our king, the Holy One of God but he is also, as they also acclaim, a "prophet" (21:11). The prophet-king, like the prophets of Israel, did not seek his own glory, did not follow his own will. Rather, he humbly, obediently spoke and enacted the will of God.

In an odd sense, we thus derive a rather Johannine experience from our encounter with today's Gospel. That is, we have noted, in the Sundays of Lent, how people keep coming to Jesus thinking that they see him, but they do not see. In John's Gospel, Jesus is persistently rearranging preconceptions of Messiahship. Matthew does much the same in this Palm Sunday Gospel. Jesus is the "king" the crowds proclaim him to be, but not the king we expected. In his words and actions during the last week of his earthly ministry, we shall see where his kingdom leads. Are we willing to follow?

Notes

1. Gail R. O'Day, *Revelation In the Fourth Gospel* (Philadelphia: Fortress Press, 1983) 1-10.
2. Alan Culpepper, *Anatomy of the Fourth Gospel* (Philadelphia: Fortress Press, 1983) 179.
3. Gail R. O'Day, *Revelation in the Fourth Gospel* (Philadelphia: Fortress Press, 1986) 76.
4. Bill Wylie Kellermann, *A Keeper of the Word: Selected Writings of William Stringfellow* (Eerdmans, Grand Rapids, Michigan, 1994) 193.
5. This is an adaptation of pp. 27–28 of my book, with Stanley Haurewas, *Where Resident Aliens Live* (Nashville: Abingdon Press, 1996).
6. Karl Barth, *The Faith of the Church* (New York: Scribner's, 1959) 145.

HOLY WEEK

GAIL R. O'DAY

HOLY WEEK, AS ITS VERY NAME SUGGESTS, is the most sacred sequence of days in the liturgical life of the church. It is the week toward which the Lenten season has been moving the worshiping community, the week of Jesus' passion and death. The week begins with the worshiping community's waving of palm branches in a reenactment of Jesus' Palm Sunday entry into Jerusalem, and ends with the Saturday evening vigil, in which the community waits and watches together for the first glimpse of the light of the resurrection. As these two framing events show, the definitional character of Holy Week is that in these days, the church lives out the events of Jesus' passion. It is not a week in which we simply remind ourselves of what happened to Jesus and his disciples "back then," but is a week in which we become part of the story and the story becomes part of us. We shout both "Hosanna" and "Crucify him" on Palm/Passion Sunday; we eat the bread and drink the wine that Jesus offers us on the night of his betrayal; we stand at a distance and watch the death of Jesus on the cross; we sit in the darkness of the tomb and rejoice at the inbreaking of light. In Holy Week, the "old" story becomes an ever-new story, as we experience once again what it means to be a community whose very life and identity derives from this week's journey to the cross.

IN HOLY WEEK, THE "OLD" STORY BECOMES AN EVER-NEW STORY, AS WE EXPERIENCE ONCE AGAIN WHAT IT MEANS TO BE A COMMUNITY WHOSE VERY LIFE AND IDENTITY DERIVES FROM THIS WEEK'S JOURNEY TO THE CROSS.

SUNDAY OF THE PASSION PALM SUNDAY

MARCH 28, 1999

Revised Common	Episcopal (BCP)	Roman Catholic
Matt. 21:1-11	Matt. 21:1-11	Matt. 21:1-11
Ps. 118:1-2, 19-29	Ps. 118:19-29	
Isa. 50:4-9a	Isa. 45:21-25 or Isa. 52:13—53:12	Isa. 50:4-7
Ps. 31:9-16	Ps. 22:1-21 or 22:1-11	Ps. 22:8-9, 17-20, 23-24
Phil. 2:5-11	Phil. 2:5-11	Phil. 2:6-11
Matt. 26:14—27:66 or 27:11-54	Matt. (26:36-75), 27:1-54, (55-66)	Matt. 26:14—27:66 or 27:11-54

The double name of this Sunday indicates that it has two roles in the liturgical calendar. As Palm Sunday, it is the day that celebrates Jesus' triumphal entry into Jerusalem, and one Gospel lesson assigned for the day tells this story (Matt. 21:1-11). As Passion Sunday, it marks the transition from Lent into Holy Week, and the other designated Gospel lesson rehearses the full scope of Jesus' passion and death in anticipation of the days ahead (Matt. 26—27).

THE NON-NEGOTIABLE CALL AND RESPONSIBILITY OF THIS SUNDAY IS TO FIX THE CONGREGATION'S FOCUS UNWAVERINGLY ON JESUS AS HE MOVES TOWARD GOLGOTHA.

Some in the congregation will participate in all of the Holy Week services, but others will move from this Sunday service straight to Easter, so that this will be their only experience of Jesus' passion and death before they celebrate his resurrection. The preacher's multiple responsibilities on this Sunday can be challenging, and the preacher may feel overwhelmed by the superabundance of riches the lessons for this Sunday provide. The preacher may be helped in navigating these riches if he or she remembers that the non-negotiable call and responsibility of this Sunday is to fix the congregation's focus unwaveringly on Jesus as he moves toward Golgotha.

PALM SUNDAY GOSPEL

MATTHEW 21:1-11

Interpreting the Text

The Gospel lesson appointed for Palm Sunday is Matthew's account of Jesus' entry into Jerusalem. Half the story (vv. 1-6) is devoted to preparation for the entry. The detailed account of the preparation communicates that this entry is not simply a whim on Jesus' part but is essential to the fulfillment of his ministry. Matthew's citation of scripture as commentary on Jesus' instructions (vv. 4-5, a blend of Isa. 62:11 and Zech. 9:9) reinforces this understanding of the entry. (Matthew seems to have misunderstood the Greek version of Zechariah 9:9 to refer to two animals, not just one. He thus describes Jesus as riding on a donkey and a colt simultaneously!)

Verses 7-11 describe the entry itself and are very similar to the version of this story found in Mark (11:1-10). The main difference between Mark and Matthew is in the ending of the story. In Mark, after Jesus is greeted by the "Hosannas" of the crowd, he quietly enters the temple precinct (Mark 11:11). In Matthew, by contrast, when Jesus entered Jerusalem, the "whole city was in turmoil, asking, 'Who is this?'" (v. 10). It is a wonderful image—this strange parade, consisting of a man riding a donkey (and a colt!), accompanied by crowds who take off their cloaks and cut branches for him to ride over. It is the topic of conversation for the entire city. According to Matthew, all the eyes of Jerusalem are turned toward Jesus as the events of this crucial week get underway.

WE NEED TO BE JOYOUS AND SLIGHTLY RIOTOUS IN OUR EXCITEMENT, BECAUSE SOMETHING OUT OF THE ORDINARY IS HAPPENING HERE, SOMETHING THAT HAD THE WHOLE CITY OF JERUSALEM BUZZING.

Responding to the Text

Even though we know how quickly the mood of anticipation and celebration of this story will turn sour, it is important that we give this mood its due. The children in a congregation, who become so excited at the thought of waving branches around in church, provide a good bellwether here. We need to be joyous and slightly riotous in our excitement, because something out of the ordinary *is* happening here, something that had the whole city of Jerusalem buzzing. If we are to feel the full impact of the betrayal, cowardice, and fear that mark the rest of the week, then we must exult fully at its start, so that we can experience how quickly our own voices can turn from cries of "Hosanna" to "Crucify him."

Palm Sunday Psalm

PSALM 118:1-2, 19-29

See William H. Willimon's comments under Palm Sunday/Passion Sunday, pp. 224-25, in the Season of Lent, and my comments below under The Great Vigil of Easter, p. 283.

First Reading

ISAIAH 50:4-9a (RCL/RC)

Interpreting the Text

This lesson from Isaiah is the third of four "Servant Songs" in Second Isaiah (Isa. 40-55). The other three are Isaiah 42:1-4; 49:1-6; and 52:13—53:12, and the four form the heart of the Old Testament lessons for Holy Week (see the first lessons for Monday, Tuesday, and Wednesday of Holy Week, as well as Good Friday). Given the prominence of these Songs in the Holy Week lectionary, it is important to provide a general orientation to these texts.

Second Isaiah was written near the end of the Israelite captivity in Babylon. The Babylonian exile had begun in 587 B.C.E., and was brought to an end by the Persian conquest of Babylon by King Cyrus in 538 B.C.E. The poet/prophet of Second Isaiah speaks of Cyrus by name and points to him as God's anointed one who will assist in Israel's release (Isa. 44:24—45:13). The central theme of Second Isaiah, appropriately nicknamed the "Book of Consolation," is to revive the Israelites' hopes of a new life and a fresh future, hopes that flagged in the years of captivity.

The Servant Songs provide a slightly different perspective on the themes of consolation and hope. In these four songs, the focus rests more on the cost of restoration and the responsibilities that accompany fresh hopes. The servant occupies the central place in the description of these costs, but the four songs differ among themselves in their representation of the servant—sometimes the servant is described in individualistic terms (52:13—53:12), sometimes in autobiographical terms (50:4-9a), sometimes in corporate terms (42:1-4). It seems best to honor the diversity of representation in these songs, and to interpret the servant as all the things the songs say that he is. That is, the poet/prophet of Second Isaiah seems to be calling the nation to the recognition that restoration will require acts of justice and self-giving on the parts of individuals and the nation, that God has anointed both the leaders and the nation to be God's chosen agents of new possibilities. The early church used the servant songs to help interpret the life and work of Jesus, a practice that continues in contemporary lectionaries.

The Servant Song appointed for Passion Sunday focuses on the relationship between God and the servant, and the ways in which that relationship sustains the servant in the enactment of his vocation. God teaches the servant (vv. 4-6), and the metaphors used to describe that teaching are vivid—"the tongue of a teacher," "wakens my ear," "opens my ear." God's presence in the servant's life and work makes a new kind of hearing and speaking possible, a hearing and speaking that can withstand the protests of naysayers (v. 6). God also helps and vindicates the servant in the face of his opponents (vv. 7-9a). The servant speaks with a clear and unshakable conviction that God's support is unfailing, and so the servant can face all adversity and strife.

Responding to the Text

When read on Passion Sunday, this Servant Song helps the Christian community to enter into Jesus' experience at his passion and death. Indeed, one can almost imagine Jesus speaking these same words as he approaches his own time of trial. Like the servant who speaks in Isaiah 50:4-9a, Jesus, too, is able to enact his ministry with confidence, because he knows that he has been taught by God. Jesus, too, can set his "face like flint" (v. 7), because the jeers and taunts that will greet him this week cannot weaken the help of God.

If we listen carefully to the servant's self-description in this song, the servant's confidence in God should move us to silenced awe. In this Servant Song, and in the application of this song to Jesus at the beginning of Holy Week, we are brought into the sacred presence of a life turned completely toward God, a life that can hope in the face of unimaginable adversity: "It is the Lord God who helps me; who will declare me guilty?" This awesome confidence belongs to Jesus, but it also is offered to the worshiping community throughout the trials of Holy Week.

ISAIAH 45:21-25 (BCP)

Interpreting the Text

This additional Old Testament reading in the Episcopal lectionary comes from Second Isaiah. Unlike the other Holy Week readings from Second Isaiah, however, it is not one of the Servant Songs (see above), but a song that celebrates God's triumph over the nations. Isaiah 44:24—45:25 consists of two oracles ("thus says the Lord"). Isaiah 44:24—45:13 announces God's choice of Cyrus, the Persian king, to be the shepherd (44:28) and anointed one who will assist God in bringing an end to Babylon's tyranny over the people of Israel and hence to exile. Isaiah 45:14-25 contains an even more stunning announcement—the nations will acknowledge Israel's God as the one true God.

Isaiah 45:21-25 is the conclusion of this oracle about the conversion of the nations, and its focus is on the singularity of Israel's God. Verses 21, 22, 24, and 25 all stress the unique character and position of Israel's God: "There is no other god besides me, a righteous God and a Savior; there is no one besides me" (v. 21); "For I am God, and there is no other" (v. 22); "only in the Lord . . . are righteousness and strength" (v. 24); "In the Lord . . ." (v. 25). Yet the power of this oracle comes not only from these affirmations about Israel's God, but from its announcement in v. 23 of the effect of the righteousness of God on the nations. The nations will bow before Israel's God, and their tongues will sing God's praises. What a remarkable transformation—the nations that once held Israel captive and so mocked Israel's God will now join Israel in the worship of this same God.

Responding to the Text

The note of celebration and exultation in this lesson from Isaiah 45 makes it an appropriate companion to the Palm Sunday Gospel. It, like the story of Jesus' triumphal entry, celebrates God's sovereignty and the wonder of a world where this God reigns. This lesson enables the faith community to share in the joy of worshiping a God whose righteousness is beyond compare. Yet this lesson also has an explicit connection with the Passion Sunday lessons. Philippians 2:10-11 is an expansion of Isaiah 45:23, and reading Isaiah 45 in that context places its note of triumph in a different light. The triumph of God that is celebrated in Isaiah 45 comes only at the end of a long period of suffering and exile for God's people. It is not a triumph that runs roughshod over the complexities of human life, but one that is known only in and through those complexities and sufferings. This lesson (Isaiah 45) thus encapsulates the tensions and double responsibilities of Palm/Passion Sunday in one text: the need to sing the praise of God and the need to acknowledge the suffering and despair that accompanies that praise.

ISAIAH 52:13—53:12 (BCP)

See my comments for the first lesson for Good Friday, pp. 269–71.

PSALM 31 (RCL)

Interpreting the Text

Psalm 31:9-16 is a cry for deliverance that echoes many of the themes from Isaiah 50:4-9a. The psalmist's situation of distress is described in even more detail than that of the servant, however. The psalm opens with an appeal to God's graciousness (v. 9a) and moves immediately to a recital of the psalmist's distress (vv. 9b-13). The psalmist's honesty in placing his distress before God makes his statement of confidence in God all the more compelling (vv. 14-16). That the psalmist is not naïve about the scope of his suffering means that he is also not naïve about his trust in God. He trusts in God in the midst of his sufferings, not apart from them.

Responding to the Text

Like the Servant Song of Isaiah 50:4-9a, this psalm allows the worshiping congregation to participate in both the sufferings and hopes of Passion Sunday. This is especially the case in those Christian traditions in which corporate speaking or singing of the psalms is a part of liturgical practice. These words become ours in the moment of speaking or singing them aloud. We become one with the psalmist, and we hear ourselves place our complaints and hopes before God. Holy Week is an important time to be reminded that our relationship with God is not an antiseptic one—we do not have to present our "best faces" to God, but we can place the complexities of our struggles and sufferings before God in prayer and worship. Indeed, the more honest our speech before God, the more deeply grounded is our hope and trust in God.

WE DO NOT HAVE TO PRESENT OUR "BEST FACES" TO GOD, BUT WE CAN PLACE THE COMPLEXITIES OF OUR STRUGGLES AND SUFFERINGS BEFORE GOD IN PRAYER AND WORSHIP.

PSALM 22 (BCP/RC)

See the comments on the psalm for Good Friday, p. 272.

SECOND READING

PHILIPPIANS 2:5-11

Interpreting the Text

The epistle lesson for Passion Sunday is the Pauline text commonly referred to as the "Philippians hymn." It receives this name because verses 6-11 are understood to be a pre-Pauline Christ hymn, which Paul quotes here. This hymn celebrates the entire Christ story and focuses on three aspects of that story: the preexistence of Christ (v. 6); the incarnation and death of Jesus (vv. 7-8); the subsequent exaltation of Christ (vv. 9-11). To speak of the preexistence of Christ is to speak of the ongoing relationship between God and Christ that began before the incarnation and continues after Jesus' death. The incarnation gives the world access to this relationship between God and Christ, but it is not the beginning of that relationship (see also John 1:1).

The pivot of this hymn, and what makes it an appropriate lesson for Passion Sunday, is verses 7-8. The vocabulary of these verses makes the contrast between preexistence and incarnation unmistakably clear—"form of God" and "equality with God" give way to "form of a slave," "born in human likeness," "human form." Christ Jesus gave up what made him one with God and different from us to become completely one with us. And as if that were not enough, he embodied his human identity so completely that he remained obedient to this identity "to the point of death—even death on a cross." It was this obedience, even to the ignominious death of crucifixion, that results in the exaltation and doxology with which the hymn ends.

The Philippians hymn is one of the most exquisitely beautiful texts in the New Testament. With disciplined economy of language, it rehearses and celebrates the heart of the Christian story. Jesus' life and ministry are compressed into two events—his birth and death—which highlight his humanity. The streamlining of the Jesus story into these two events is all the more noticeable given that they are framed by verses that focus on Christ's heavenly existence with God. The hymn's structure highlights the movement of having, letting go, and receiving again.

Responding to the Text

The epistle lesson provides a suggestive lens through which to read all the Passion Sunday lessons. This lens is found in Paul's own words that precede his quotation of the hymn, "Let the same mind be in you that was in Christ Jesus" (v. 5). The exhortation of this verse, Paul's urging of the Philippian

Christians, positions the Christ hymn as the key to how they are to live their own lives. Note carefully that Paul does not exhort them to live Christ's life, but, if we translate the Greek a bit more literally, to think with Christ's mind. The mind of Christ is exemplified by the hymn that follows—humility, obedience, a refusal to grasp for power.

For us to think with the mind of Christ is to think and act in ways that are in striking contrast to accepted cultural and societal norms of how we relate to one another. To think with the mind of Christ is to put aside competition, self-seeking ambitions, advancement at any cost. To think with this mind is to imagine living in a world shaped by the movement of this hymn, a world where relinquishing one's power is the first step in receiving multifold blessings. To think with this mind is to live in a world shaped by the cross and a full embrace of what it means to be human. Philippians 2:5-11 suggests a way in which the story of Holy Week becomes our story—in living into the events celebrated in this hymn, we can begin to see the world through the mind of Christ.

TO THINK WITH THE MIND OF CHRIST IS TO LIVE IN A WORLD SHAPED BY THE CROSS AND A FULL EMBRACE OF WHAT IT MEANS TO BE HUMAN.

Gospel

MATTHEW 26:14—27:66

Interpreting the Text

The Gospel lesson for Passion Sunday is the passion narrative in Matthew. The option to read only Matthew 27:11-54 allows for an abbreviated version of this story, but to choose that option is to offer the congregation the "condensed version" of the story from which their life and identity come. As time-consuming as it can be to read all of Matthew 26 and 27, what could be more pressing in the Sunday morning liturgy than to hear together the most sacred of our stories?

Matthew follows the Markan version of the passion narrative very closely; indeed, the sequence of events in Matthew is identical to that found in Mark. In Matthew's recasting of this material, however, the focus of the story seems to shift toward the drama that is being played out between Jesus and his disciples. Each of the events leading up to Jesus' trial before Pilate (27:11-26) is punctuated by references to the betrayal, denial, and desertion of Jesus by his disciples (see, for example, 26:14-16, 20-25, 31-46, 51, 56, 58, 69-75; 27:3-10). More space is devoted to the failure of Jesus' disciples in Matthew 26 than to Jesus' own actions. Once the trial before Pilate begins, those characters whom the reader of Matthew has come to think of as Jesus' disciples disappear from the story altogether. In their place, other disciples appear: Simon of Cyrene who carries Jesus' cross; the centurion who names Jesus as the Son of God; Jesus' women followers who, alone among all of Jesus' disciples, keep vigil at the cross; Joseph of Arimathea who buries the body of Jesus. The story of discipleship in Matthew's passion story is not one of complete failure, but it is one in which surprising characters act with boldness and compassion.

Responding to the Text

The preacher's task in handling the Matthean passion story is deceptively simple. It is to get out of the way so that this story can be heard in all its dignity, pathos, pain, and power. That is, whatever words the preacher speaks in response to this story must not be an attempt to reduce this story to what it "means," to identify its "contemporary relevance," or worse, to override the story with one's own sense of what is important for the day. On Passion Sunday, the worshiping community, preacher and congregation alike, is invited to reenter the story of Jesus' suffering and death, to hear it not only as Jesus' story, but as our story—to hear it as the story that orients us to our relationship to God and to our place in the world.

THE PREACHER'S TASK IN HANDLING THE MATTHEAN PASSION STORY IS DECEPTIVELY SIMPLE. IT IS TO GET OUT OF THE WAY SO THAT THIS STORY CAN BE HEARD IN ALL ITS DIGNITY, PATHOS, PAIN, AND POWER.

To hear this story on Passion Sunday, to hear it read aloud in the company of one's brothers and sisters in faith, is to come home. It is, like all homecomings, an experience fraught with pain and some peril, but it is a homecoming nonetheless. This story is where we are called to live, where we experience anew who we are and what we hold holy.

MONDAY IN HOLY WEEK

MARCH 29, 1999

REVISED COMMON	EPISCOPAL (BCP)	ROMAN CATHOLIC
Isa. 42:1-9	Isa. 42:1-9	Isa. 42:1-7
Ps. 36:5-11	Ps. 36:5-10	Ps. 27:1-3, 13-14
Heb. 9:11-15	Heb. 11:39—12:3	
John 12:1-11	John 12:1-11 or Mark 14:3-9	John 12:1-11

THE LESSONS FOR THE MONDAY OF HOLY WEEK take a step back from the intensity of Passion Sunday and create a space in which the worshiping community can reflect on the experience of God made available to it in the life and death of Jesus. The lessons from Isaiah and the psalms celebrate God's faithfulness and graciousness toward God's people. The lesson from Hebrews reflects on how Christ's death brings into being a new relationship with God and one another. The Gospel lesson from John is a story of limitless love that reminds us of the love that lies at the heart of the passion narrative.

FIRST READING
ISAIAH 42:1-9

Interpreting the Text

This lesson contains two distinct units: In verses 1-4 is the first of the four Servant Songs in Second Isaiah; verses 5-9 are the beginning of a longer section (42:5-17) that celebrates God's work in creation and Israel's history. In both units, the voice that is speaking is God's. (A general introduction to the Servant Songs is included in the comments on Palm/Passion Sunday, pp. 232-33).

In Isaiah 42:1-4, God introduces the servant to the nation. The closeness of the relationship between God and the servant is emphasized by the frequent use of the first person singular in verse 1: "my servant, whom I uphold, my chosen, in whom my soul delights." In addition, the servant is anointed with

God's own spirit, making clear that the servant will do God's work. Verses 1-4 detail three interrelated traits of the vocation for which the servant is anointed—he will work and teach for justice; he will work patiently and not quit until justice is established; his mission for justice is not parochial, but is global in scope ("to the nations," "in the earth," "the coastlands"). Whether one understands the servant as an anointed individual or as the anointed nation does not change the impact of God's words here. The vision is of a new world, shaped by God's justice, that will be brought into being by God's servant's unfailing work.

In verses 5-9, God reminds Israel who their God is, what God has done in creation. These verses provide an important backdrop to the work of the servant. When the servant is anointed to work for God's justice, he is anointed to work for the vision of life that is contained in the wonder of God's acts of creation (v. 5) and in the faithfulness of God's covenant (v. 6). Israel's God is beyond compare with other gods (v. 8), because God is the one who makes all things new (v. 9). Verse 7 supports the corporate reading of the servant, because in this verse God stresses the covenantal responsibilities of all of God's people to do justice.

Responding to the Text

This lesson is a reminder that the community itself, as recipient of God's goodness at creation, is called to be an instrument of God's justice in the world. Although Holy Week rightly turns the community's eyes toward Jesus as God's anointed one, this lesson from Isaiah also calls us to accountability about our own work for justice. Yes, we look to Jesus as the one who gives sight to the blind and release to those imprisoned (cf. Matt. 11:4-6; Luke 4:18-19), but Isaiah 42:7 asks us to remember our own responsibilities as members of God's covenant people.

The portrait of God in this lesson also provides a powerful image of hope in the midst of Holy Week. The language about God here is simultaneously cosmic in scope ("who created the heavens and stretched them out") and intensely intimate ("I have taken you by the hand and kept you"). In the struggles and trials of Holy Week, we can turn to this God in prayer and know that nothing is too small or too great for God's sovereign care.

Responsive Reading

PSALM 36 (RCL/BCP)

Interpreting the Text

It is important to place vv. 5-11 in the broader context of Psalm 36. This hymn of praise (vv. 5-9) and prayer for safekeeping (vv. 10-11) are framed by words about the wicked (vv. 1-4, 12). The full context of Psalm 36 makes the appointed verses a very fitting psalm for Holy Week, because it suggests that the lavish praise of God in verses 5-9 is offered when the psalmist feels under threat, not when all is well.

It is useful to examine Psalm 36:5-11 alongside Isaiah 42:5-9. The two share similar affirmations about the character of God, especially God's boundless righteousness and justice, but the speaking voices of the two texts are different. Whereas Isaiah 42 is presented as the voice of God, in Psalm 36 it is the psalmist who speaks—and the psalmist is even more effusive in praising God than God's own voice in Isaiah! Verses 5-6 are an excellent example of the psalmist's exuberant praise of God.

Responding to the Text

This psalm can be sung in a loud voice or prayed in a still, small voice; it matters not. What matters is that the worshiping community gives itself over to the joy and confidence of this psalm. This psalm does not contain words of "cheap grace." The psalmist knows what it feels like to be stepped on by the foot of the arrogant and self-serving (vv. 2, 11), but the psalmist also knows that God's steadfast love is without bounds, and that indeed, the universe is supported by that love (v. 5).

THE PSALMIST KNOWS THAT GOD'S STEADFAST LOVE IS WITHOUT BOUNDS, AND THAT INDEED, THE UNIVERSE IS SUPPORTED BY THAT LOVE.

PSALM 27 (RC)

See Robert H. Smith's comments on the psalm under the Third Sunday after the Epiphany, pp. 124–25.

SECOND READING

HEBREWS 9:11-15 (RCL)

Interpreting the Text

This lesson from Hebrews is the opening verses of a much longer treatment of the meaning of Christ's sacrifice (Heb. 9:11—10:18). To understand the perspective of Hebrews, contemporary readers must make a vast imaginative leap in order to hear its vocabulary and imagery of sacrifice and cult in the context of the levitical religious system of ancient Israel and not in the context of modern uses of the word *sacrifice.* The Letter to the Hebrews thus should always be read with the text of Leviticus close at hand.

To make or offer a sacrifice is an explicit religious rite. *Sacrifice* always and only has a religious and, more specifically, a cultic meaning in ancient Israel. It is not simply about giving something up, as contemporary usage of *sacrifice* usually suggests, but of giving something to God in worship in order to render it holy. The sacrificial system in Israel was a system of atonement, in which the priest offered the blood of animals as a means to effect reconciliation for wrongs before God and one another. It was a public act that was at the heart of the temple liturgy (see Lev. 16:1-34; 17:11). The sacrificial system enacted the important theological and pastoral recognition that serious human transgressions cause a major rupture in the fabric of humanity's relationship with God and one another, and that this rupture cannot be ignored but reparation needs to be made.

The sacrificial system came to an end in Israel with the destruction of the Jerusalem temple by the Romans in 70 C.E. This fact, too, is important for understanding the lesson from Hebrews, because it means that at the end of the first century C.E., Jews and Christians alike were engaged in renegotiating how one thinks about making reparation and atonement before God. For the author of Hebrews, the answer was obvious—Christ's death is the one true sacrifice that renders the former (now defunct) sacrificial system obsolete, but it is important to remember that Hebrews is only one of many New Testament negotiations of that issue.

When read against this background, the logic of the Hebrews lessons is fairly straightforward. Verses 11-14 contrast the temple sacrificial system and the sacrifice of Christ (vv. 11-12; 13-14) and verse 15 offers a theological interpretation of this contrast. Verses 11-12 compare elements from one system with that of the other—and find Christ's sacrifice more efficacious. The greater and perfect tabernacle of Christ the high priest is contrasted with the temple that was made of human hands. Christ's offer of his own blood, so that he is both priest and sacrificial victim, is contrasted with the blood of goats and calves. The contrast in verses 13-14 works on the logical premise of arguing from the lesser ("for if the blood of goats and bulls") to the greater ("how much more will the blood of Christ"). Verse 15 explains the significance of these contrasts: Christ's death mediates a new covenant, one that is eternal and cannot be erased by time.

Responding to the Text

How are contemporary Christians to negotiate this seemingly archaic text, whose core presuppositions are centuries removed from the world in which we live? The simplistic appropriation of this text ("Israel's sacrifices were empty formal acts, but Christ's sacrifice is the real thing") is both wrong and dangerously anti-Semitic. The sacrificial system of the Jerusalem temple was not a bankrupt religious system, but as noted above, contained an acknowledgment of the serious rupture that sin can cause in human community. Was it "mere ritual" in its actual practice? The Old Testament prophets indicate that the answer to that question was sometimes "yes," but Christian liturgical practices, including the Eucharist, can also often become empty, formal acts.

For the contemporary Christian, then, this text is not about the contrast between Jewish and Christian systems of sacrifice, but about what it means to interpret the death of Christ in the images of Israel's sacrificial system. These images help us to think about Christ's death as a way of restoring the brokenness that human sin can cause in our lives. These images position Christ's death as the act of restitution that restores the balance in our lives with God, so that we can "worship the living God" (v. 14).

THIS TEXT IS NOT ABOUT THE CONTRAST BETWEEN JEWISH AND CHRISTIAN SYSTEMS OF SACRIFICE, BUT ABOUT WHAT IT MEANS TO INTERPRET THE DEATH OF CHRIST IN THE IMAGES OF ISRAEL'S SACRIFICIAL SYSTEM.

HEBREWS 11:39—12:3 (BCP)

See the comments on the second lesson, Hebrews 12:1-3, under Wednesday in Holy Week, pp. 256–57.

GOSPEL

JOHN 12:1-11

Interpreting the Text

Although the sequence of Gospel lessons for Holy Week positions this lesson from John after the entry into Jerusalem, that is not its location in the Fourth Gospel narrative. In John, the story of the anointing is the third of three interrelated stories that precede Jesus' Palm Sunday entry into Jerusalem; the other two are the raising of Lazarus (11:1-44) and the Sanhedrin's decision to kill Jesus (11:45-54). Together, these three stories function like a musical overture to the events of Holy Week. That is, when one listens carefully to these stories, one hears the first hints of themes that will be played out more fully in the passion narrative.

The opening verses of the anointing story already contain the many notes that are simultaneously sounded in this story. Verses 1-2 can be read as a simple description of the place and location of a dinner party, but they communicate much more than that. Passover, the time of Jesus' death, is near, and Jesus returns to Bethany, a town in close proximity to Jerusalem. Lazarus sits at table with him—and it was Jesus' raising of Lazarus from the dead that led to the Sanhedrin's official decision to kill him. The undercurrents of the threats to Jesus' life are everywhere.

The dinner party is interrupted by an astonishing act—Mary, one of Jesus' hosts, anoints Jesus' feet with perfume. She uses a pound of expensive perfume, so that the whole house is full of the fragrance (v. 3). The rest of the story is well known—Judas protests Mary's act, and Jesus silences Judas's protest—but perhaps not so well understood. Most readings of this story, in large part influenced by the story of an (other) anointing in Matthew and Mark (Mark 14:3-9; Matt. 26:1-13), take the exchange between Judas and Jesus as the key to the story. But the Fourth Evangelist goes out of his way in this story to tell the reader that Judas is an unreliable interpreter of events—Judas is the betrayer (v. 4) and a thief (v. 6). The key to the story is in Mary's act itself.

On the face of it, Mary's actions are a bit peculiar. In addition to the extravagant amount of perfume she uses, she wipes the perfume off of Jesus' feet with her hair as soon as she has anointed them. To many commentators, Mary's actions here make no sense and are explained as an echo of the woman's actions in the anointing story of Luke 7. Yet a careful reading of the wording of verse 3 suggests that Mary's wiping of Jesus' feet is actually central to the story. The verb for "wipe" here is the same verb used at 13:5 to describe Jesus' wiping of his disciples' feet at the footwashing. Mary does for Jesus what Jesus will soon do for his disciples; she acts in love toward Jesus as he will soon demonstrate for the rest of his disciples. In Mary's anointing and wiping of Jesus' feet, then, we hear the beginnings of a theme that will play more fully at the footwashing—extravagant love as an expression of discipleship and relationship with Jesus. (For a discussion of the footwashing in John 13, see my comments on the Gospel lesson for Holy Thursday, pp. 266–68.)

Responding to the Text

The story of Mary's anointing of Jesus is a stunning story that points toward some of the major themes of Holy Week—Jesus' impending death, Jesus' love for his disciples. It also looks beyond Holy Week to the newness that the events of Holy Week will make possible. The extravagance of Mary's love for Jesus, symbolized by both the amount and quality of the perfume, provides a model for faithful discipleship. In Mary's act, she holds nothing back in expressing her love for Jesus, her love for the man who brought her brother back from the dead, for the man who makes all things new. As Judas's protest suggests, such extravagant expressions often may seem to contradict what we take to be the norms of social behavior. Was it sensible or prudent for Mary to spend an entire year's salary on the perfume with which she anointed Jesus? No and no, but neither sensibility nor prudence is what is called for in one's response to Jesus' outpouring of his life for us in love. The only appropriate response to such an extravagant outpouring is an outpouring equally extravagant in its own way.

NEITHER SENSIBILITY NOR PRUDENCE IS WHAT IS CALLED FOR IN ONE'S RESPONSE TO JESUS' OUTPOURING OF HIS LIFE FOR US IN LOVE.

Mary expressed her love and discipleship toward Jesus in the symbolic act of his anointing. Later in the Gospel of John, Jesus will suggest another way to express this love and discipleship—by loving one another as he has loved us. When we love one another—and act toward one another in love—with the same extravagance that Mary embodies in her anointing of Jesus, then we begin to experience the fullness of life that the life, death, and resurrection of Jesus make possible. Mary held nothing back; Jesus held nothing back. It is our call and vocation as recipients of that extravagant gift to hold nothing back as well.

TUESDAY IN HOLY WEEK

MARCH 30, 1999

REVISED COMMON	EPISCOPAL (BCP)	ROMAN CATHOLIC
Isa. 49:1-7	Isa. 49:1-6	Isa. 49:1-6
Ps. 71:1-14	Ps. 71:1-12	Ps. 71:1-6, 15, 17
1 Cor. 1:18-31	1 Cor. 1:18-31	
John 12:20-36	John 12:37-38, 42-50 or Mark 11:15-19	John 13:21-23, 36-38

THE TEXTS FOR THE TUESDAY OF HOLY WEEK return to the themes of Passion Sunday, as each of the texts provides an interpretive angle on the suffering and death of Jesus. The Old Testament lesson is another Servant Song and focuses on the servant's vocation. Psalm 71 is a lament psalm spoken in a time of distress and persecution. The epistle lesson (1 Cor. 1:18-31) is one of Paul's most eloquent treatments of the meaning of the cross, and the Gospel lesson (John 12:20-36) also reflects on the meaning of Jesus' death.

FIRST READING
ISAIAH 49:1-7

Interpreting the Text

This lesson is the second of the four Servant Songs in Second Isaiah. (Introductory remarks on the Servant Songs in general and their place in Isaiah can be found in the comments on the Old Testament lesson for Palm/Passion Sunday, pp. 232–33.) Whereas in the first Servant Song (Isa. 42:1-4; see the Monday of Holy Week) God speaks and introduces the servant, in Isaiah 49:1-7 it is the servant himself who speaks. Yet importantly, the servant uses much of the same language used by God in the first Song. For example, Isaiah 42:4 ends with God's statement that the coastlands wait for the servant's teaching; Isaiah 49:1 opens with the servant's direct address to the coastlands. God introduces the servant with the words, "Here is my servant, whom I uphold, my chosen" (Isa. 42:1), and those terms reappear in the servant's words (Isa. 49:3, 4, 5, 7). That God and the servant use the same language to speak of the servant's mission communicates to the reader of Second Isaiah both the continuity between God's perception of the servant's work and the servant's self-perception, and the servant's acceptance of God's definition of his vocation.

This Servant Song divides into two parts. Verses 1-4 articulate the servant's acceptance of his call and vocation. These verses are very similar to prophetic call texts elsewhere in the Old Testament. In particular, verse 1 is an exact parallel to Jeremiah's description of his call (Jer. 1:5; see also Paul's description of his call in Gal. 1:15 and the announcement of John the Baptist's prophetic vocation before his birth in Luke 1:13-17). The focus on the servant's difficulties in enacting his vocation (v. 4a) and the emphasis on the role of the spoken word (v. 2) also recall other Old Testament prophets (for example, Jer. 1:9, 20:7-13; Amos 7:14).

The "and now" with which verse 5 begins introduces a surprising twist into the prophetic vocation of the servant. In verse 5, the servant himself articulates the assumption that his call falls within the conventional framework of one of Israel's prophets—to restore Israel ("to bring Jacob back to him"). At verse 6, however, the voice of God interrupts the servant's self-presentation, and the effect of this interruption is to dislodge this conventional understanding. The servant is not simply to restore Israel; that is "too light a thing." Rather, the servant's mission is one of universal salvation and restoration before God. Not only Israel, but all the nations are to be the recipients of the servant's light. The language of verse 7, which recalls Israel's situation in exile ("abhorred by the nations," "the slave of the rulers"), suggests that the reader should understand the servant as a corporate image. All of Israel will be testimony to the nations of who God is.

Responding to the Text

Perhaps one of the most suggestive aspects for Holy Week of this Servant Song is the way it pushes the church to think beyond privatized and sectarian understandings of God's redemption. As sacred and important as the servant's vocation toward Israel was, this text quite pointedly states that "it is too light a thing" for the servant's work to have only a parochial focus. This probably came as surprising and not altogether good news to many people in Israel, who felt that their "reward" after the sufferings of exile should be restoration to their privileged place as God's chosen people. Instead, that place is to be shared with all the nations, thus rendering "chosen" and "privilege" rather meaningless terms.

This same dynamic is apparent in Jesus' ministry. According to Luke, when Jesus preached at the Nazareth synagogue, the congregation was transfixed and amazed at the graciousness of the words of Jesus' sermon at first (Luke 4:20-22)—until he told them that the good news of God's redemption was to be offered to the Gentiles, too, not to Israel alone (4:23-27). At those words the congregation was "filled with rage" and tried to throw Jesus off a cliff (4:28-29)! It is often difficult to learn that God's graciousness is actually larger than our own, that God's definition of human family and community knows no bounds, because we somehow are afraid that this largesse will mean that we will not get our "fair share," that the "undeserving" will get what we have earned.

Holy Week is an important time to remember that we have not earned any privileged spot in God's plan for the redemption and reconciliation of the world. By virtue of Jesus' life and death we have a place in that plan, but we cannot call that reconciliation ours alone. That is indeed "too light a thing."

Responsive Reading
PSALM 71

Interpreting the Text

Psalm 71 is a psalm of individual lament, in which the petitioner places his or her life in God's hands and asks for refuge and rescue from troubles. When one reads all of Psalm 71, the rhythmic quality of its structure and contents is striking. In most lament psalms, the movement of the psalm is from plea to praise, from complaint to comfort (see Psalm 13 as a classic example of this form). In Psalm 71, however, the petitioner prays a prayer that does indeed begin with plea (vv. 1-4), but does not simply make a straightforward progression to praise and comfort. Instead, the petitioner interlaces his or her calls for help from God with stunning affirmations of the petitioner's lifelong experience of God's help (vv. 5-7, 14-17, 22-24). As a result, the reader of the psalm experiences the very thing about which the psalmist sings—the ongoing and dependable rescue and refuge of God. At every turn in life, the psalmist has known God to be "my rock and my fortress," and the movement of this psalm makes that experience available to others who share in this psalm.

Responding to the Text

Psalm 71 is placed in the Holy Week lectionary because it is a psalm of individual lament. Its cries for help and deliverance from enemies and the unjust allow the worshiping community to express the agony and anguish of Jesus' trials during Holy Week. But as the exegesis above suggests, this psalm is also a powerful and celebrative psalm of praise and trust, and this trust, too, needs to be voiced in Holy Week. God fails neither Jesus nor us in the struggles of this week.

1 CORINTHIANS 1:18-31 (RCL/BCP)

Interpreting the Text

The epistle lesson from First Corinthians lays out the heart of Paul's understanding of how the cross of Christ completely transforms our relationship with God and one another. The occasion that generates these words from Paul is a situation of quarreling and dissension in the Corinthian Christian community that threatens to tear the community apart (1:10-17). In response to this situation, Paul speaks directly to the Corinthian community about "the word of the cross" (1:18).

Although most contemporary Christians take language about the "word" or "message" of the cross for granted, that was not the case for Paul and his listeners. What Paul is attempting to do in these verses is to provide an explicit interpretive framework through which the Corinthians—relatively young Christians—could understand what difference the death of Jesus on a cross makes in their lives as individuals and more importantly, as a community. To do this, Paul begins with experiences and concepts that the Corinthians bring with them to their new lives as Christians, both Jews and Gentiles, and shows how the cross confounds those prior experiences and replaces them with something more compelling.

For Paul, the impact of the cross can be seen most clearly in the ways in which cultural understandings of wisdom and power have been subverted. Paul lays out two common ways of looking at the world apart from the cross, one defined by "signs," impressive demonstrations of power and might, and another defined by "wisdom," impressive displays of eloquence and knowledge. He challenges the Corinthians by saying in effect, "This may be what you are looking for, but this is all you are going to get from us: Christ crucified. If you insist on your old categories of wisdom and power, you are going to miss out on what is offered in the cross, and you will end up weak and foolish." By the world's conventions, how could death by a means reserved for criminals possibly be anything wise or powerful? It cannot, and that is precisely Paul's point. The death of Jesus on a cross does not fit the world's categories and standards; it shakes them to their very core. Life is not to be measured and assessed according to human standards and expectations, because life can come only from God. The world may call this foolishness, but "God's foolishness is wiser than human wisdom, and God's weakness is stronger than human strength" (1:25).

LIFE IS NOT TO BE MEASURED AND ASSESSED ACCORDING TO HUMAN STANDARDS AND EXPECTATIONS, BECAUSE LIFE CAN COME ONLY FROM GOD.

Responding to the Text

These words of Paul here are a radical call to a new way of inhabiting the world. Everything that we took as a measure of how the world is to be ordered before the cross has to be thrown away in favor of the new categories inaugurated by Jesus' death on a cross. Human self-sufficiency—that we can know enough, be strong enough, be rich enough to make our own way in the world—is rendered void by Paul's interpretation of the cross. When weakness is really strength and foolishness is really wisdom, then we have to start all over again and reorganize our priorities for human community. Paul asked the newly Christian Corinthians to try to shape their community life according to what they saw in the cross. Every situation had to be measured by this standard, "What are we affirming as strength here? What are we valuing as knowledge? Does what we are doing look like the cross?"

This text poses the same questions to us today, and perhaps at no time more acutely than at Holy Week. We have the cross of Jesus in front of us, and we are called to ask ourselves the hard questions about the expectations and categories according to which we live. Do we allow ourselves to be lulled into the path of least resistance and accept the world's definitions of wisdom and strength? Or do we take the harder path and insist on the foolishness and weakness of the cross?

Gospel
JOHN 12:20-36 (RCL)

Interpreting the Text

The Gospel lesson is a series of teachings in which Jesus interprets the significance of his own death. The specific occasion that evokes these teachings is the desire of "some Greeks" to see Jesus (vv. 20-21). The arrival of these Greeks, symbolic of the world outside of Jerusalem and Judea, confirms the Pharisees' unconscious prophecy of 12:19 ("Look, the world has gone after him!"). Yet their arrival also marks a turn in Jesus' ministry. In the Old Testament, the spread of God's promises to the Gentile world was one of the images of the arrival of God's new age (for example, Isa. 56:6-8; 60:1-14). The arrival of the Greeks testifies to the eschatological significance of Jesus' death. Jesus' death, and all that follows from it, will bring in God's promised new age.

Jesus uses three different metaphors to speak about his death in this passage. These metaphors are unique to the Gospel of John, and the significance of Jesus' words will be lost if these distinctive expressions are not understood. First, Jesus speaks of "the hour" (vv. 23, 27). In John, Jesus' "hour" refers to the critical moment of his death, resurrection, and ascension (see 2:4; 7:30; 8:20; 13:1; 17:1). Second, "glorification" (vv. 23, 27, 28) is another Johannine idiom to refer to Jesus' death, resurrection, and ascension. The moment of glorification is the moment when God's glory will be revealed in Jesus, that is, when Jesus will reveal the identity and character of God most fully. For John, that moment is the inseparable constellation of events that begins with the crucifixion and ends with the ascension. The arrival of the hour in which the Son of Man will be glorified, then, means the arrival of the hour in which Jesus will die (vv. 23, 27-28), and the final acts of his mission in the world will be played out.

The third metaphor is the expression "lifted up" (v. 32). This expression occurs three times in John as a way of speaking of the crucifixion (see also 3:14; 8:28). The verb *lift up* has a double meaning. In addition to meaning "to lift up physically" (as on the cross), it also means "to exalt" and thus is another way of speaking of Jesus' death on the cross as the beginning of the moment of glorification. The arrival of the hour of glorification and lifting up is the arrival of the moment when God's new age, God's promises for God's people, come to fulfillment.

The arrival of the moment of eschatological possibility is also the arrival of the moment of eschatological reckoning. In these teachings of Jesus, therefore, the focus on Jesus' death is balanced by a focus on people's response to Jesus' death (vv. 25-26, 32, 35-36). The world will be judged in its response to Jesus' hour. As the universal language of verse 32 ("all people") makes clear, there are no limits on the offer of new possibilities. The only limits are those people set for themselves in their response.[1]

Responding to the Text

The location of this lesson in the Holy Week lectionary mirrors its location in the Fourth Gospel narrative—it immediately follows Jesus' Palm Sunday entry into Jerusalem (12:12-19) and precedes Jesus' final meal with his disciples (John 13-17). The Holy Week lectionary thus does the same thing for the worshiping community as the Fourth Evangelist does for the Gospel reader—provides an opportunity for explicit reflection on the meaning of the death of Jesus as a prelude to telling that pivotal story.

This lesson pushes us to the heart of the most basic and most difficult claim of Holy Week—that Jesus' death is a source of new life for us. The language of growth in 12:24 underscores this link between death and life, as does the language about loving and hating life in verses 25-26. The most direct statement of this claim comes in 12:32, when Jesus says that when he dies on the cross, he "will draw all people to myself." But how can death be the source of life? It is this seemingly contradictory and impossible claim with which the Christian church is called to grapple, Holy Week after Holy Week.

John 12:20-36 offers a slightly different perspective on this claim than that with which Christians may be most familiar. It does not speak of Jesus' death as a sacrifice (in contrast, for example, to the author of Hebrews; see epistle commentary for the Monday of Holy Week, pp. 242-43). Instead, John 12:20-36 points to Jesus' death as a source of new life because in it, we have the boldest expression of God's and Jesus' love for one another and the world and of the power of God's promises. In death, Jesus is not a sacrificial victim, but the grain of wheat that dies to bring forth fruit (12:24). Jesus' death is an act of abundant giving of life in love (see especially John 10:16-18).

Jesus' death is a source of new life because it opens up for us a new way of knowing God, a way based in the limitlessness of love and the transformative power of community grounded in that love. The faith community consists of those who redefine the meaning of life on the basis of Jesus' death (12:24-26). Life is now defined and shaped by Jesus' love—and it is the community's responsibility to show forth that love to the world (see John 13:34-35). Life can come from death, then, because death is rendered powerless in the face of the love of God. That is what Jesus means in this text when he says that "now the ruler of this world will be driven out" (v. 32). Jesus' death on the cross shows the church the power of the love of God; with this love, there are no limits that cannot be defeated, no impossibilities.

JOHN 12:37-38, 42-50 (BCP)

Interpreting the Text

The Gospel lesson in the Episcopal lectionary draws from John 12:37-50, the epilogue to Jesus' public ministry. Verses 37-38 are part of the Fourth Evangelist's commentary on the effects of Jesus' public ministry; verses 44-50 are a summary discourse by Jesus.

The two parts of this passage work together to place before the Gospel reader the need to make a faith decision about Jesus. The Evangelist's commentary reflects on a dilemma experienced by many early Christians: How can one explain that Jesus' presence did not bring all people to faith? Verse 38 addresses that dilemma through the lens of the servant song of Isaiah 53 (see the Old Testament lesson for Good Friday).

The discourse by Jesus in verses 44-50 takes another approach to the question of faith and belief. It provides a summary of the basic theological themes of Jesus' public ministry in John—that Jesus makes God known (v. 44) and that Jesus says and does nothing on his own but speaks the words that God has given him to say (vv. 49-50). The discourse also restates one of the central christological claims of the Gospel: Jesus has come into the world as the light of the world in order to save the world (v. 46). It also confronts the reader with the paradoxical nature of judgment in John: Jesus comes not to judge, but to save, but his presence will evoke judgment by the way that people respond to him (vv. 47-48).

Responding to the Text

This Gospel lesson is unsettling to encounter in Holy Week, because we want to turn all our attention to the events of Jesus' life and death, but this lesson forces us to examine ourselves. Instead of allowing us to lose ourselves in the reexperience of the events of Jesus' passion, this lesson from John asks us instead whether we give our assent to the revelation of God in Jesus. Instead of allowing us to lose ourselves in story, this lesson pushes us to think about what the events of the story mean. It is not enough to walk the streets of Jerusalem with Jesus this week; this lesson calls us to claim our belief that we do come to know God in Jesus. Do we believe in Jesus as the incarnate Word of God or not? The question that this lesson puts before us is both that simple and that stark. It is a question that echoes behind all the events of Holy Week.

JOHN 13:21-23, 36, 38 (RC)

See the Gospel for Wednesday in Holy Week, pp. 258-59.

WEDNESDAY IN HOLY WEEK

MARCH 31, 1999

REVISED COMMON	EPISCOPAL (BCP)	ROMAN CATHOLIC
Isa. 50:4-9a	Isa. 50:4-9a	Isa. 50:4-9
Psalm 70	Ps. 69:7-15, 22-23	Ps. 69:8-19, 21-22, 31, 33-34
Heb. 12:1-3	Heb. 9:11-15, 24-28	
John 13:21-32	John 13:21-35 or Matt. 26:1-5, 14-25	Matt. 26:14-25

THE TEXTS FOR THE WEDNESDAY OF HOLY WEEK bring the worshiping community closer to Jesus' betrayal and death. The Gospel lesson, which focuses on Judas, is an uncomfortable reminder of the ease with which betrayal and evil can enter into our relationships with one another and with God. Yet this message of human betrayal is balanced in the other lessons by affirmations of the trustworthiness of God and Jesus. The church thus is led to contemplate the contrast between human infidelity and divine fidelity.

FIRST READING
ISAIAH 50:4-9a

This Old Testament lesson (the third of the Servant Songs from Second Isaiah) is also the Old Testament lesson for Palm/Passion Sunday. *See my comments on pp. 232–33.*

RESPONSIVE READING
PSALM 70 (RCL)

Interpreting the Text

Psalm 70 is a brief personal lament psalm. Its form and content recall many other lament psalms. More specifically, it is almost identical to Psalm

40:13-17, and scholars are divided in their opinion over which of these two psalms borrowed from the other.

Psalm 70:1 opens with a prayer for God's help and deliverance, and verse 5 closes the psalm with the explicit affirmation that God is "my help and my deliverer." In between this frame, the psalmist contrasts two types of people—the psalmist's enemies, who seek his life and mock him (vv. 2-3), and those who seek God and rejoice in God (v. 4). The psalmist's opening and closing affirmations about God's deliverance indicate that the psalmist is in the latter group. As with Psalm 71 (see my comments for Tuesday of Holy Week, p. 248), the structure of this psalm reinforces its contents—that God is the source of help and deliverance.

Responding to the Text

Psalm 70 expresses in condensed form the dynamics of the worshipper's life with God during Holy Week. It models a powerful form of prayer, in which both the petitioner's needs in a situation of extreme hardship and duress, and the petitioner's unshakable faith in God even in this extreme situation are brought before God. One can imagine Jesus praying such a prayer on the Wednesday of his own Holy Week, but perhaps more importantly, this prayer reminds the community that authentic religious life is not simply a cheery affirmation of God's goodness, but involves trusting God enough that one can honestly and openly ask for help in times of distress.

PSALM 69 (RC/BCP)

Interpreting the Text

Like Psalm 70, Psalm 69 is a personal lament psalm that prays for deliverance from enemies. Psalm 69 is one of the longest lament psalms in the psalter, and consists of two main parts: verses 1-29, the psalmist's petitions and complaints, and verses 30-36, the psalmist's turn to praise of God. The Episcopal lectionary includes only verses from the first section; the Roman Catholic lectionary adds a few verses from the thanksgiving section.

Responding to the Text

Of all the verses of this long psalm, verse 21 is probably most well known to Christian readers, as it is quoted in the crucifixion narratives of all four Gospels (Matt. 27:34; Mark 15:36; Luke 23:36; John 19:29). Its use in all the Gospels suggests that the early Christians found Psalm 69 to be a helpful lens through which to interpret the death of Jesus (note also Paul's use of Ps. 69:22-

23 in Romans 11:9). The psalmist's situation of suffering is narrated in vivid detail and rich metaphors in Psalm 69, which gave the early Christians a language that they could use to tell their own foundational story of distress and suffering. Psalm 69 provided confirmation to these first believers that Jesus' death on the cross was not a rupture in the fabric of their relationship with God, but had a place in that story. The use of this psalm in the Holy Week lectionary reinforces for contemporary believers what it taught the first Christians—God is present in the depths of this week.

Second Reading
HEBREWS 12:1-3 (RCL)

Interpreting the Text

The epistle lesson from Hebrews is a transitional section in the Letter to the Hebrews, as the "therefore" with which verse 1 begins suggests. It draws on what precedes, the list of the faithful in Hebrews 11, and at the same time moves from the past to the present and the future by making explicit the way in which that "old" story is in fact our own story. At the center of this transition is Jesus, "the pioneer and perfecter of our faith" (v. 2).

Verse 1 contains one of the most exquisite metaphors for Christian community found anywhere in scripture, "since we are surrounded by so great a cloud of witnesses." The image is irresistibly compelling: the lives and testimony of the faithful—Abraham (Heb. 11:17), Isaac (11:20), Jacob (11:21), Joseph (11:22), Moses (11:23-29), Joshua (11:30), Rahab (11:31), prophets and kings (11:32-34), and the unnamed host (11:35-40)—are not just names and stories from the past, recorded for our edification. Rather, this myriad of heroes and heroines of the faith form the very air we breathe and the very atmosphere in which we move. They are a cloud that surrounds us, and even when their forms are not clearly discernible, they are there, supporting us and making our lives possible. This is confirmed by the rhetorical structure of verse 1; the author of Hebrews positions the "cloud of witnesses" as the foundation upon which his first exhortation is based. He can exhort his community to lay aside every weight and to run the race with perseverance because the very air that fills their lungs as they run is permeated with the strong testimony of the faithful.

At the center of that cloud stands Jesus. The story of the cross, which the author summarizes in verse 2, is the crowning example of the faith to which the author calls his community. In many ways, the language of verse 2 recalls the Christ hymn of Philippians 2:6-11 (see comments at Palm/Passion Sunday). Jesus disregarded the shame of the cross (cf. Phil. 2:6-8) because he had confidence in God's future ("for the sake of the joy that was set before him"). Verse 2 celebrates Jesus' faithfulness to the unseen promises of God (see Heb. 11:1-3), and it is that faithfulness that results in his exaltation (cf. Phil. 2:9-11).

By naming Jesus as the "pioneer and perfecter of our faith," the author of Hebrews points to Jesus as the one who opens the way from the past into the community's own present and future. Jesus went before the community into the region shaped and claimed by God's promises, and the community can follow in confidence. The race may seem long, and the road strewn with pitfalls, but because of Jesus and the cloud of witnesses in which he takes his place, the community need not "grow weary or lose heart" (v. 3).

Responding to the Text

There could be no more apt lesson for Holy Week than this epistle text from Hebrews. With memorable metaphors and economy of expression, this text helps us to see how our own lives belong to the ongoing story of Christian faith. We never stand before God alone, even in the moments of most extreme and isolating suffering and hardship, but always stand surrounded by a cloud of witnesses. Those witnesses extend across time and space; they are our ancestors in the faith and they are our contemporary colleagues in the faith. We may not always be able to call the names of all these witnesses, but they are always there with us and we with them. This is what it means to live in a faith community.

IN ENDURING THE SHAME AND AGONY OF THE CROSS, JESUS BECAME COMPLETELY ONE WITH US, BECAUSE OUR LIVES, TOO, ARE MARKED BY SEEMINGLY UNENDURABLE AGONIES.

At the center of these witnesses is Jesus, and it is to him in particular that the author of Hebrews directs our attention ("looking to Jesus," v. 2; "consider him," v. 3). His death on the cross shows us the unlimited power of faith. Even the shame of the cross pales before the power of faith in God's promises for the future. This faith, those promises, and that future should form the heart of our Holy Week reflections. In enduring the shame and agony of the cross, Jesus became completely one with us, because our lives, too, are marked by seemingly unendurable agonies. In looking to him as pioneer and perfecter of our faith, we can in turn become completely one with him, because his strength can become our strength, his faith and hope our faith and hope.

HEBREWS 9:11-15, 24-28 (BCP)

See pp. 242–43, the Second Reading for Monday in Holy Week.

GOSPEL

JOHN 13:21-35 (RCL/BCP)

Interpreting the Text

The Gospel lesson narrates Jesus' final prediction in John of his betrayal by Judas (see also 6:64, 71; 12:4; 13:2, 11). The scene occurs in the context of Jesus' washing of his disciples' feet (13:1-20) and his teachings to them on the meaning of love and community (13:1—16:33). This context is crucial to grasping the full pathos of this scene, because it reinforces that Jesus is not betrayed by a stranger, but by one of his closest followers.

The core of this scene, Jesus' announcement of his betrayal by one of his own, coupled with his disciples' response, is recounted at the Last Supper scene in all of the four Gospels (see also Matt. 26:21-25; Mark 14:18-21; Luke 22:21-23). The questioning of Jesus by his disciples after his announcement of betrayal is narrated in much more detail in John than in the other Gospels. The two disciples who play the pivotal role in the questioning are Peter and the "disciple whom Jesus loved." This latter disciple makes his first appearance in the Fourth Gospel here and will be a main character throughout the story of the events that surround Jesus' death (19:26-27; 20:2-10). He is never named, but instead is identified always and only by the nature of his relationship to Jesus.

THE REAL PLAYERS HERE ARE JESUS AND THE DEVIL, NOT JESUS AND JUDAS, AND THE REAL STRUGGLE HERE IS BETWEEN GOOD AND EVIL, BETWEEN THAT WHICH IS OF GOD AND THAT WHICH IS OPPOSED TO GOD.

The heart of this story occurs in the exchange between Jesus and Judas in verses 26-30. Jesus' words and actions reinforce that the betrayer is one of Jesus' intimates; he is one to whom Jesus offers food and hospitality. The reference to Satan in verse 27 (see also 13:2) reminds the reader that Judas's betrayal of Jesus is not simply the result of a disagreement among friends. Rather, the real players here are Jesus and the devil, not Jesus and Judas, and the real struggle here is between good and evil, between that which is of God and that which is opposed to God. That it is Judas who enacts the evil, however, is a crucial reminder that the seemingly smallest gestures can often embody great evil.

After Judas leaves the meal, the evangelist reports "And it was night" (v. 30). This notation has a much more important function than simply telling the reader what time of day it is. One of the core elements of Jesus' teaching throughout John has been that he is the light of the world (8:12; 9:5), and that day and light mark the presence of his work in the world (9:4; 11:10; 12:35-36). Judas's actions of betrayal usher in the time that brings Jesus' presence as the light of the world to an end. The lectionary's inclusion of verses 31-32 in this unit makes this point especially clear. A reference to Judas's departure sets up Jesus' announcement to his remaining disciples that "Now the Son of Man has been glorified, and God has been glorified in him" (v. 31). The move to the new and final part of the story is underway; the time for Jesus' death and his ultimate revelation of God to the world has arrived. (For a discussion of "glorification" as a metaphor for Jesus' death, resurrection, and ascension in John, see comments on John 12:20-36 for Tuesday in Holy Week, pp. 250–51. For Responding to the Text, see below under Matt. 26:1-5, 14-25.)

MATTHEW 26:1-5, 14-25 (RC/BCP)

Interpreting the Text

The Matthean version of this betrayal story provides the Gospel lesson for the Roman Catholic lectionary and an alternate Gospel lesson for the Episcopal lectionary. The story is constructed quite differently in Matthew than in John. For John, the story of the betrayal has two pivotal elements: (1) the intimacy of the relationship between Jesus and Judas, and (2) the cosmic dimension to the betrayal, expressed in the references to Satan. Matthew, in contrast, narrates the betrayal much more as a business transaction between Judas and the Pharisees. It is not the direct expression of evil that leads to the betrayal, but Judas's greed and opportunism (Matt. 26:14-16). Indeed, at the supper table in Matthew's story, Judas responds to Jesus' words about the betrayer with an opportunistic act of dissembling (26:25). He is a cowardly and untrustworthy man, but not explicitly evil in Matthew. Because of the way Matthew portrays Judas, it is possible for him later to include a story in which Judas repents of his actions (Matt. 27:3-10). No similar repentance is possible in John, because the focus is on the bigger struggle in which Judas is only one player. In Matthew, then, the pathos of the betrayal comes from its very ordinariness. For the right price, anything is possible.

Responding to the Text

The Gospel lesson of the announcement of Judas's betrayal of Jesus brings the worshiping community to one of the lowest points in the storytelling of the faith. The stories in Matthew and John eat away at the smug self-confidence any of us may have that we could never betray Jesus, but they do so in quite different ways.

By ascribing a clearly identifiable motive to Judas's betrayal—greed and opportunism, Matthew at least suggests a way in which Judas's actions make sense. But that sense is not at all reassuring to the contemporary believer, because we are all too well aware that we also may have a price. As hackneyed and moralistic as this sentiment may appear in contemporary North American culture, it nonetheless takes on new weight when reflected upon in the light of the Judas story. How often do we sell Jesus out for not much more than Judas's thirty pieces of silver? How often is our own gain and well-being more attractive than the acts of faithfulness and courage it may take to go all the way down the road with Jesus? The ordinariness of Judas's act is the key to its insidiousness. Judas was not a criminal mastermind; he was an ordinary man who saw what he took to be an easy—and self-enhancing—way out.

If we stir uncomfortably in our pews when we hear again the story of Judas, it may be because it asks us to clarify our own choices. Will we choose the way of evil and death, or will we embrace what Jesus gives us?

The story of Judas in John haunts us in a different and perhaps even more disturbing way. John does not give the reader a motive for Judas's betrayal. The only details about Judas that have any relevance for the Fourth Gospel are those that pertain to his relationship with Jesus. The reader is forced to grapple with what it means that one of Jesus' intimates betrayed him. Because no ulterior motives are ascribed to Judas's betrayal of Jesus, the modern reader is forced to contemplate the reality of evil in the world. Greed or opportunism seems like an attractive alternative to what the Fourth Evangelist asks the reader to accept; that in Judas's betrayal we see the human surrender to the power of evil.

The power of evil will not win in the larger story. Jesus' victory over death in the resurrection defeats the power of evil (14:30; 16:33), but that does not take away the sting of the story of Judas. Judas, one of Jesus' closest associates, chose to side with evil and death, even when he was within arm's reach of the one who offered fullness of life. If we stir uncomfortably in our pews when we hear again the story of Judas, it may be because it asks us to clarify our own choices. Will we choose the way of evil and death, or will we embrace what Jesus gives us?

MAUNDY THURSDAY
HOLY THURSDAY

April 1, 1999

Revised Common	Episcopal (BCP)	Roman Catholic
Exod. 12:1-4, (5-10), 11-14	Exod. 12:1-14a	Exod. 12:1-8, 11-14
Ps. 116:1-2, 12-19	Ps. 78:14-20, 23-25	Ps. 116:12-13, 15-18
1 Cor. 11:23-26	1 Cor. 11:23-26, (27-32)	1 Cor. 11:23-26
John 13:1-17, 31b-35	John 13:1-15 or Luke 22:14-30	John 13:1-15

Maundy Thursday is the beginning of the liturgical celebration known as the "Easter Triduum," the three days of Maundy Thursday, Good Friday, and Holy Saturday Vigil. These are the days in which the church moves with Jesus through the story of his passion and resurrection. The worshiping community will move together from the warm intimacy of a supper table to the dark loneliness of a tomb. The texts for Maundy Thursday begin this journey by focusing on three communal celebrations—the Passover meal (the Old Testament lesson); the eucharistic meal (the epistle lesson); and the footwashing (the Gospel lesson).

First Reading
EXODUS 12:1-14

Interpreting the Text

The Old Testament lesson for Maundy Thursday relates the instructions for the institution of the festival of Passover. The narrative context of this text is important: It occurs as Israel's days of slavery in Egypt are moving toward their dramatic conclusion. More specifically, the Passover narrative (12:1-28) serves as an interlude between the announcement of the tenth and final plague (Exod. 11:1-10) and its enactment (12:29-32). In this interlude, the character of the Exodus narrative shifts from storytelling to liturgical instruction. Indeed, the liturgical instructions for the feast of Passover precede the recounting of the event that the festival will now commemorate. The liturgical instructions, framed as God's words to Moses and Aaron (v. 1), are a bold reminder that deliverance from Egypt is not simply about the past, but is always about the present identity of the community who tells this story.

Once the significance of the context of the Passover instructions is recognized, the instructions themselves are fairly straightforward. Verses 2-11 provide detailed and precise instructions for how the lamb, the centerpiece of the feast, is to be prepared and eaten. The Passover is explicitly presented as a feast of the community ("the whole congregation"). Where having one's own lamb would be a financial hardship for a small household, households should combine (vv. 2-4). The instructions for selecting and killing the lamb are quite specific (vv. 5-6). The blood of the slaughtered lamb is to be smeared on the lintels and doorposts (v. 7); the household is to eat the roasted lamb (vv. 8-9); and what cannot be eaten in the evening is to be destroyed rather than allowed to rot. The meal is to be eaten "hurriedly," by people dressed and ready for travel (v. 11).

Verses 12-13 give the explanation for these rituals. The night of the feast is the evening of the "passover of the Lord," in which the tenth plague, the destruction of the firstborn, will be executed. The blood on the houses is a sign to God that his own people are within. It is the night of the boldest demonstration of God's power over Egypt's gods and protection of his own people.

The instruction in verse 14 points explicitly from the present that is still underway in the Exodus narrative (the deliverance of Israel) to the future in which the worshiping community now lives. This statement, coupled with verses 12-13, anticipates the outcome of the deliverance story before it is completed.

Responding to the Text

The importance of this lesson as a reading for Maundy Thursday cannot be overstated. First, there is the traditional connection between the celebration of the Passover and the events of Holy Week. In the Synoptic Gospels, the last meal that Jesus eats with his disciples is the Passover meal, and it is crucial that Christians carry the associations and significance of this meal into our celebration of Maundy Thursday. The Passover feast, as 12:14 makes explicit, is a day of remembrance, in which the worshiping congregation remembers God's deliverance of them from slavery. The feast brings to active memory both their old life as slaves (that they must eat the lamb in haste) and their new life as liberated people of God. It is as this people that Jesus and his disciples gathered to celebrate the Passover together, and this affirmation of God's deliverance is an essential part of the Maundy Thursday observance.

Second, this text reminds the worshiping community of the power of liturgy to shape identity and to keep the "old stories" of the faith current. Israel was not instructed simply to retell one another the story of the Passover; rather, it was instructed to relive with one another their experience as a people delivered by God. It is in the practice of the faith stories, as well as the retelling, that the community is nurtured in its identity. As Christians on Maundy Thursday, we do not simply tell ourselves the stories of this night, but we, too, live out these stories.

Third, what may be most overwhelming about this Passover narrative is its affirmations about the victory of God in advance of that victory. The community is told how to celebrate the night of God's passing over before the passing over has even happened. The Passover liturgy, then, is a deeply eschatological text in which confidence in God's future, even when that future is not visible in the present moment, is the defining reality for the present. This, too, speaks powerfully to the Maundy Thursday liturgy. Even at the moment of betrayal, when the present appears bleak and dark, we announce through our participation in this liturgy our confidence in God's future.

Responsive Reading
PSALM 116 (RCL/RC)

Interpreting the Text

Psalm 116 is a thanksgiving psalm; note the words of love and devotion to the Lord with which the psalm begins (vv. 1-2). The occasion that prompts the thanksgiving seems to have been the psalmist's recovery from a life-threatening illness (vv. 3-11), but the psalm moves beyond that private circumstance to become a prayer of community thanksgiving. Verses 12-19 make quite explicit that the setting for the recital of this psalm is in the community's worship in the Jerusalem temple (vv. 13, 14, 17-19).

This psalm, along with Psalms 113–118, formed a separate hymnal that was incorporated into the Passover liturgy at a very early date. This psalm was sung in the temple when the Passover lambs were slaughtered by the priests (see Exod. 12:6), and was also part of the family celebrations around the Passover dinner table. Perhaps because of the reference to the cup of salvation in verse 13, it was sung as a blessing over the fourth cup of wine.

Responding to the Text

In reading Psalm 116 on Maundy Thursday, the Christian worshiping community places itself in continuity with one of Judaism's most ancient

Passover traditions. If one engages in an act of liturgical imagination, one can envision Jesus and his disciples sitting at the Passover table, singing this psalm together. This psalm, with its gratitude for God's deliverance and its recognition of the thanks and praise that are to be returned to God, reminds the Christian church of the character and identity of the God who is at the center of its life in these holy days. It also reminds the Christian church that it stands in a long line of worshiping communities who give thanks to and who owe their identity to this God.

PSALM 78 (BCP)

Psalm 78 is a historical psalm that recites the crucial moments in Israel's life with God. The verses selected for the Maundy Thursday reading retell parts of the Exodus story, in particular the story of Israel's sojourn in the wilderness (vv. 14-20) and God's gracious feeding of the people with manna (vv. 23-25). The use of this reading in the Maundy Thursday liturgy adds an image of another communal meal to that of the Passover and the Eucharist, and so provides yet another example of God's care and deliverance.

SECOND READING
1 CORINTHIANS 11:23-26

Interpreting the Text

The epistle lesson is Paul's recounting of the institution of the Lord's Supper. This is the oldest version of the institution recorded in the New Testament, since Paul's epistle to the Corinthians antedates the written accounts of the Synoptic Gospels (Matt. 26:26-29; Mark 14:22-25; Luke 22:14-20) by several decades. In the Gospels, the account of the institution of the Eucharist is part of the ongoing storytelling of the events of Jesus' last days. In First Corinthians, by contrast, Paul tells the story of the Lord's Supper in an attempt to correct an abuse of the practice in the Corinthian church. The celebration of the Lord's Supper, which seems to have occurred every time the community gathered for worship (vv. 17-18), has become an occasion for community division and separation, rather than unity. Since the Lord's Supper was eaten as part of a meal, it appears that the rich members of the Corinthian church were eating first and more abundantly than the poorer members of the church (vv. 21-22). As Paul states quite directly, this communal gathering was no longer really the Lord's Supper (v. 20).

Paul attempts to correct this abuse by reminding the Corinthians of the sacredness of the traditions they have received and of the ritual in which they participate. The language of verse 23a ("received from the Lord," "handed on") reinforces that the celebration of the Lord's Supper stems from Jesus himself, and that Paul and the Corinthians stand as recipients of that tradition. Verses 23b–25 recite the story of the institution, locating it in the events of Jesus' passion ("on the night when he was betrayed") and highlighting the communal dimensions of the meal and its inseparable connections to Jesus' life and death. Verse 26 provides Paul's commentary on the significance of the Eucharist by pointing toward the Eucharist's role in shaping the community's vision of the future.

Responding to the Text

Perhaps most striking in the context of the Maundy Thursday readings are the theological and liturgical similarities between these Pauline liturgical instructions and those in Exodus 12. In both texts, the community's celebration is explicitly and absolutely linked with a particular event in the past, and the shape of the liturgical celebration derives from that event. The liturgical celebration is not simply a rehashing of that "old" event, however, but is the creation of something new. Both the Exodus instructions and those in 1 Corinthians emphasize the pivotal role of remembrance to create something new by actively bringing the past into the present (Exod. 12:14; 1 Cor. 11:24, 25). The community becomes who it is through its participation in this liturgical act of remembrance, whether that be Passover or the Lord's Supper. That is why the Corinthians' abuse of the Lord's Supper is so contemptible to Paul—the community's very identity is at risk because it does not honor the liturgical practice that makes it one with its past.

THE CELEBRATION OF THE LORD'S SUPPER, LIKE THAT OF THE PASSOVER, POINTS THE WORSHIPING COMMUNITY TOWARD ITS HOPES FOR THE FUTURE AS CLEARLY AS IT GROUNDS THE COMMUNITY IN THE DECISIVE EVENTS OF ITS PAST.

Yet the Passover and eucharistic instructions do not look only to the relationship between the past and the present. They both also look to the future. The eschatological dimension of the Passover instructions was noted above, and there is a comparable dimension to Paul's eucharistic instructions. Just as Exodus 12:14 expresses confidence in God's victory before the event, 1 Corinthians 11:26 expresses confidence in God's ultimate victory before the event. The Lord's Supper is indeed a remembrance of the night of betrayal and of Jesus' death, but it is also an announcement of Jesus' future coming, of a time when the world will live out the victory of God that is revealed in the death and resurrection of Jesus. The celebration of the Lord's Supper, like that of the

Passover, points the worshiping community toward its hopes for the future as clearly as it grounds the community in the decisive events of its past. "For as often as you eat this bread and drink this cup," Paul writes; "throughout your generations you shall observe it as a perpetual ordinance," Exodus 12:14 declares. The continuity of the liturgical celebrations is a sign of the community's unwavering faith in God and hope in God's future.

Gospel

JOHN 13:1-17, 31b-35

Interpreting the Text

What is most obviously striking about the Johannine account of Jesus' last meal with his disciples is that there is no account of the institution of the Lord's Supper. It is critically important that the preacher respect the absence of this account from the Johannine narrative and resist the temptation to harmonize the Gospel accounts, that is, to tell the story of Jesus' last meal with his disciples as if there were both a eucharistic meal and a footwashing. This can be a difficult balancing act, given the liturgical celebrations of Maundy Thursday that often include both a Eucharist and a footwashing, but the church loses an important perspective on the night of Jesus' betrayal if the distinctiveness of the Johannine portrait is muted.

Two overview observations can be made. First, the Gospel of John does contain an account of the eucharistic meal and its implications for the ongoing life of the Christian community—but it is lodged in the discourse that follows the feeding miracle in John 6, not in the Holy Week narrative. Such freedom in the handling of traditions is a regular trait of the Gospel of John (cf. the location of the cleansing of the temple narrative at the beginning of Jesus' ministry in John 2:13-22 rather than during Holy Week). For the Fourth Evangelist, the Eucharist belongs as much to the incarnation and life of Jesus as it does exclusively to his death, and so he presents the eucharistic traditions in a way that fits with his understanding of the cruciality of the incarnation and the pervasive sacramentality of the believer's life with Jesus.[2] Second, by placing the footwashing at the center of Jesus' last meal with his disciples, the Fourth Evangelist has chosen to narrate the farewell meal in a way that highlights his understanding of the events of Jesus' hour as the full expression of Jesus' love.

The story of the footwashing divides into two parts: verses 1-11, which narrate the footwashing; and verses 12-20, which contain a discourse by Jesus on service. John 13:1 introduces Jesus' hour, and hence the larger narrative of the events of Jesus' death, resurrection, and ascension (see comments on John 12 lesson for the Tuesday of Holy Week), but it also introduces the specific events of the Last Supper. Perhaps most important in this introduction is the notation that Jesus loved his disciples "to the end." Jesus' love for his own will be demonstrated in the footwashing, but it will receive its full and final expression in his gift of his life (15:13).

Verses 2-3 introduce the footwashing; verses 4-5 narrate the footwashing proper. In the ancient Mediterranean world, footwashing was a way of welcoming one's guests. The footwashing was normally performed by the guests themselves, or by servants at the behest of the host, so that footwashing as service is closely linked with footwashing as hospitality. When Jesus washes his disciples' feet, he combines the roles of servant and host.

The Fourth Evangelist provides two different, but related, interpretations of the meaning of the footwashing. The interpretation with which the contemporary church is most familiar is the second interpretation (vv. 12–17) that presents the footwashing as an act of service to be imitated by the disciples. But the first interpretation (vv. 8b–10), in which Jesus speaks of the footwashing as an act that the disciples are to receive from Jesus, needs to be recognized and reclaimed by the church.

THE CHURCH LOSES AN IMPORTANT PERSPECTIVE ON THE NIGHT OF JESUS' BETRAYAL IF THE DISTINCTIVENESS OF THE JOHANNINE PORTRAIT IS MUTED.

In verse 8 Jesus' washing of Peter's feet is described as a necessary condition for Peter's "share" with Jesus. To have a "share" with Jesus is to have fellowship with Jesus, to participate fully in Jesus' life. The footwashing draws the disciple into the love that marks God and Jesus' relationship to one another and to the world (3:16, 35; 14:23, 31; 17:23, 24, 26). The footwashing unites the believer with Jesus and marks the believer as one of Jesus' own. To have Jesus wash one's feet is to receive from Jesus an act of hospitality that decisively alters one's relationship to Jesus and, through Jesus, to God.

Both interpretations of the footwashing are necessary to understand fully Jesus' love commandment in 13:31-35. These words are not simply words about love as service, but they are words about love as the embodied expression of one's relationship with God and Jesus. The love of which Jesus speaks in these verses is not a generalized emotion, but is a love that receives a very specific content from Jesus' gift of his own life in love.

As noted above, there is a tendency in contemporary church appropriation of the footwashing narrative to begin and end one's interpretation of this text with verses 12-17. That is, in most conversations about this text within the church, the footwashing is held up as an example of humble service that those who follow Jesus are called to imitate. While there is no question that John 13:12-17 does present the footwashing as a model for communal service, those verses are one piece of a much larger picture.

The call to service in this text cannot be separated from the call to participation with Jesus in verses 1-11. One can follow Jesus' example (v. 15) only if one has already experienced Jesus' loving service for oneself. This is critically important for the church to remember at every juncture in its life, but acutely so during Holy Week. In 13:1-11, Jesus asks nothing of the disciples other than that they place themselves completely in his hands (cf. 13:3), that they allow their relationship with him to be defined by God's love and God's love alone. Peter's initial responses (vv. 6, 8) and the mention of Judas's betrayal in this story (vv. 2, 11) make clear that we often resist this gesture of love and hospitality. To move with Jesus in the last days and hours of his life, however, we cannot keep our distance, but must allow ourselves to be drawn in.

The footwashing story reminds us that we are not separated from the events we recall this week; rather we must be active participants in the story if we are to share in its blessings and claim our identity as people of these stories. Just as the Old Testament and epistle lessons remind us of the crucial importance of being an active participant in the creation and recreation of the community's identity, so, too, does the footwashing text. We cannot love others as Jesus loves us until we risk letting Jesus love us first.

GOOD FRIDAY

APRIL 2, 1999

REVISED COMMON	EPISCOPAL (BCP)	ROMAN CATHOLIC
Isa. 52:13—53:12	Isa. 52:13—53:12 or Gen. 22:1-18 or Wisd. 2:1, 12-24	Isa. 52:13—53:12
Psalm 22	Ps. 22:1-21 or 22:1-11 or 40:1-14 or 69:1-23	Ps. 31:2, 6, 12-13, 15-17, 25
Heb. 10:16-25 or 4:14-16; 5:7-9	Heb. 10:1-25	Heb. 4:14-16; 5:7-9
John 18:1—19:42	John (18:1-40); 19:1-37	John 18:1—19:42

WHEN THE CHURCH ARRIVES AT GOOD FRIDAY, it arrives at the most somber and dark day in its communal life. The church is asked to look without blinking at the suffering and death of Jesus, and through it to face the reality of suffering and death in the world in a way that it may try to avoid at other times.

The lessons for Good Friday allow for no avoidance of suffering, however. Through the decisive lens of the death of Jesus, the lessons appointed for this day invite the church to enter into the seemingly conflicting realities of suffering and the presence and providence of God. The centerpiece of these lessons is the story of Jesus' trial before Pilate from John 18–19.

FIRST READING
ISAIAH 52:13—53:12 (RCL/RC/BCP)

Interpreting the Text

The Old Testament lesson is the last of the four Servant Songs in Second Isaiah. This Servant Song is the traditional Old Testament lesson for Good Friday; it is the assigned lesson in all three years of the lectionary cycle. Indeed, this Song is so clearly identified in Christian tradition with the suffering and death of Jesus that it is often difficult to remember that its original meaning had nothing to do with that context. This song was written to the Judean community in exile in Babylon around 539 B.C.E., and the sufferings and indignities enumerated in this song are the sufferings of the people Israel, removed from their homeland and the subjects of foreign domination. (A general introduction to the Servant Songs is included in the comments on the Old Testament lesson for Palm/Passion Sunday, pp. 232–33). In order to understand how this Song provides Christians with a lens through which to view the death of Jesus and a voice to speak about this death, the interpreter must first try to hear this Song in its own terms as a response to exile.

The first three Servant Songs are spoken either in the voice of God (Isa. 42:1-4) or the voice of the servant (Isa. 49:1-6; 50:4-9). The fourth Servant Song begins and ends with the voice of God (52:13-15; 53:11b-12), but the middle of the song is spoken in the voice of the community who observes and recounts the drama of the servant's life and death (53:1-11a). The introduction of this new voice into the Servant Songs is an effective poetic device, because it positions the reader as a member of this community. The servant is the subject of the Song, but never speaks himself. The focus of the poetry is not on how the servant experiences the suffering, but on the aspect of the drama that the reading and worshiping community can experience for themselves—the effect of the servant's suffering and death on them.

What is particularly striking about this poem is that the servant's suffering and death are not presented as a failure and defeat, but as the successful culmination of God's plan for the salvation of God's people. The Song opens with God's promise of the servant's exaltation (52:13) and the reversal of fortune for those who despise the servant (52:14-15). The community's recital of the events of the servant's life—his undistinguished appearance (53:1-2); his status as one despised and rejected (53:3)—points not to exaltation, but humiliation, yet the Song shows conclusively that looks and expectations can be deceiving. The key to the exaltation and dramatic reversal in the story line seems to lie in the servant's vocation as the one who "has borne our infirmities and carried our diseases" (53:4), who takes on himself the iniquities and transgressions of this community. At the servant's trial and death, it becomes clear to the speaking community that the servant's death is a "perversion of justice"—not because the legal system is skewed, but because he was the innocent one and they the guilty ones. In that realization lies exaltation, because the people are finally able to see both their transgressions and the healing work that has been effected for them.

Responding to the Text

One of the most frequent affirmations spoken in the Christian church about the death of Jesus is, "Christ died for our sins." Indeed, so common is this affirmation, that we often do not stop to reflect on why vicarious suffering and death is salvific, and it is here that the fourth Servant Song is especially helpful and important in Good Friday observances. The language and imagery of vicarious suffering is different from the language of priestly sacrifice that is prominent in the lesson from Hebrews appointed for Good Friday (see below and the epistle lesson for Monday of Holy Week, pp. 242–43). Unlike the priestly imagery in Hebrews, the dominant imagery in Isaiah is legal imagery, and guilt and innocence here are not primarily cultic categories, but legal ones. The servant's death is decided by the justice system, not the temple system.

What, then, is the logic behind the saving grace of the servant's vicarious suffering and death if it is not that of the temple sacrifice? It is that the trial, condemnation, and execution of an innocent man serves as a kind of mirror for the community, in which the servant's innocence reflects back the community's guilt. The community members had all turned to their own ways (53:6), but not the servant. The community watches while an innocent man, whom they have actively scorned and rejected, silently suffers through the indignities and punishments that are rightly theirs. They rejected him, but he, even at the point of suffering and death, does not reject them, but instead "was wounded for our transgressions." This vicarious suffering and death was salvific for the community, because through the servant's fate—the unjust suffering of an innocent man—they were able to see clearly, as if for the first time, their own sin and abandonment of God. Unlike the priestly sacrifice, the servant's death is vicarious not because it takes something away from the people, but because it puts something on them—the recognition of their own sinfulness and guilt. This recognition is ultimately salvific, because it leads the people back to God. Through the servant's death on their behalf, the community sees what it has become, how alienated from God their life is, that an innocent man has to die for their transgressions. When they see this, new life with God is possible.

THE DEATH OF CHRIST ON THE CROSS CAN FUNCTION FOR THE WORSHIPING COMMUNITY AS A MOMENT OF RECOGNITION OF ITS OWN GUILT AND ALIENATION FROM GOD AND ONE ANOTHER.

The reading of this Servant Song on Good Friday invites the church to have the same response to Christ the servant as the Judeans had to the servant of this song. The death of Christ on the cross can function for the worshiping community as a moment of recognition of its own guilt and alienation from God and one another. This moment of recognition is salvific, because in recognizing our sin, the way to reconciliation is opened.

RESPONSIVE READING

PSALM 22 (RCL/BCP)

Interpreting the Text

The selection of Psalm 22 as the psalm for Good Friday is governed by Jesus' quotation of Psalm 22:1 from the cross in Matthew and Mark (27:46; 15:34). Psalm 22 is a psalm of complaint and petition, and as is typical of that type of psalm, contains an opening section of complaint to God (vv. 1-11, 12-21) followed by a section of praise of God (vv. 22-31).

The opening verse of the psalm captures well the intensity of the petitioner's complaint and trust. The petitioner's complaint is stark and unyielding—"Why have you forsaken me? Why are you so far from helping me?"—yet even in this intense complaint, the petitioner's faith in God is evident. Note the opening address to God: "My God, my God." The God to whom the petitioner speaks is no stranger, but is One to whom the petitioner speaks with intimacy and with whom the petitioner claims a relationship—you are my God. From the very opening verse of this complaint, then, the petitioner's deep faith is already evident. The complaint of verses 2-21 makes clear that the suffering and duress the petitioner is experiencing is acute, yet even in the middle of this suffering, the petitioner addresses God as "my God."

The alternate psalms for the Episcopal lectionary, Psalm 40:1-14 or 69:1-23, and the psalm for the Roman Catholic lectionary, Psalm 31, all also demonstrate the mix between complaint and thanksgiving in psalms of petition for deliverance.

Responding to the Text

When the worshiping community sings or says together Psalm 22 on Good Friday, it begins to experience for itself the intimacy of relationship with God that enables the psalmist—and Jesus from the cross—to turn to God with equal words of complaint and trust. The portrayal of Jesus speaking these words at his crucifixion compellingly communicates the intensity of Jesus' suffering and of his confidence in God. It is a remarkable trait of the Psalter that its hymns provide the worshiping community with a way to turn to, rather than away from, God in times of despair and suffering. Both the trust of the words, "My God, my God," and the abject despair of "Why have you forsaken me?" belong to the religious experience of the psalmist and to everyone who joins in the words of this psalm.

Second Reading

HEBREWS 10:16-25 (RCL/BCP)

Interpreting the Text

The lesson from Hebrews 10 looks beyond Good Friday itself and moves the worshiping community from the intensity of the events of Good Friday to a theological reflection on the effects of those events on the life of the community. That is, in this lesson, the focus shifts from looking at the suffering and death of Jesus to looking at the gifts that the community receives for its life as a result of this death.

The lesson combines verses from two different sections in Hebrews: verses 16-18 are the conclusion to a discussion of the sacrifice of Christ that began at 9:1, and verses 19-25 introduce a new section of exhortations directed toward the community's current situation. The quotation of Jeremiah 31:31-34 in verses 16-18 articulates Hebrews' understanding of the lasting significance of Christ's death: his death brings the promised new covenant in which forgiveness of sins is assured and absolute. This new covenant ushers in a new relationship between God and the worshiping community, in which the community has complete access to the presence of God (vv. 19-20), a privilege formerly reserved for the priests. Because Jesus is the great priest, the people themselves now can enter the house of God (v. 21).

This remarkable situation carries with it new responsibilities, of which the writer reminds his readers in verses 22-25. Unlimited, guaranteed access to the presence of God does not mean that the community is free of religious duties to God and one another. On the contrary, as the three exhortations of verses 23-25 make clear ("let us approach with a true heart," "let us hold fast to the confession of hope without wavering," "let us consider how to provoke one another to love and good deeds"), the community must respond in kind to the privilege it now enjoys. The community is urged to live out its new relationship with God fully and at all times, guided by a heart that always bears the marks of forgiveness (v. 22), by a faith and hope that are as unwavering as the promises of God brought to completion in Jesus (v. 23), and by a communal ethos that is marked by love and good deeds (vv. 24-25).

> If we tell the Good Friday story, but do not "hold fast to the confession of our hope," the story remains only a story, not the beginning of a new life.

Responding to the Text

While the rest of the Good Friday lessons invite us to reexperience the story of Jesus' suffering and death and thereby claim it as our own, the Hebrews lesson offers a different entry point into that story. Because the writer of Hebrews insists upon the once-and-for-all quality of Jesus' death, our access to the story cannot really be in the repetition of it, because what happened cannot and need not be repeated. Rather, the author of Hebrews suggests that our access to the story of Jesus' death is through the way we live out the effects of that death as a community. The Hebrews lesson thus reminds the community that Jesus' death has made us new, because it has given us a new relationship with God. The ongoing significance of Jesus' death is experienced when we live our lives guided and shaped by that new relationship. If we tell the Good Friday story, but do not "hold fast to the confession of our hope," the story remains only a story, not the beginning of a new life. If we neglect to meet together in worship (v. 25), opting instead for individualistic encounters with God, then we cannot "provoke one another to love," and the Good Friday story loses its future.

The Hebrews lesson reminds the church that the last chapters of the Good Friday story are written in the "pages" of the community's own behavior and religious life. We have been given unlimited access to the presence of God by the death of Jesus; whether we enter into God's presence and live as a community shaped by that presence is up to us.

HEBREWS 4:14-16; 5:7-9 (RCL/RC)

Interpreting the Text

These verses, excerpted from the longer section of Hebrews 4:14—5:14, could be considered the "classic" Good Friday lesson from Hebrews. The contents and emphasis of Hebrews 4:14-16 are very similar to those found in the lesson from Hebrews 10:16-25 discussed above. Two aspects of the life and death of Jesus are intertwined: the new reality created by Jesus the great high priest and the demands this new reality places on the believing community. In both Hebrews 4:14-16 and Hebrews 10:16-25, the reality of Jesus as the high priest who has immediate and unlimited access to the presence of God ("who has passed through the heavens," 4:14; cf. 10:19-21) is the indicative on which the imperative of new community behavior is based ("let us hold fast," 4:14; "let us therefore approach the throne of grace with boldness," 4:16; cf. 10:22-25).

This lesson also introduces an element not found in the Hebrews 10 lesson:

the depth of Jesus' suffering as an expression of his full humanity. One of the distinguishing marks of Jesus the great high priest is that he is not set apart from the weaknesses and sufferings of human life, but is rather one who "in every respect as been tested as we are." This high priest provides us with access to God *and* knows fully the needs and sufferings that we bring to God. Hebrews 5:7-9, which can be viewed as the Hebrews version of the Good Friday story, is the definitive illustration of this characteristic of Jesus the high priest. These verses recount the agonies Jesus experienced in the "days of his flesh," and make unambiguously clear the extent of Jesus' "testing." He was tested to the point of death (cf. Phil. 2:5-11 and the discussion of this text on Passion Sunday). Hebrews 5:7-9 thus relate the story on which the theological claims of Hebrews 4:14-16 are grounded. We can approach God boldly in our time of need (4:16), because of the life and death of our great high priest.

Responding to the Text

Once again the lesson from Hebrews reminds the worshiping community of its responsibilities in response to the Good Friday story (see also comments on Heb. 10:16-25 above). Jesus has done his work—he has been tested and suffered, died, and been exalted to God's presence—and now we are left with the work of faith. The exhortations to hold fast to the confession of faith (4:14) and to approach the throne of grace with boldness (4:16) are in essence synonymous exhortations, because at the heart of the confession of faith is the claim that we can indeed approach the throne of grace with boldness and confidence. These exhortations are urgent ones, for if we ignore them, then we lose our access to the new life with God that Jesus' death opens up for us.

HEBREWS 10:1-25 (BCP)

Interpreting the Text

The epistle lesson for the Episcopal lectionary comes from the discussion of Christ's sacrifice that runs from Hebrews 9:1—10:18. Unlike the other lessons from Hebrews, it does not contain exhortations for the community's life, but instead focuses wholly on the description of Jesus as high priest. For a discussion of the assumptions about the levitical sacrificial system that shape this text, see the treatment of Hebrews 9:11-15, Monday of Holy Week, pp. 242–43.

GOSPEL

JOHN 18:1—19:42

Interpreting the Text

The Gospel lesson provides the narrative and theological center point around which all the other lessons of Good Friday revolve. One finds a basic similarity in the stories of Jesus' death in all four Gospels. Each narrates Jesus' betrayal, arrest, trial, crucifixion, and burial, yet they also have many details in common—all the Gospels narrate Jesus' retreat with his disciples to a garden and the subsequent arrival of Judas, and the crowd's demand for the release of Barabbas, to cite two examples. Yet there are also significant differences among the four Gospels, and it is the preacher's responsibility to allow those differences to be heard and honored, and not to attempt to present a hybrid account of Jesus' death, formed by merging all the diverse elements into one common story. The New Testament canon preserves these four different versions because each one of them teaches us something distinctive yet essential about the death of Jesus, and if we overlook the differences, we diminish our own experience of what it means to be the heirs of these traditions.

John 18:1—19:42 is the Johannine account of the arrest, trial, crucifixion, and burial of Jesus. It can be divided into five units: (1) 18:1-12, the arrest; (2) 18:13-27, the interrogation of Jesus by Annas; (3) 18:28—19:16a, the trial before Pilate; (4) 19:16b-37, the crucifixion and death; and (5) 19:38-42, the burial. This long unit begins and ends in a garden, and as the outline makes clear, the centerpiece of John 18–19 is the trial before Pilate. Not only is it the literal center of these chapters, but it is also their longest sustained scene. Indeed, this trial narrative is the Fourth Evangelist's literary and theological masterpiece. One cannot even begin to do justice to the majestic richness of John 18–19 in the brief space allotted in this volume. Of the many dimensions of this story that could be mentioned, only two will be noted here, both of which are crucial if the preacher is to understand the Johannine perspective on the death of Jesus.

First, throughout the story of the arrest, trial, and death, Jesus is portrayed by John as being in complete control of the events around him. Jesus goes to his death neither as sacrificial victim nor martyr, but as one who willingly chooses his death. Note, for example, the way that Jesus goes forward to meet the soldiers in the garden. He does not wait for Judas' kiss to identify him (cf. Matt. 26:47-50; Mark 14:43-46), but declares himself to the soldiers with the bold words, "I am" (18:4-6). This is the moment toward which his whole life has been moving, and he embraces his death freely. The exchange between Pilate and Jesus in 19:10-11 about power and authority gives explicit expression to his theme. Pilate claims to have power to crucify Jesus, but Jesus' answer to him makes clear that he has no such power. The power over Jesus' life and death rests with Jesus and God, not Pilate. The narrative of Jesus' death thus illustrates Jesus' words from 10:17-18, "No one takes it [my life] from me, but I lay it down of my own accord." These words are given a pointed illustration when Jesus carries the cross to Golgotha himself (19:17), and the restrained language used to describe the moment of Jesus' death also underscores their truth, "he handed over his spirit" (19:31). The reconciling power of Jesus' death does not come from his role as sacrifice (cf. the readings from Hebrews throughout Holy Week), but from the depth of his love, in that he chooses to lay down his life for his friends (cf. 15:12).

Second, the theological themes of Jesus as king and judge that have been present throughout the Gospel are brought to their dramatic and powerful conclusion in the trial before Pilate and the crucifixion. John's story of the trial and crucifixion deliberately pits the world's conventional understandings of kingship and power against Jesus' embodiment of those realities (for example, 18:33-39; 19:1-5, 8-12, 15-16, 19-22). The mock enthronement of Jesus as king at 19:1-4, the placard that Pilate places above the cross—all point to the true shape of Jesus' kingship. Jesus' kingship is not defined by political might, but by his willingness to lay down his life. Throughout the trial, Pilate is the character ostensibly acting as judge and with the authority of the king ("emperor," 19:12), but the unfolding of the drama of the trial shows the reader that Jesus is really the judge, and that Pilate and those who bring Jesus to trial stand under Jesus' judgment. Jesus' death judges the world by revealing the distance between the world and the love of God, just as surely as it establishes his kingship.[3]

JESUS' DEATH JUDGES THE WORLD BY REVEALING THE DISTANCE BETWEEN THE WORLD AND THE LOVE OF GOD, JUST AS SURELY AS IT ESTABLISHES HIS KINGSHIP.

Responding to the Text

The Gospel of John provides a perspective on the meaning of the death of Jesus that often goes unheard in contemporary conversations about atonement and the saving power of Jesus' death. For the Fourth Evangelist, the death of Jesus is not primarily an act of sacrifice or ransom for our sins. Rather, Jesus' gift of his life on the cross is exactly that—pure gift. It was not required of him, but he gave it freely, so that the world could see the full extent of God's love. Jesus lays down his life in love for those whom he loves, and the meaning of both life and love changes.

The poignancy of Jesus' death on a cross is a reminder that when we speak of God's love, we are speaking about more than sentimentality, emotion, or affection. Love defines the very core of character and identity. To speak of the love of God and Jesus is to speak of love without limits, even the limit of death. It is this love that stands behind Jesus' commandment to his disciples, "Just as I have loved you, you also should love one another" (13:34). Jesus is not commanding that we be "nice" to one another, but that we love one another as fully as Jesus has loved us, that is, that we love deeply enough to be willing to give our life, our all, for one another.

It is not always clear what the enactment of such love would look like day-to-day. Jesus does not provide detailed instructions to accompany the love commandment, because it is the overarching character of this love grounded in his love that has to set the course for community life, not a behavior manual. For the Christian community to live out the love of God that is made known in Jesus' life and death is to love without restraint and to give without counting the cost. This is no easy goal, but it is the hope and promise to which the Good Friday story in John summons us.

THE GREAT VIGIL OF EASTER HOLY SATURDAY

April 3, 1999

Revised Common	Episcopal (BCP)	Roman Catholic
Gen. 1:1—2:4a	Gen. 1:1—2:2	Gen. 1:1—2:2 or 1:1, 26-31
Gen. 7:1-5, 11-18 8:6-18; 9:8-13	Gen. 7:1-5, 11-18	
Gen. 22:1-18	Gen. 22:1-18	Gen. 22:1-18 or 22:1-2, 9-13, 15-18
Exod. 14:10-31; 15:20-21	Exod. 14:10—15:1	Exod. 14:15—15:1
Isa. 4:2-6	Isa. 54:5-14	
Isa. 55:1-11	Isa. 55:1-11	Isa. 55:1-11
Bar. 3:9-15, 32:1—4:4 or Prov. 8:1-8, 19-21; 9:4b-6	Bar. 3:9-15, 32:1—4:4	
Ezek. 36:24-28	Ezek. 36:24-28	Ezek. 36:16-28
Ezek. 37:1-14	Ezek. 37:1-14	
Zeph. 3:14-20	Zeph. 3:12-20	
Psalm 114	Psalm 114	Ps. 118:1-2, 16-17, 22-23
Rom. 6:3-11	Rom. 6:3-11	Rom. 6:3-11
Matt. 28:1-10	Matt. 28:1-10	Matt. 28:1-10

The celebration of the Holy Saturday Easter Vigil is the most liminal moment in the church's life, and from that liminality the celebration derives its power. The worshiping community truly stands suspended between two realities—the reality of Jesus' death and the reality of his resurrection. As Holy Saturday begins, it is the reality of the death that governs, but by the end of the evening, it will be the reality of the resurrection that holds sway. This move from one reality to another is expressed in many aspects of the Holy Saturday liturgy—for example, from the service's beginning in darkness to the lighting of the Easter candle, the baptism of new Christians, the renewal of baptismal vows. The core lessons for the Vigil service guide the community into the new reality that dawns with the resurrection. The lesson from Romans celebrates the transforming power of baptism; the psalm praises God's work of deliverance in bringing God's people to a new life; and the Gospel lesson recounts Matthew's story of the first Easter.

EPISTLE

ROMANS 6:3-11 (RCL/RC/BCP)

Interpreting the Text

The focus of this passage from Romans is on baptism, and the ways in which baptism draws Christians into the story of Jesus' death and resurrection. As such, it is the perfect text for the Easter Vigil, in which the rites of baptism play a role in celebrating Christ's Easter victory over death.

Verses 3-5 articulate the perspective that shapes the entire passage. The governing imagery is the language of the Good Friday/Easter event—death, burial, resurrection—but Paul is not concerned here simply to remind his readers of that story. Instead, he uses that story to help the community at Rome reenvision their own lives as baptized Christians. Note the recurrence of language of participation in these verses—"baptized into Christ Jesus"; "baptized into his death"; "buried with him"; "just as Christ was raised . . ., so we too . . ."; "united with him in a death like his, we will certainly be united with him in a resurrection like his." For Paul, baptism is more than simply a rite of initiation into a new community; it is a rite that makes us participants in the events of Good Friday and Easter. Those events did not simply happen at some distant point in time, at which we can look back in calm reflection. The events of Good Friday have an ongoing present and an unlimited future, because the body of Christ lives on as the body of the church (cf. 1 Cor. 12).

THE EVENTS OF GOOD FRIDAY HAVE AN ONGOING PRESENT AND AN UNLIMITED FUTURE, BECAUSE THE BODY OF CHRIST LIVES ON AS THE BODY OF THE CHURCH.

Paul's understanding of baptism depends on a somewhat complex use of the terms "death" and "life." Paul uses these terms with literal and metaphorical meanings, and it is essential that the interpreter of these verses recognize both dimensions of the terms. Death, for example, can have its literal meaning, the cessation of life, as when Paul refers to Christ's death in verse 3. But death also has a range of metaphorical and symbolic meanings. One metaphorical usage of death is to define death not simply as the cessation of life, but as life governed by sin and the power of death, so that life without the death and resurrection of Christ is not life at all. Rather, such a life is death. Life is always defined by the resurrection of Jesus and the end to the power of sin and death that the resurrection inaugurates. The Christian's "life" thus begins only when "our old self was crucified with him, so that the body of sin might be destroyed." There is a certain circularity to Paul's thought here—as sin is by definition that which blocks life, and the death of sin is by definition the beginning of life—and intentionally so, because only one thing can unlock that circle for Paul: dying and rising with Christ.

The balance between death and life is eloquently articulated in verses 10-11. The crucifixion is a death to sin and is "once for all," since death is absolute. But "the life he lives, he lives to God," which means that the life is everlasting and ongoing. Thus, for Paul, the opposite of death and sin is really God, because God makes all life possible. We can consider "ourselves dead to sin and alive to God in Christ Jesus," because we are baptized into that death and that new life.

Responding to the Text

In the early church, as in some churches today, baptism was practiced by submerging a person in water to enact the drama of dying and rising. In this form of baptism, one has the physical experience of death and darkness; the moment of reentering the light looms as a possibility, but is not yet a known reality. In that helpless moment when one is submerged under water, everything hinges on whether life will overcome death, or whether death is really the end of the line.

When the person was submerged in the water, he or she was at a liminal point similar to that of the church at the Easter Vigil. One of the powerful dimensions of the Easter Vigil as a celebration of the resurrection is that the liturgy does not take place on a bright and shining Sunday morning, but in the ambiguity of darkness, in which it is possible to wonder, at least for a moment, if the light ever will shine again. Romans 6:3-11 gives us directions on how to negotiate the darkness and how and why to look for the new life. Contemporary Christians, particularly those with generations of heritage in the church, often have little sense of the wonder of the first-time experience of passing from the power of death into the possibility of new life. Paul reminds his readers—first-century and contemporary—that baptism is not something conventional, something that simply happens by rote each time there is a new baby or a new communicant in the church body. Baptism is a tangible reminder of the death and resurrection of Christ, and of our participation in those events. The death and resurrection of Christ completely altered the configuration of life and death, and baptism is a sign that this alteration remains the defining reality of our identity as Christians.

RESPONSIVE READING

PSALM 114 (RCL/BCP)

Interpreting the Text

Psalm 114 is a poem that extols the wonders of God's deliverance of Israel in the exodus. The poem combines a recital of the pivotal events in Israel's history—the escape from Egypt (v. 1), the crossing of the sea (vv. 3, 5), the wilderness sojourn (vv. 4, 6), and the entrance into the Promised Land (v. 2)—with a call to praise the majesty of God (vv. 7-8). The events of Israel's deliverance are not recounted in chronological order, but are pieced together like a memory quilt, in which scattered bits of memory come together to form the whole picture of the exodus. The poem celebrates the end of captivity and the beginning of new life, and God's power to cause this to happen.

Responding to the Text

Psalm 114 is an appropriate and moving text for the Easter Vigil, because it is a reminder that what we celebrate at Easter is in continuity with God's acts of salvation toward and for God's people throughout time. The God we celebrate at Easter is the one who brings freedom from captivity and life from death—whether that captivity be slavery in Egypt or the burial tomb. This psalm is celebratory from beginning to end, and its thankful exuberance also makes it an appropriate community response to the events of Easter. It helps the worshiping community remember that the main actor here is God, and that it is God's indomitable power for life that we celebrate at the Easter Vigil.

Psalm 114 also suggests another interesting connection with the events celebrated at the Easter Vigil. In verse after verse of this brief poem, its rich metaphors highlight the cosmic dimensions of God's actions—the sea fled, the mountains and hills (which could have been formidable obstacles in the wilderness) skipped like rams and lambs. In verse 7, it is the earth itself that is exhorted to tremble "at the presence of the Lord." This trembling at God's presence is echoed in the Gospel lesson from Matthew 28, in which an earthquake accompanies an angel's descent from heaven to Jesus' tomb (28:2). There is a global, cosmic dimension to God's acts of deliverance.

PSALM 118:1-2, 16-17, 22-23 (RC)

Interpreting the Text

Psalm 118 is a psalm of thanksgiving for national deliverance, perhaps from battle. Verses 1-2 begin the psalm with an explicit call to thanksgiving, in which God's steadfast love is declared twice (note the continued repetition of this affirmation about God in vv. 3-4). Verse 2 makes clear that this is a hymn of communal thanksgiving ("Let Israel say"). Verse 16 gives one of the reasons why thanksgiving is in order. The right hand of the Lord, a metaphor for the deliverance of God that recalls the exodus from Egypt (see Exod. 15:6, 12), has prevailed. Verses 17 and 22 are probably the reason that this psalm is associated with the Easter Vigil liturgy. The affirmation of verse 17 resounds as an Easter-like proclamation. The stone saying of verse 22 was picked up in the New Testament and interpreted as a symbol of the rejection and subsequent exaltation of Christ (for example, Matt. 21:42; Acts 4:11; 1 Pet. 2:7).

Responding to the Text

Even though the stone saying may be the primary reason Psalm 118 found its way into the Easter Vigil liturgy, the appropriateness of this psalm for this occasion is not limited to this verse. Rather, like Psalm 114 (see above), this psalm's thanksgiving and celebration of the strength and deliverance of God provide a compelling response to the events of Easter. What else can the community do when facing into the wonder of the empty tomb than turn to God in thanksgiving? Moreover, the joy and purpose for life that the psalmist finds in recounting the deeds of the Lord (v. 17) is a wonderful refrain for the Easter season. It also contains an important reminder that the events celebrated at Easter do not come to rest with the impact of the resurrection on me and my life, or on us and our lives, but that the Easter celebration must always circle back to God and praise the author of our lives.

THE EASTER CELEBRATION MUST ALWAYS CIRCLE BACK TO GOD AND PRAISE THE AUTHOR OF OUR LIVES.

GOSPEL

MATTHEW 28:1-10 *Interpreting the Text*

Matthew 28:1-10 contains two units from Matthew's resurrection narrative: the appearance of the angel at the tomb (vv. 1-8) and the first appearance of Jesus (vv. 9-10). (Verses 11-15, the bribing of the guards, and vv. 16-20, Jesus' meeting with the gathered disciples in Galilee, conclude the resurrection narrative in Matthew.) Two women, Mary Magdalene and "the other Mary," are the first witnesses of Christ's resurrection in this lesson, for it is to them alone that the angel and Jesus appear.

Verse 1 sets the scene for the story that follows, providing the conventional storytelling details of character (Mary Magdalene and the other Mary), time (dawn of Sunday morning), and place (the tomb). This fairly ordinary story beginning immediately gives way to a series of events that are far from ordinary—a great earthquake and the descent of an angel from heaven, whose actions and appearance are described in great detail (vv. 2-3). The earthquake and the angel are intended to remind the reader of the cosmic and world-changing character of the events of the crucifixion and resurrection (see comments on Ps. 114 above). Whereas in the other three Gospels the women simply discover that the stone has been rolled away from the tomb (see, for example, Mark 16:3-4; Luke 24:2; John 20:1), Matthew makes the angel's rolling back of the stone a key element in his telling of the story. This is another way of reinforcing for the reader that the events that transpired at Jesus' tomb do not belong to the realm of everyday experience, but instead spring from a decisive intervention by God. Matthew imbues the opening of the resurrection story with a sense of awe at the power and presence of God, even before the resurrection is announced. The guards' response to the angel (v. 4) reinforces the awesomeness of the moment.

The angel's words (vv. 5-7) consist of four parts: opening words of reassurance, the affirmation of the reality of the death of Jesus ("who was crucified"), the Gospel's first announcement of the resurrection, and a commissioning of the women as the first evangelists of the good news of the resurrection ("go quickly and tell . . ."). The women respond immediately to the angel's words ("they left the tomb quickly"), and are rewarded for their faithfulness by an appearance of the risen Jesus. This resurrection appearance has none of the drama of mistaken identity that one finds in the first resurrection stories in Luke (24:13-35) and John (20:1-18). Instead, the women recognize Jesus immediately and begin to worship him (v. 9). Jesus' words to them repeat the words of the angel, with the important difference, of course, that it is now the risen Jesus himself who speaks directly to the women.

Responding to the Text

This lesson from Matthew 28:1-10 is an appropriate Gospel lesson for the Easter Vigil, because while it contains the story of Jesus' first appearance, it also has a note of expectancy and promise (vv. 7, 10) that fits the Vigil setting. The Vigil service has taken the worshiping community from darkness into light, from a tomb sealed shut to the tomb whose seal has been broken, from grief and mourning to the joyous recognition of the reality of resurrection. Yet it also has a note of more to come, because the Vigil inaugurates the Easter season in which the promise of the resurrection is celebrated and explored in depth. At the Vigil, it is enough to stand in awe at the wonder of God who defeats the power of death with new life.

The exegesis of Matthew 28:1-10 noted many ways in which Matthew invites the reader to enter into the awesomeness of this moment at the tomb, and the preacher may do the same thing for his or her congregation. Matthew 28:1-10 depicts two very different responses to the presence of God at Jesus' tomb, and in these two responses the worshiping community can see the options before it as it attempts to live into the promise of the resurrection.

The first response is that of the guards. At the sight of the angel, they are so overcome with fear, that they "shook and became like dead men." This description of the guards as "like dead men" cannot be accidental on Matthew's part. At the tomb of Jesus, in the presence of the angel who rolls away the stone and brings the first announcement of the resurrection, the guards are so afraid that they become more dead than alive. The guards' fear shuts them off from the new life that is now available. Instead of seeing the wonder of God in the awesomeness of the moment, they see only something to dread.

> FEAR CAN CLOSE OUR HEARTS TO WHAT GOD OFFERS US, BUT IF WE LISTEN FOR GOD'S COMFORT AND ALLOW OURSELVES TO LOOK FOR THE RISEN JESUS, THEN THE EASTER LIFE IS TRULY POSSIBLE.

The response of the women stands in marked contrast to that of the guards, a contrast highlighted by Matthew's use of language. Both the guards and the women are described as experiencing fear, yet the women's fear is combined with another response—"great joy." The women were able to heed the angel's assurance, "Do not be afraid," and so were able to see in the events of the resurrection something at which they could rejoice. Their joy did not obliterate completely their fear (note that Jesus also speaks words of assurance in the face of fear to the women, v. 10), but because their fear is tempered with great joy, the women open themselves to the possibility of new life, rather than locking themselves away in a world of death.

These two responses provide powerful object lessons for the church as it stands at the cusp of the Easter season. One can be so afraid of the newness that is offered in the Easter season, that instead of embracing God's remarkable invitation to new life, one can become "like dead men," shaped by the reality of death and the sealed tomb, existing in a closed world without the hope-filled promises of God. Or one can be like the women, who saw in the earth-shattering events of that morning at the tomb an occasion to rejoice at the presence of God. The women run quickly after they heard the angel's news—they are not "like dead men," but instead have exuberance for life.

The story from Matthew 28 suggests that the difference between "living" in fear and living in joy is the reassuring word of God and the experience of the risen Jesus who is willing to meet us on the road. Fear can close our hearts to what God offers us, but if we listen for God's comfort and allow ourselves to look for the risen Jesus, then the Easter life is truly possible.

Notes

1. The complexities of this text cannot be addressed adequately in this brief treatment of John 12:20-36. For a fuller discussion, see Gail R. O'Day, *John,* The New Interpreter's Bible, Volume 9 (Nashville: Abingdon Press, 1996), 710–15.

2. For a much more detailed discussion of this complex Johannine approach, see ibid., 604-15.

3. For a fuller treatment of the themes of king and judge in John 18–19, see ibid., 811-30, and the bibliography cited there.